The Bible Speaks Today
Series editors: Alec Motyer (OT)
John Stott (NT)
Derek Tidball (Bible Themes)

The Message of
Sonship

The Bible Speaks Today: Bible Themes series

The Message of the Living God
His glory, his people, his world
Peter Lewis

The Message of the Resurrection
Christ is risen!
Paul Beasley-Murray

The Message of the Cross
Wisdom unsearchable, love indestructible
Derek Tidball

The Message of Salvation
By God's grace, for God's glory
Philip Graham Ryken

The Message of Creation
Encountering the Lord of the universe
David Wilkinson

The Message of Heaven and Hell
Grace and destiny
Bruce Milne

The Message of Mission
The glory of Christ in all time and space
Howard Peskett and Vinoth Ramachandra

The Message of Prayer
Approaching the throne of grace
Tim Chester

The Message of the Trinity
Life in God
Brian Edgar

The Message of Evil and Suffering
Light into darkness
Peter Hicks

The Message of the Holy Spirit
The Spirit of encounter
Keith Warrington

The Message of Holiness
Restoring God's masterpiece
Derek Tidball

The Message of Sonship
At home in God's household
Trevor Burke

The Message of Sonship

At home in God's household

Trevor J. Burke

Professor of Bible
Moody Bible Institute

Inter-Varsity Press

INTER-VARSITY PRESS
Norton Street, Nottingham NG7 3HR, England
Email: ivp@ivpbooks.com
Website: www.ivpbooks.com

First published 2011

British Library Cataloguing in Publication Data
A catalogue record for this book is available from the British Library.

ISBN: 978–1–84474–538–8

Set in Stempel Garamond
Typeset in Great Britain by Servis Filmsetting Ltd, Stockport, Cheshire
Printed and bound in Great Britain by Ashford Colour Press Ltd,
Gosport, Hampshire

*Inter-Varsity Press publishes Christian books that are true to the Bible
and that communicate the gospel, develop discipleship and strengthen the
church for its mission in the world.*

*Inter-Varsity Press is closely linked with the Universities and Colleges
Christian Fellowship, a student movement connecting Christian Unions
in universities and colleges throughout Great Britain, and a member
movement of the International Fellowship of Evangelical Students.
Website: www.uccf.org.uk*

To three of God's children I cherish most
Yvonne
Luke and Simeon

Contents

7

GENERAL PREFACE

THE BIBLE SPEAKS TODAY describes three series of expositions, based on the books of the Old and New Testaments, and on Bible themes that run through the whole of Scripture. Each series is characterized by a threefold ideal:

- to expound the biblical text with accuracy
- to relate it to contemporary life, and
- to be readable.

These books are, therefore, not 'commentaries', for the commentary seeks rather to elucidate the text than to apply it, and tends to be a work rather of reference than of literature. Nor, on the other hand, do they contain the kinds of 'sermons' that attempt to be contemporary and readable without taking Scripture seriously enough. The contributors to *The Bible Speaks Today* series are all united in their convictions that God still speaks through what he has spoken, and that nothing is more necessary for the life, health and growth of Christians than that they should hear what the Spirit is saying to them through his ancient – yet ever modern – Word.

ALEC MOTYER
JOHN STOTT
DEREK TIDBALL
Series editors

Author's preface

This book arose from an earlier one I wrote entitled *Adopted into God's Family*. During the writing of that volume D. A. Carson, in the course of written correspondence, made the insightful remark that the notion of sonship was probably the larger biblical concept of which adopted sonship was a part. Dr Carson's comments were an important seed-thought which blossomed into the book you now hold in your hands. The contents, however, are entirely my responsibility.

A word about the title: 'The Message of Sonship' should not be taken to exclude females; indeed, it would have better to have used the word 'children', but 'The Message of the Children of God' did not have the same ring as 'sonship' nor did it fit with the mostly one-word titles of the other volumes in the Bible Speaks Today series. I have tried to be as inclusive as possible and so when I use the term 'son' males *and* females are usually intended, except in the case of Paul's adoption term where males only are in view – females could not be adopted as they were unable to carry on the family name.

My reasons for writing this book are to inform, but also to encourage, edify and strengthen the faith of all Christians who are part of the church, the family of God. I have pastors in mind in the hope that they will preach some of these important texts and I trust the book will be useful for individual and group Bible study of what is an overlooked and neglected biblical theme. One legitimate way of 'doing' biblical theology is through narrative and I have endeavoured to use the metaphor of sonship as a means of understanding the biblical story. With this in mind, I would recommend the book is read right through; if a chapter is chosen to be read, however, I would encourage the reader to first turn to the introductory chapter which sets the context for the rest of the book.

Other New Testament letters could have been considered (e.g. 1 Peter and Galatians), but the constraints of space meant it was not possible to discuss all of them; in any case, a discussion of Galatians can be found in my earlier book, *Adopted into God's Family*.

I owe a huge to debt to a number of people. I am particularly grateful to my employer, Moody Bible Institute, who granted me a sabbatical year (2010–11) during which most of the material was written. Thanks to Derek Tidball for his initial positive response to consider including this book in the Bible Speaks Today series and for the time he took to read the manuscript, as well as his encouragement throughout. I am grateful to Phil Duce at Inter-Varsity Press for reading the book and for his editorial comments which have also resulted in an improved volume. Alison Walley must also be thanked for the sterling work she has done with the copy-editing and proof checking. Thanks are due to three busy pastors, Ed Searcy, Derek Hutchison and Lewis Clark, who took the time to read and provide feedback on parts of the manuscript. Many students have provided feedback, including a number formerly at Moody Bible Institute – some of whom are now in pastoral work or engaged in further training to serve the church of Jesus Christ – including Joseph Ananias, Brandon Hovey, Peter Stonecipher and Matt and Lindsay Tully.

Joe Cataio, a librarian at Moody Bible Institute and a fund of knowledge on all kinds of subjects, has been unstinting in his support in ordering any bibliographical materials I needed, in many cases actually getting the books or articles the same or next day.

My greatest debt, as always, is to my wife Yvonne, who read and commented on most, if not all, of the material and engaged in conversations on the topic. And I am grateful to our two sons, Luke and Simeon, who read some of the material and showed an interest by frequently asking 'how's the book going?' It is to Yvonne, Luke and Simeon to whom this book is affectionately dedicated.

Trevor J. Burke
Chicago
January 2011

Abbreviations

AB	Anchor Bible
AnBib.	Analecta Biblica
AOTC	Apollos Old Testament Commentary
BDAG	W. Bauer, F.W. Danker, W. F. Arndt and F.W. Gingrich, *A Greek-English Lexicon of the New Testament and Other Early Christian Literature* (Chicago: Chicago University Press, 2000)
BECNT	Baker Exegetical Commentary on the New Testament
BNTC	Black's New Testament Commentary
BTCL	Biblical Theological Classics Library
Bib Sac	*Bibliotheca Sacra*
BST	The Bible Speaks Today
BTB	*Biblical Theology Bulletin*
DBI	Leland Ryken, James C. Wilhoit, Tremper Longmann III (eds.), *Dictionary of Biblical Imagery* (Downers Grove/Leicester: InterVarsity Press, 1998)
ESV	English Standard Version
Gk	Greek
HCOT	Historical Commentary on the Old Testament
IBC	Interpreter's Bible Commentary
IBS	*Irish Biblical Studies*
ICC	International Critical Commentary
IVPNTC	IVP New Testament Commentary
JB	Jerusalem Bible
JETS	*Journal of the Evangelical Theological Society*
JSNTS	*Journal for the Study of the New Testament Supplements*
KJV	King James Version
LBT	Library of Biblical Theology
LNTS	Library of New Testament Studies
LXX	The Septuagint
NAC	New American Commentary
NCBC	New Century Bible Commentary

NIB	New Interpreters Bible
NIBC	New International Biblical Commentary
NIDB	New Interpreters Dictionary of the Bible
NICNT	New International Commentary on the New Testament
NICOT	New International Commentary on the Old Testament
NIGTC	New International Greek Testament Commentary
NIV	New International Version
NIVAC	New International Version Application Commentary
NovT	Novum Testamentum Supplements
NRSV	New Revised Standard Version
NSBT	New Studies in Biblical Theology
OBT	Overtures in Biblical Theology
PAST	Pauline Studies
PNTC	Pillar New Testament Commentary
SJTOP	Scottish Journal of Theology Occasional Papers
SP	Sacra Pagina
St.BL	Studies in Biblical Literature
TDOT	G.Johannes Botterweck and Heinz-Josef Fabry (eds.), *Theological Dictionary of the Old Testament* (Grand Rapids: Eerdmans, 1974–).
TEV	Today's English Version
TNIV	Today's New International Version
TNTC	Tyndale New Testament Commentary
TOTC	Tyndale Old Testament Commentary
TynBul	*Tyndale Bulletin*
WBC	Word Biblical Commentary
ZAW	Zeitschrift für die neutestamentliche Wissenschaft
ZEC	Zondervan Exegetical Commentary

Select bibliography

Balla, Peter, *The Child-Parent Relationship in the New Testament and its Environment* (Tübingen: Mohr Siebeck, 2002).

Banks, Robert, *Paul's Idea of Community: The Early House Churches in their Cultural Setting*, 2nd ed. (Peabody: Hendrickson, 1994).

Bunge, Marcia J. (ed.), *The Child in the Bible* (Grand Rapids: Eerdmans, 2008).

Burke, Trevor J., 'Pauline Paternity in 1 Thessalonians', *TynBul* 51.1 (2000), pp. 59–81.

—— *Family Matters: A Socio-Historical Study of Kinship Metaphors in 1 Thessalonians*, JSNTS 247 (London: T&T Clark, 2003).

—— 'Paul's role as "Father" to his Corinthian "Children" in Socio-historical Context', in Trevor J. Burke & J. Keith Elliott (eds.), *Paul and the Corinthians: Studies on a Community in Conflict. Essays in Honour of Margaret Thrall*, NovT 109 (Leiden: Brill, 2003).

—— *Adopted into God's family: Exploring a Pauline Metaphor*, NSBT 22 (Nottingham: Apollos, 2006).

—— 'Adopted as Sons: The Missing Piece in Pauline Soteriology', in Stanley E. Porter (ed.), *Paul: Jew, Greek and Roman*, PAST 5 (Leiden: Brill, 2008).

—— 'The Holy Spirit as the Controlling Dynamic in Paul's Role as Missionary in 1 Thessalonians', in Trevor J. Burke and Brian S. Rosner (eds.), *Paul as Missionary: Identity, Activity, Theology and Practice,* LNTS 420 (London: T&T Clark, 2011), *forthcoming.*

Burke, Trevor J. and J. Keith Elliott (eds.), *Paul and the Corinthians: Studies on a Community in Conflict. Essays in Honour of Margaret Thrall*, NovT 109 (Leiden: Brill, 2003).

Burke, Trevor J. and Brian S. Rosner (eds.), *Paul as Missionary: Identity, Activity, Theology and Practice,* LNTS 420 (London: T&T Clark, 2011), *forthcoming.*

Byrne, Brendan, *'Sons of God' – 'Seed of Abraham': A Study of the Idea of the Sonship of All Christians in Paul Against the Old Testament Background* (Rome: Biblical Institute Press, 1979).

Carson, D. A., 'God is Love', *Bib Sac* 156 (1999), pp. 131–142.

Colijn, Brenda, *Images of Salvation in the New Testament* (Downers Grove: IVP, 2010).

Collins, Raymond C., *The Power of Images in Paul* (Collegeville: Liturgical Press, 2008).

deSilva, David A., *Honor, Patronage, Kinship and Purity* (Downers Grove: IVP, 2000).

Fee, Gordon D., *Pauline Christology: An Exegetical-Theological Study* (Peabody: Hendrickson, 2008).

—— *The First and Second Letters to the Thessalonians*, NICNT (Grand Rapids: Eerdmans, 2009).

Ferguson, Sinclair B., 'The Reformed Doctrine of Sonship', in Nigel de S. Cameron and Sinclair B. Ferguson (eds.), *Pulpit and People: Essays in Honour of William Still on his 75th Birthday* (Edinburgh: Rutherford House, 1986).

—— *Children of the Living God* (Edinburgh: Banner of Truth Trust, 1989).

Francis, James M. M., *Adults as Children: Images of Childhood in the Ancient World and the New Testament* (Bern: Peter Lang, 2006).

Gaventa Roberts, Beverly, *Our Mother St. Paul* (Louisville: Westminster John Knox Press, 2007).

Hahn, Scott, *A Father Who Keeps His Promises: God's Covenant Love in Scripture* (Cincinnati: St Anthony Messenger Press, 1998).

Hellerman, Joseph H., *When the Church was a Family: Recapturing Jesus' Vision for Authentic Christian Community* (Nashville: Broadman and Holman, 2009).

Hess, Richard and M. Daniel Carroll (eds.), *Family in the Bible: Exploring Customs, Culture, and Context* (Grand Rapids: Baker Academic, 2003).

Köstenberger, Andreas and David W. Jones, *God, Marriage and Family: Rebuilding the Biblical Foundation*, 2nd ed. (Wheaton: Crossway Books, 2010).

Malherbe, Abraham J., 'God's New Family in Thessalonica', in Michael L. White and O. Larry Yarbrough (eds.), *The Social World of the First Christians: Essays in Honour of Wayne A. Meeks* (Philadelphia: Fortress Press, 1995).

Packer, J. I., *Knowing God* (London: Hodder and Stoughton, 1973).

15

Peterson, Eugene H., *Practice Resurrection: A Conversation on Growing up in Christ* (Grand Rapids: Eerdmans, 2010).

Ryken, L., J. C. Wilhoit and T. Longmann (eds.), *Dictionary of Biblical Imagery* (Downers Grove/Leicester: IVP, 1998).

Schmidt, John J., 'Israel as Son of God in Torah', *BTB* 24 (2004), pp. 69–73.

Scott, James M., *Adoption as Sons of God: An Exegetical Investigation into the Background of HUIOTHESIA in the Pauline Corpus* (Tübingen: Mohr/Siebeck, 1992).

Smail, Thomas M., *The Forgotten Father: Rediscovering the Heart of the Christian Gospel* (London: Hodder and Stoughton, 1980).

Strange, W. A., *Children in the Early Church: Children in the Ancient World, the New Testament and the Early Church* (Carlisle: Paternoster, 1996).

Stibbe, Mark, *From Orphans to Heirs: Celebrating our Spiritual Adoption* (Oxford: The Bible Reading Fellowship, 1999).

—— *I Am Your Father: What Every Heart Needs to Know* (Oxford: Monarch, 2010).

Thompson, Marian Meye, *The Promise of the Father: Jesus and God in the New Testament* (Louisville: Westminster John Knox Press, 2000).

Walterstorff, Nicholas, *Lament for a Son* (Grand Rapids: Eerdmans, 1987).

Wright, Christopher J. H., *God's People in God's Land: Family, Land and Property in the Old Testament*, BTCL 14 (Carlisle: Paternoster Press, 1997).

—— *Knowing God the Father through the Old Testament* (Oxford: Monarch, 2007).

Introduction: sonship as a biblical metaphor

'The Bible is more than a book of ideas: it is also a book of images and motifs. Everywhere we turn we find concrete pictures and recurrent patterns'.[1] Who could forget, for example, Amos's graphic description of the people of God as 'a basket of ripe fruit' (Amos 8:2), a reminder that the axe of God's judgment is about to fall on the nation of Israel? Or take the prophet Ezekiel, 'easily the most bizarre of all the prophets',[2] who turns hairdresser and then tosses some of the strands of his locks into the air which the wind blows in all directions, a vivid reminder that God is about to disperse his own people to the corners of the earth (Ezek. 5:1–2). The pages of the New Testament are similarly populated with colourful imagery. The Gospel evangelists portray Jesus as *the* consummate communicator who uses the ordinary, everyday objects of sheep (Luke 15:3–7) and seed (Luke 8:4–8), water (John 7:37–38) and wine (Luke 5:37) – imagery which would have resonated in a subsistence, peasant context – in order to teach profound truths about the kingdom of God. Or we might think of the apostle Paul whose context of ministry was the city and whose language throbs with the imagery of the metropolis. Paul draws from the realms of banking and commerce (Rom. 6:23), buildings and architecture (1 Cor. 3:10), sea travel (Eph. 4:14) and masonry (2 Tim. 2:15)[3], all of which would have immediately connected with his more sophisticated cosmopolitan hearers. It is an inescapable fact that the biblical authors not only teach, narrate, prophesy,

---

[1] 'Introduction', in *DBI*, p. xiii.

[2] Christopher J. H. Wright, *The Message of Ezekiel: A New Heart and a New Spirit*, BST (Leicester: IVP, 2001), p. 11.

[3] For more on these metaphors see David J. Williams, *Paul's Metaphors: Their Character and Context* (Peabody: Hendrickson, 1999).

exhort and warn, but they often do so by painting pictures in our minds.

A careful reading of the metaphors and figures of speech listed above, however, will reveal that they all have to do with inanimate or impersonal objects. There are other metaphors in Scripture, however, which are of a much more personal and relational nature. One familial image[4] that looms large on the landscape of the Bible and which will be the focus of this book is that of *sonship*. The term sonship – and by this we mean sons *and* daughters – is one with which we can easily and immediately identify and are all too familiar. We think we know what this term means based on our modern perceptions of what it means to be a son, but sonship in biblical times was radically different to our twenty-first-century Western individualistic understanding. One important difference, for example, is that society in ancient times was much more structured, communally oriented and patriarchal than our more egalitarian, fragmented Western social order at the beginning of the third millennium. Thus, it is a mistake of some magnitude to read our modern understanding of what it means to be a son into ancient presuppositions associated with this term, and we shall be especially alert to these aspects as we proceed to grapple with the biblical texts.

Sonship is a powerful and striking metaphor but it may not be the first expression that springs to mind when thinking of important biblical themes, so perhaps some justification needs to be given for our study. As we do so, it is worth noting that no full-length book has been written on the theme of sonship from the perspective of biblical theology. This book is not a full-blown study of a biblical theology of sonship but has the more modest aim of serving as a brief introduction to an important and overlooked theme in Scripture. As we unpack this theme we will spend much time reflecting on what lies behind it, namely, the relationship between that of a father and a son where the former was the dominant member and if anything was to happen it took place at his instigation. However, I also wish to be sensitive to looking at this relationship from *the perspective of the child, a son or a daughter*,[5] not least for the fact that this is a book

---

[4] I am convinced that one cannot understand the Scriptures without due consideration of the importance which familial language has to play. Unlike our twenty-first-century fragmented society, the family in both Testaments was the basic building block of ancient society.

[5] Because of the patriarchal structure of society in Old and New Testament times the father was the dominating figure in the household and one cannot discuss sonship without reference to the parent. Most studies of the family in antiquity have focused more on the parent than the child in the parent-child relationship For a recent study which also focuses on the *child* as opposed to the parent, see Peter

about sonship but also because this metaphor is an unusual one with which to describe anyone, especially when we realize that children in the ancient Near East were the least important members of the family and were often viewed as being on its margins.[6] Children in the ancient world were seen and not heard and by choosing to use the image of 'son' or 'child/ren' the biblical authors use a filial term associated with social inferiority, which is interesting, if not significant, for the fact that it is one that is taken and infused with new meaning as an expression for spiritual formation.[7]

Remember Jesus' action when he chided his disciples as they disputed over who would be the greatest in the kingdom by calling a little child to stand in the middle of them? 'Whoever humbles himself like this child', he rebuked them, 'is the greatest in the kingdom of heaven' (Matt. 18:4). Jesus is always the subversive, challenging the status quo. Moreover, we need to pay careful attention to the metaphor 'son/daughter' since it is distinct from other biblical images (e.g. servant) and is full of symbolism, signifying as we shall see not only a call to relationship with God, but also within that filial relationship the need to grow together, change and be renewed. Several words in the last sentence are important as far as an understanding of the metaphor is concerned because sonship throws important light on our understanding of *salvation* ('call to relationship'), *community* ('grow together') and *morality* ('change'). Thus, as we encounter this metaphor we will be particularly alert to these factors and the message which the biblical authors are trying to convey.

There is good reason for the study of the use of this filial term in the Bible – the expression 'son' is used with remarkable diversity in Scripture and has a broad spectrum of meanings. In the Old Testament, for example, 'son' sometimes denotes the physical relations that exist within a family (Gen. 4:25; Exod. 2:2; cf. Matt.1:21; Mark 1:19) or describes human rulers and judges (Ps. 82:6). Even Satan is called one of the sons of God (Job 1:6[8])! But equally, if not more important, are those occasions where 'son' is used

Balla, *The Child-Parent Relationship in the New Testament and Its Environment* (Tübingen: Mohr, 2002).

[6] For example, this was symbolized by the way that children were sometimes buried under the foundations and at the very extremity of the structure of the house. Marianne Meye Thompson puts it well: 'the data does testify, that on the whole, children, and especially those particularly vulnerable, were viewed as less than fully human and, therefore, sometimes treated virtually as trash to be disposed of if inconvenient in any way'; see her 'Children in the Gospel of John', in Marcia J. Bunge (ed.), *The Child in the Bible* (Grand Rapids/Cambridge: Eerdmans, 2008), p. 205.

[7] See the excellent volume by James L. Resseguie, *Spiritual Landscape: Images of the Spiritual Life in the Gospel of Luke* (Peabody: Hendrickson, 2004), p. 55.

[8] This is clear in the ESV, the NIV gives 'son' in its footnote to the verse.

metaphorically throughout Scripture to denote the relationship of divine sonship between believers and God as 'Father'. Of course the idea of 'son' can also be understood in a real sense 'for the predication that God is "father" is a literal statement. God is the Father of Israel as its founder'[9] but the term rules out any pagan notion of a metaphysical relationship between God and believers as his spiritual offspring.

'The motif of God's son or sons is a frequent one in the Old Testament'[10] where, as regards the former, God is repeatedly (in the singular) described as 'Father' over the nation of Israel his 'son' (Exod. 4:22; Deut. 32:6). This individual aspect also applies to David, king of Israel, where the dynastic promise is couched in filial terms: 'I will be his Father and he will be my son' (2 Sam. 7:14). On other occasions the Israelites (plural) are described as 'sons' or 'children' of Yahweh, especially in contexts where there is a responsibility of loyalty, obedience and holiness to God (Deut. 14:1–2; Isa. 1:2).[11] And in the New Testament, where the expression occurs more frequently, Christians are most often identified in the plural as 'sons' (Matt. 5:45; Rom. 8:14) or 'children of God' (John 1:12) where there is a moral duty for believers to honour their heavenly Father (e.g., Rom. 8:13–14; 1 John 3:1–3), texts to which we shall return later.

As noted already, when we use the term 'son,' we do not intend to exclude believers who are God's 'daughters'; likewise, when we think of God as 'father' this does not exclude maternal expressions, which are also used by the biblical writers to describe God's relationship with people. Indeed, it is also more accurate to view God as *parent* because Scripture does not refer to God in exclusively masculine terms; rather paternal and maternal imagery are both used to express Yahweh's relations with his people. While 'son' is the more frequently occurring metaphor to describe believers in Scripture, Yahweh refers to Israel 'my . . . daughter my people' (Jer. 14:11) where, as John Goldingay points out, 'the expression is a term of endearment suggesting the tender relationship of father to daughter'.[12] Regarding maternal imagery, the prophet Isaiah, in some of the most tender words of Scripture, reminds Israel how God is inextricably tied to believers, like a 'mother . . . hard-wired

---

[9] Marianne Meye Thompson, *The Promise of the Father: Jesus and God in the New Testament* (Louisville: Westminster John Knox, 2000), p. 41.

[10] G. Braumann, 'Huios' in Colin Brown (ed.), *New International Dictionary of New Testament Theology*, vol. 1 (Grand Rapids: Zondervan, 1986), p. 290.

[11] Christopher J. H. Wright, *God's People in God's Land: Family, Land, and Property in the Old Testament*, BTCL 14 (Carlisle: Paternoster, 1990), pp. 16–20.

[12] John Goldingay, *Old Testament Theology*, vol. 2, *Israel's Faith* (Downers Grove: IVP and Milton Keynes: Paternoster, 2006), p. 175.

for caring':[13] 'Can a mother forget her baby at her breast and have no compassion on the child she has borne? Though she may forget, I will not forget you!' (Isa. 49:15).[14] Here, as elsewhere in Isaiah, 'God is a tender mother, whose fierce maternal love outstrips that of every human mother for her children'.[15] We even find an author mixing maternal and paternal imagery together when he depicts Yahweh as castigating his child for deserting 'the Rock, who fathered you; you forgot the God who gave you birth' (Deut. 32:18).[16] The prominence of this female imagery has prompted one scholar to conclude that a better designation for Yahweh might be 'a motherly father'.[17]

Perhaps what is most striking about all this language, and the filial language in particular, is that it is part of the wider notion of God's people as a community, a *family* or *household* comprising sons and daughters, in which Yahweh is the father *and* mother – the parent *par excellence* – of his spiritual progeny. Israel is even described as a household: 'Hear this word that the LORD has spoken against you, O people of Israel – against the whole family I brought up out of Egypt. You only have I chosen of all the families of the earth' (Amos 3:1). And in Galatians, for example, after Paul describes the Christians as 'sons' (Gal. 4:5, *huioi*) he later portrays them as 'the family of believers' (Gal. 6:10, *tous oikeious tēs pisteōs*). The metaphor of sonship is therefore an important way of helping us to think about and understand community.

Moreover, the maternal references above are of particular significance and ought not to be lightly passed over, as they demonstrate occasions when an author is breaking with the normal social expectations of culture and custom, and by so doing adding nuances of meaning that complement God's paternal care for believers. Even though 'father' may be the more prominent[18] designation, paternal and maternal references to describe God do not contradict each other; rather they are complementary aspects of God's parental responsibilities toward his spiritual offspring and we shall be sensitive to both roles as we proceed.

---

[13] Ibid., p. 112.

[14] M. Daniel Carroll, 'Family in the Prophetic Literature', in Richard S. Hess and M. Daniel Carroll (eds.), *Family in the Bible: Exploring Customs, Culture, and Context* (Grand Rapids: Baker Academic, 2003), pp. 100–124, however, rightly observes: 'Unlike the metaphor of Yahweh as father ... the image of God as mother does not have any punitive elements attached to it' (p. 119).

[15] Jacqueline E. Lapsley, ' "Look! The Children and I are as Signs and portents in Israel": Children in Isaiah', in Bunge (ed.), *Child in the Bible*, p. 102.

[16] For other examples of maternal imagery in relation to God see Isa. 42:14; 66:13.

[17] Goldingay, *Israel's Faith*, p. 110.

[18] Also, Scripture nowhere explicitly refers to God as 'Mother'.

1. Sonship as a central biblical theme[19]

Sonship is an important metaphor for understanding the grand meta-narrative of the Bible. We could even go as far as to say that sonship functions as an *inclusio* or as bookends to the whole of the biblical canon. The narrative of Scripture[20] is, in one sense, a story of sonship, a story with a single plotline with many twists and turns along the way: Adam, the first human being, is identified as a 'son of God' (Luke 3:38) and it is this same filial designation which brings Scripture to a triumphant conclusion in the penultimate chapter of the Bible with the resounding words: 'He who overcomes will inherit . . . I will be his God and he will be my son' (Gk *huios*, Rev. 21:7). Put succinctly, *'sonship to God is the apex of creation* and *the goal of redemption'*.[21] The storyline of the Bible is therefore clear in that 'God is . . . making for himself a family of sons and daughters [who] will serve him and praise him and reign with him in his kingdom forever'.[22] Of course, there are many other references to sonship sandwiched in between (e.g., Exod. 4:22–23; Deut. 8:5; 14:1–2; 2 Sam. 7:12–16; Jer. 31:9; Luke 1:36; 4:1–11; Rom. 8:12–17; 1 John 3:1–13) and these will be the substance of much of this book.[23] C. S. Lewis, the Belfast-born Christian apologist, was probably not over-stating the point when he wrote: 'when the Bible talks of . . . Sons of God . . . this brings us up against the very centre of Theology'.[24]

That 'sonship' has an important trajectory running throughout the entire canon of Scripture has caused D. A. Carson rightly to comment: 'There is a score of *dominant themes* that form the sinews holding the Bible's rich diversity of history and forms together – temple, people of God, sacrifice, *sonship* and many more – and a host of minor ones.'[25]

---

[19] I am indebted here to Sinclair B. Ferguson's fine article, 'The Reformed Doctrine of Sonship', in Nigel M. de. S. Cameron and Sinclair B. Ferguson (eds.), *Pulpit and People: Essays in Honour of William Still on his 75th Birthday* (Edinburgh: Rutherford House, 1986), p. 84.

[20] For the recovery of story in biblical studies see N. T. Wright, *The New Testament and the People of God* (London: SPCK, 1997), pp. 41–42, 139–142; Craig G. Bartholomew and Michael W. Goheen, *The Drama of Scripture: Finding our Place in the Biblical Story* (Grand Rapids: Baker Academic, 2004).

[21] Sinclair B. Ferguson, *Children of the Living God* (Edinburgh: Banner of Truth, 1989), p. 6 (italics original).

[22] 'Family', in *DBI*, pp. 264–267.

[23] We will not be considering the writings of Philo, the Qumran community, Rabbinic Judaism or Greco-Roman authors where sonship language is also found.

[24] C. S. Lewis, *Mere Christianity* (London: Fontana, 1980), p. 134.

[25] Cited from the online interview with D. A. Carson for InterVarsity (USA) for

If sonship is one of the more dominant themes of Scripture it merits closer scrutiny and study than has been given thus far. In doing so, we shall sketch the biblical thread of this theme as it unfolds throughout the Bible, noting how the metaphor functions typologically and follows an Adam-Israel-David-Christ-Christians trajectory.

a. Sonship: the focus of creation

In his autobiography *Open*, André Agassi tells how he was invited to a photo shoot with Canon, the photography company. Agassi was to drive a luxury car, a Lamborghini, dressed in a white suit, with the instructions to step out of the car, look directly at the camera, lower his sunglasses and say *Image is everything*.[26] This is how it is in today's world, but in another sense (as we shall see) for those who are God's children image really is everything. It is an often overlooked fact that Adam, the first man, is described in filial terms as 'Adam, the son of God' (Luke 3:38). The story of Adam initiates a pattern of sonship that continues throughout the larger biblical storyline. Adam's sonship has been usually understood solely in creaturely terms, a sonship which all people share by virtue of being born into the human race. But here more is probably intended for several reasons: first, 'to be a son, in the language of Genesis was to be made in the image and likeness of one's father'.[27] Scripture itself makes this very point when it records the birth of Seth to his parents, Adam and Eve, in the following terms: 'When Adam had lived 130 years, he had a son in his own likeness, in his own image' (Gen. 5:3). It is significant how the same expression is used to describe the relationship between God and Adam in Genesis 1:26: 'Then God said, "Let us make man in our image, in our likeness" (cf. Gen 5:1–2). In these texts, the implied conclusion is obvious: Seth is to Adam as Adam is to God, that is, a son. Certainly, sonship and likeness are not exactly the same reality, but they are nevertheless tightly linked together to the extent that if we were asked to explain the former the answer lies (at least in part) in what it means to be made in the likeness and image of God.

A second reason why the sonship of Adam does not reside merely in terms of him being a part of creation is the parallel which exists

---

the New Studies in Biblical Theology. The emphasis, however, is mine. The link is <http://www.ivpress.com/spotlight/2600.php>.

[26] Material taken from *Open: The Autobiography* (St Ives: HarperCollins, 2010), p. 131, italics original.

[27] Ferguson, *Children of the Living God*, p. 6.

between Adam and Christ. This is evident in the testing period of Adam in the Garden of Eden and the testing of the Second Adam, Jesus the Son of God, in the wilderness. Even though differences lie in the bountiful provision made for Adam in the garden over against the barren wasteland which is the context of Jesus' testing, what is important to note is the *timing* of the temptations – the son of God Adam's testing takes place at the inception of creation whereas Jesus' filial test takes place at the inauguration of his public ministry (Matt. 4:1–11, esp. vv. 3 and 5; Luke: 4:1–13, esp. vv. 3 and 9).[28] As a result of Adam's sin and failure to obey God's command, his sonship was lost and the image shattered, whereas in the case of Jesus, and as a result of his obedience to the voice of his Father, his sonship was authenticated (Matt. 3:17). The latter is a defining moment in the historical career of Jesus, and as a consequence of his obedience to his Father *this* Son of God is now ready to embark on his public ministry to be God's emissary to a needy world (Matt. 4:12). Also, Jesus' role as Son is unique and unmatched as he is the conduit through whom many other sons and daughters will be brought into God's household. What is interesting as regards this idea is that the apostle Paul in his letters is acutely aware of these important connections between sonship and image when he brings them both together to remind the Roman believers that God's goal for them as sons and daughters (Rom. 8:14), through Jesus, is to be 'conformed to the likeness of his Son' (Rom. 8:29).

b. Sonship: a metaphor for salvation

The book of Exodus recounts the epic story of God's people languishing in bondage to the mighty Egyptians and how Yahweh raises up a leader, Moses, whom he charges with the responsibility of confronting the tyrannical domination of the Pharaoh. What immediately strikes us here is the manner in which Moses is asked to do this, namely, by reminding Pharaoh of the special filial relationship that God is about to inaugurate between himself and the nascent nation of Israel: 'Israel is my firstborn son ... let my son go, so that he may worship me' (Exod. 4:22–23). Notably, only two chapters later the nation's filial relationship to God and its future emancipation from bondage is described in salvific terms:

---

[28] Both evangelists, Matthew and Luke, show that the devil's temptations centre on Jesus' filial relationship as Son to his Father – 'If you are the *Son of God*, tell these stones to become bread' (Matt. 4:3, 6; Luke 4:3, 9). Scholars call this a first class conditional clause and it is better translated 'Since' and not 'if'. Satan knew full well of Jesus' identity as the Son of God.

'I am the LORD, and I will bring you out from under the yoke of the Egyptians. I will free you from being slaves to them, and I will redeem you with an outstretched arm' (Exod. 6:6). Of course, and most importantly, the sin from which Yahweh rescues his son, Israel, is not their own but the sin of *their oppressors*[29] but '*God gave birth* to the nation *through God's saving act*, thereby establishing the father-child relationship'.[30] God's sovereignty is seen in the ensuing Exodus event and shows, as J. A. Motyer rightly insists, that '*sonship* and *salvation* are indissolubly linked'.[31] Looking back on this incident, the narrator of Deuteronomy describes the saving significance of the event in filial terms: 'you saw how the LORD your God carried you, as a father carries a son, all the way you went until you reached this place' (Deut. 1:31). So, when 'God redeems his people in the Old Testament, it is the filial model which most eloquently describes the relationship between the Lord and his people'.[32]

Sonship is also the saving centre of Jesus' message, a point made clear by the evangelist at the beginning of the fourth Gospel when he identifies who God's true progeny are. John makes it abundantly clear that the climactic purpose of the incarnation – the coming of God's son – was for salvation, a rescue he is careful to couch in terms of sonship: 'He came to that which was his own, but his own did not receive him. Yet to all who received him, to those who believed in his name, he gave the right to become children of God – children not born of natural descent, nor of human decision or a husband's will, but born of God' (John 1:12–13; cf. 1 John 3:1–2). Receiving Jesus, believing in his name, is salvation here expressed by John in terms of sonship.

The apostle Paul strikes a similar chord when he uses his own unique filial term 'adopted as son' (*huiothesia*)[33] which he immediately juxtaposes alongside the metaphor of slavery in order to underscore the saving significance of the death of Jesus Christ. In Galatians 4:1–7, and within a wider context of a discussion on the

---

[29] Israel's sin and wayward life as a disobedient son will manifest itself a little later in the Exodus narrative.

[30] R. Alan Culpepper, 'Children of God', NIDB, vol. 1 A–C (Nashville: Abingdon, 2010), p. 590.

[31] J. A. Motyer, *The Message of Exodus*, BST (Leicester: IVP, 2005), p. 91.

[32] Ferguson, 'Reformed Doctrine', p. 85.

[33] The Greek word *huiothesia* is used five times by Paul in three of his letters, two of them in capital epistles (i.e., Gal. 4:5; Rom. 8:15, 23; 9:4; Eph. 1:5). It should also be noted that sonship is the larger biblical category under which is subsumed the notion of adopted sonship in Paul. For a fuller treatment of this latter term see Trevor J. Burke, *Adopted into God's Family: Exploring a Pauline Metaphor*, NSBT 22 (Nottingham: IVP, 2006).

Torah, Paul illustrates,[34] by drawing on Roman law,[35] that a son who is a minor (*nēpios*) is little different to a slave. A change in the minor's position could take place, not because of anything he could do, but only because of everything the father had done ('until the time set by the father', v. 2b). The paternal emphasis should not be overlooked. In verses 3–7 Paul begins to apply the illustration by saying that just as the human father was solely responsible for determining when the minor should come of age, so God the Father has a divine timescale in mind. It was when 'we were children . . . in slavery' (v. 3) that God decisively and climactically intervened in salvation-history in the last days by sending his Son. Paul then uses two purpose clauses (Gk *hina)* to emphasis the intentionality of God the Father's action: 'But when the set time had fully come, God sent his Son, born of a woman, born under the law, to (*hina*) redeem these under the law, that (*hina*) we might receive adoption to sonship . . . so you are no longer slaves, but God's children' (Gal. 4:4–7, TNIV). The coming of the Son of God into the world is not only incarnational but sacrificial – Jesus was born to die and in so doing redeems us so that we might be adopted into God's household. No longer slaves to sin, but adopted sons and daughters of the living God – that too, for Paul, is salvation.[36]

---

[34] James M. Scott, *Adoption as Sons of God: An Investigation into the Background of HUIOTHESIA* (Tübingen: Mohr, 1992), pp. 121–186 is very much in the minority when he understands this passage within the framework of Egyptian typology. Rather than viewing Gal. 4:1–2 as illustration and 4:3–7 as the application, Scott argues these verses allude to Israel's period of bondage for forty-three years in Egypt and subsequent exodus and adoption to sonship. The former is a type of the eschatological adoption effected by Christ, which Christians partake of. However, careful scrutiny of Gal. 3 – 4 clearly shows that the whole sweep of Paul's argument is not the Egyptian period of slavery as such but upon the *following* period of bondage and captivity that was inaugurated with the introduction of the Torah.

[35] One recent interesting and significant addition in the TNIV translation has been to include a footnote for each of the Pauline adoption passages (Gal. 4:5; Rom. 8:15, 23; 9:4; Eph. 1:5) with the following comment: 'The Greek word for adoption to sonship is a legal term referring to the full legal standing of an adopted male heir in Roman culture.'

[36] See Robert A. Peterson, *Adopted by God: From Wayward Sinners to Cherished Children* (Phillipsburg: P&R Publishing, 2001), pp. 28–29, for a pastorally sensitive approach to adoption. See also Mark Stibbe, *From Orphans to Heirs: Celebrating our Spiritual Adoption* (Oxford: Bible Reading Fellowship, 1999), pp. 170–171. Mark Stibbe's book is an excellent popular treatment of adoption and is also interesting because he writes (often very movingly) as one who was adopted himself. For a more academic approach see Trevor J. Burke, 'Adopted as Sons: The Missing Piece in Pauline Soteriology', in Stanley E. Porter (ed.), *Paul: Jew, Greek and Roman*, PAST 5 (Leiden: Brill, 2008), pp. 259–287.

c. Sonship: the moral obligation

Undergirding the father-son relationship in Scripture is a whole raft of normal social expectations associated with how fathers and sons were supposed to behave. Sonship is essentially 'a functional category in the Bible'[37] and the old adage 'like father like son' was etched into the *psyche* of the ancient mind and was every bit (if not more) as important in antiquity as it is in society today. In ancient times, sons usually worked at the same occupation as their father: indeed, Jesus was a 'chip off the old block' (if you can excuse the pun) since he was probably a worker of wood, like Joseph. And James and John, sons of Zebedee, also earned their livelihood from fishing, from which Jesus called them in order to fish for people. Moreover, sons were expected to take their sense of identity from their father and to live in such a way as to honour him, in order not to bring his name or that of the household into disrepute.

Foundational to the father-son relationship was the ancient principle of reciprocity: fathers were expected to demonstrate authority, educate their offspring and be an example for their sons to follow; sons on the other hand, were expected to conduct themselves accordingly by being obedient, by imitating and by honouring their father and the family name. With this in view, God in Deuteronomy 14:1–2 – probably the oldest reference to father-son relations in the Old Testament[38] – reminds the Israelites of their filial status: 'You are children of the Lord your God', after which the author draws out the moral responsibility which this now brings: 'you are a people holy to the Lord your God'. As noted earlier, the description 'children of God' in the plural is to be distinguished from other references to Israel the nation in the singular.[39] As regards the latter (singular), the emphasis lies with what *Yahweh* has done for Israel, but more importantly in the case of the former (Deut. 14:1–2), the focus is on *what is expected by God* from his children. This point is particularly underscored by the inversion of the word order in the original language in Deuteronomy 14:1 which reads 'children of God you are' thereby accentuating the responsibility upon the sons and daughters of God, an accountability that 'includes . . . *rigorous expectations for . . . conduct*'.[40] The point is blatantly clear: the God of the Old (and New) Testament is a holy Father seeking

---

[37] D. A. Carson, 'God is Love', *Bib Sac.* 156 (1999), p. 135.

[38] Wright, *God's People*, pp. 15–16.

[39] See ch. 2 for a discussion of the nation of Israel (singular) as God's 'firstborn son' (Exod. 4:22).

[40] Walter Brueggemann, *Deuteronomy*, AOTC (Nashville: Abingdon Press, 2001), p. 156.

holy children. Put another way, there is an ethical responsibility for God's progeny to be obedient and loyal and to live in such a way as to honour God before the nations. This is no small matter because in antiquity there was no more heinous offense than for a son to besmirch the name of his father or to tarnish the family name in the eyes of outsiders.

The same moral ramifications are also at work with respect to sonship in the New Testament, only the shift in the covenants with the appearing of Christ in the last days brings an onus for God's children to live out their Christian faith in the intervening period between the 'now' and the 'not yet'. For example, Paul addresses his converts at Thessalonica[41] as 'sons of the light and sons of the day' (1 Thess. 5:5) after which he immediately exhorts them with the words: 'So then, let us not be like others, who are asleep, but let us be alert and self-controlled . . . those who get drunk get drunk at night. But since we belong to the day, let us be self-controlled, putting on faith and love' (1 Thess. 5:6–8). Paul's converts at Thessalonica consisted mostly of Gentiles brought out of paganism (1 Thess. 1:9–10), and it is not surprising that he provides these new sons and daughters with important moral instructions on how they are to live circumspectly as member of 'God's new family'.[42] 1 Thessalonians is often viewed as Paul's major treatise on eschatology (doctrine of the last things)[43] but it is most important to note how Paul brings *ethics* and *eschatology* together in order to emphasis that God's children need to live appropriately in light of the sure return of the Lord Jesus Christ. As members of God's new household the nascent converts at Thessalonica are to put aside the old ways of drunkenness and sexual immorality and instead to put on faith and love. In this regard Chuck Colson, one-time member of the Nixon administration involved in the Watergate scandal and now a Christian writer and popular speaker in the USA, rightly makes the point that 'the task of the church is not to make men and women happy; it is to make

---

[41] For a discussion of the heavy concentration of the familial imagery of nursing mother (2:7), father (2:11–12), brothers and sisters (x19), orphan (2:17) in 1 Thessalonians, see Trevor J. Burke, *Family Matters: a Socio-Historical Study of Kinship Metaphors in 1 Thessalonians*, JSNTS 247 (London: T&T Clark, 2003). See also Beverly Roberts Gaventa, *Our Mother Saint Paul* (Louisville: Westminster John Knox, 2007).

[42] See Abraham J. Malherbe, 'God's New Family in Thessalonica', in Michael L. White and O. Larry Yarbrough (eds.), *The Social World of the first Christians: Essays in Honor of Wayne A. Meeks* (Philadelphia: Fortress Press, 1995), pp. 116–125. Two moral areas where the Thessalonians were lacking are sexual (1 Thess. 4:3–8) and work ethics (1 Thess. 4:9–12).

[43] Each chapter of 1 Thessalonians ends with a reference to the second coming of God's Son (cf. 1:10; 2:19; 3:13; 4:15–16; 5:23).

them holy'.[44] As members of the church, the family of God, God's spiritual offspring have a responsibility to live upright and holy lives that really do honour the Father who himself dwells in unapproachable light. Is it any wonder that those outside the church are sometimes rightly critical of the fact that there is little difference in lifestyle between those who profess to belong to God's family and those who do not? If our sonship is to be legitimized in the eyes of a watching world there needs to be a disdain and hatred for all sin, and Christian conduct that exalts our holy, heavenly Father.

d. Sonship: the goal of restoration

We noted earlier in this chapter how sonship spans the biblical canon from Adam to the climactic statement in Revelation 21:7. Nowhere is the goal of salvation made clearer than in Romans 8:18–25 where Paul describes God's adopted children as they are caught in the limbo period between present suffering and the future glory that awaits them. The former, the present suffering, is all too readily apparent at a personal level as we all face weak and ailing bodies, sickness, and eventual death. On a more global scale, in 2008 the horrors of the present suffering were underscored by the occurrence of two major natural catastrophes, one a devastating cyclone in Myanmar where over 138,000 people died, and another in the form of a massive earthquake in China where nearly 70,000 men, women and children perished and over 374,176 were injured. Like you, I forget these are not just statistics but are real people – devastated lives, fractured families, cracked communities – and the reality is that the whole of creation, the non-human and the human order, is suffering.

This is the subject Paul addresses in Romans 8:17–25 where *suffering* (v. 17), *sonship* (v. 23) and *salvation* (v. 24) are three very important interlocking themes. Earlier in Romans 8 Paul has reminded the Roman believers of the alpha point of their adoption as God's sons and daughters (v. 15), but in verse 23 he goes on to remind them that the omega point still lies ahead. Paul here addresses the reality of living in the intervening period between the 'now' and the 'not yet'. But what for Paul and the believer does living in this 'waiting-room' period look like? A crucial contextual clue is given in verse 17 where Paul uses a conditional clause when he writes: 'Now if we are children, then we are heirs – heirs of God

---

[44] Cited in Jeffrey A. D. Weima, 'How You Must Walk to Please God: Holiness and Discipleship in 1 Thessalonians', in Richard N. Longenecker (ed.), *Patterns of Discipleship in the New Testament* (Grand Rapids: Eerdmans, 1996), pp. 98–118.

and co-heirs with Christ, if indeed we share in his sufferings in order that we may also share in his glory.' The phrase in question in this verse is 'if indeed'. Paul is not saying here that Christians *may* suffer, rather, he is dead certain that they *will*, as Thomas Schreiner's comments on this text make clear, 'this denotes a real condition that must be met for believers to enjoy their inheritance'.[45] Since Christ has suffered, believers can expect to suffer as well, of that the apostle is sure.[46] For the Christian, then, sonship and suffering are not unusual bedfellows but are actually two sides of the one coin. One *cannot* enter into one's glorious inheritance without suffering – Paul's teaching here rules out any whiff of a health-wealth gospel.

Paul's main point in Romans 8:18–25 is that not only is the non-human order suffering (vv. 19–22) but so too is the human order (v. 23), even though the former is the passive partner in the glorious future that lies ahead, as Paul had earlier stressed: 'The creation [i.e., non-human] waits in eager expectation for the sons of God to be revealed' (v. 19). In other words, the transformation of the inanimate order is *contingent* or *dependant* upon what will happen to the adopted sons and daughters of God. The physical cosmos will indeed be transformed but so also will God's children, the major partner in this cosmic drama and the ones through whom these events will come about. But crucially Paul spells out that this transformation for the adopted sons of God is no less than a *restoration* 'to the image of his Son' (v. 29, TNIV). That image, shattered as a result of the first son of God, Adam, has been put together and restored to the even greater image of Jesus, God's perfect Son. The chief purpose of the Son of God stepping out of eternity into history was so that we, the sons of humankind, might be restored to his perfect likeness. Can there be any more glorious prospect for the children of God to look forward to than this?

2. The God who is relentlessly relational

As we bring this introductory chapter to a close, we have tried to set the 'scene' for our theme. Before we begin to discuss this further, sonship raises a number of important issues that impact us as the Christian church in practical ways. God is more than a theological construct, idea or doctrine to discuss (or cause division) – the God of Scripture above everything else is a relentlessly relational Being.

---

[45] Thomas R. Schreiner, *Romans*, BECNT (Grand Rapids: Baker, 1998), p. 428.
[46] Christ's suffering is, of course, unique in that he was sinless but died in our place and as our substitute.

The three *persons* of the Trinity, Father, Son and Holy Spirit,[47] is a community, a divine family no less, in which relationship is at the heart of who God is.

Today, our society is in danger of losing the importance of relationship; indeed, in our increasingly fractured world we reduce one another to a social security number and depersonalize one another by being known in the form of an email address. Also, travel on any form of public transport and you will invariably find people listening to their MP3 player, 'tuned in and turned on to their music' but severed socially and relationally from those sitting beside them on the train, bus, aeroplane – tuned into their own particular needs but out of tune with the 'community' around them. Moreover, in today's world, family life is becoming more and more fractured and dysfunctional.

When purchasing a house an estate agent will tell us the three most important things are location, location, location. In God's economy, however and in the life of Jesus who poured himself into a motley band of twelve disciples, the three most important aspects are relationship, relationship, relationship. Eugene Peterson in his usual fresh and provocative way in a book entitled *Practice Resurrection: A Conversation on Growing up in Christ*,[48] rightly reminds us: 'God reveals himself in personal relationship and *only* in personal relationship ... God is triply personal, emphatically personal, unrelentingly personal.'[49] Christianity is not about a philosophy, a code of practice, or a religion, but a relationship. This relational aspect is also important in another way which has to do with the emphasis on the Bible as the word of God. Today, the Bible[50] has almost been given Trinitarian status to the extent that we now worship the Father, Son and the Holy *Scriptures*. There is the danger of becoming bibliolaters – worshippers of a book – rather

---

[47] It is easier for us to conceive of the Father and Son in familial terms but the Holy Spirit is also referred to in personal terms and is the third member of the divine family. In Rom. 8:12–17, a passage dominated by the language of sonship, the personal characteristics of the Spirit are especially emphasized: the Spirit *leads* (v. 14), *bears witness* (v. 16), and a little later in the chapter (Rom. 8:26–27) *intercedes*, a ministry ascribed to Jesus Christ the Son (Rom. 8:34).

[48] Eugene H. Peterson, *Practice Resurrection: A Conversation on Growing up in Christ* (Cambridge/Grand Rapids: Eerdmans, 2010). Peterson's conversation partner is Paul's letter to the Ephesians.

[49] Ibid., pp. 86–87, 198.

[50] It has been said in jest that Protestants talk a lot about Scripture and the Bible, mostly the apostle Paul, while Catholics talk mostly about the church and it is left to the atheists to talk about Jesus, but only as a swear word. Somehow the Bible or the church and *not* Jesus – the sum and substance of the Christian faith – has become central today.

than worshippers of the God who is personal and who has chosen to communicate with us in a relational way. Some Christians, students, pastors and scholars love to study Scripture, all very necessary and important (I myself am a teacher of the New Testament) in and of itself, *but do we really love Jesus?* In this respect, John Stott, who is one of the most able expositors and life-long lovers of Scripture, sounds a warning in the following account which is worth quoting in full:

> To suppose that salvation lies in a book is as foolish as supposing that health lies in a prescription. When we are ill and the doctor prescribes some medicine for us, does he intend that we should go home with the prescription, read it, study it and learn it by heart? Or that we should frame it and hang it on our bedroom wall? Or that we should tear it into fragments and eat the pieces three times a day after meals? The absurdity of these possibilities is obvious. The prescription itself will not cure us. The whole purpose of a prescription is to get us to go to the chemist, obtain the medicine prescribed and drink it. Now the Bible contains the divine prescription for sin-sick souls. It is the only medicine which can save us from perishing. In brief, it tells us of Jesus Christ who dies for us and rose again. But we do not worship the Bible as if it could save us; we go to Christ. For the overwhelming purpose of the Bible is to send us to Christ and to persuade us to drink the water of life which he offers.[51]

More than anything else the God of the Bible, revealed as Father, Son and Holy Spirit, is a relational Being. Of course, God does not need any of us, as there is perfect harmony within the Godhead, but he entered into a relationship with us – first with his chosen son Israel, but in the last days decisively and more relationally, by sending his own Son in order that Jew and Gentile might become children in the one family of God (Eph. 2:14).

As a consequence of being God's sons and daughters, we are also related to one another on the horizontal level as brothers and sisters in Jesus Christ. Thus, the theme of sonship has important ecclesial ramifications because there is no such thing as isolated children or independent offspring in God's household. We *belong* to each other because we first belong to God through Christ. As believers in Christ we are in community with one another. Margaret Thatcher was right to emphasize the importance of personal or individual

---

[51] J. R. W. Stott, *Christ the Controversialist: A Study of the Essentials of Evangelical Christianity* (London: Tyndale Press, 1970), pp. 101–102.

moral responsibility, however she overreacted when she said 'there is no such thing as society . . . There is no such thing as a collective conscience, collective kindness, collective gentleness, and collective freedom'.[52] Robin Cook, the former Labour Foreign Secretary, in his resignation speech in the House of Commons on 17 March 2003 spoke differently when he disagreed with his own government going to war against Iraq: 'The longer I have served in this place, the greater respect I have for the good sense and *collective* wisdom of the British people.'[53] Moreover, only ten years after Margaret Thatcher's comments, when Princess Diana died in 1997, there was a huge outpouring of collective grief unprecedented in the UK. In times of great extremity there is evidence of a sense of community and collective conscience, but this is being eroded more and more in our society. Parents and children no longer sit down together at the dinner table in the evening to share a meal and to catch up on what each one has been doing during the day.

But no matter how fragmented family life and society has become, relations within the church of Jesus Christ *should* be radically different, for when God calls each of us to himself by making us his children *he also calls us into community*, a united family of believers. If sonship is about anything it is about our familial identity as God's children and our relationship to each other as siblings in Christ. Plutarch, the Greek philosopher and contemporary of the apostle Paul, reminds us that real siblings 'walking together should not let a stone come between them'.[54] Were we to *really* grasp the fact that the church is a family it would revolutionize the way we *are* and *do* church. Instead, as David deSilva rightly points out, sometimes 'Christians are less than kin and less than kind to one another'.[55]

What it really means to be members in God's household was forcefully brought home to me by my brothers and sisters in Christ in the Majority World, amongst whom I have had the privilege to live and serve. Christians in Africa and the South Pacific have taught me much about the church being a loving, caring, and sharing fellowship – a genuine 'household of faith' (Gal. 6:10). The church family in the Global South often enjoys deeper bonds of community and has a greater understanding of a sense of belonging and dependence

---

[52] <http://news.bbc.co.uk/2/hi/uk_news/politics/8488752.stm>.

[53] Margaret Cook, 'Robin, I'm so Proud of you', *Daily Mail*, 6 Feb. 2010, p. 28, emphasis added; <http://www.dailymail.co.uk/news/article-1248873/MARGARET-COOK-Im-proud-Robin--youre-man-emerge-honour-Iraq-debacle.html>.

[54] The quotation is from Plutarch's treatise 'Brotherly Love', 19/490D.

[55] David deSilva, *Honor, Patronage, Kinship and Purity: Unlocking New Testament Culture* (Downers Grove: IVP, 2000), p. 238.

on one another than the church in the West. This is because believers invest time in being together, building strong relationships, and as a result treasure and care for each other. Thus, when even the lowliest member of the church family goes through difficult times and experiences adversity of one kind or another Africans actually live out their own proverb which states: 'Whenever the big toe hurts the whole body stoops to help.' In the West, we are more often driven by the clock and concerned to move on to the next item which needs to be checked off our to-do list. As a result, our relationships are sometimes shallow and our sense of community within the family of God is the poorer as a result. The old adage 'blood is thicker than water' is true, but for each of us whom God the Father has made his sons and daughters, the bonds should (and do) run deeper – much deeper – for they will last for all eternity!

Part One
Sonship in the Old Testament

Exodus 4:22–23
1. A son is born: Israel

We begin our story proper by turning to the book of Exodus and the nation of Israel. The theme of sonship is an Old Testament idea that is deeply rooted in the soil of the Hebrew Scriptures. It is here that we must begin our study of this biblical theme and in particular in the book of Exodus, especially as it pertains to Israel, our first key player, because 'Exodus is a major witness to Israel's sonship'.[1] Early in this Old Testament book and at a strategically important moment in the history of God's dealings with his people, we read the 'stunning identity',[2] what another scholar calls 'one of the great watchwords of the exodus'[3]: *Israel is my firstborn son* (22), a divine declaration that would not only echo out to the surrounding nations at that time but which would continue to reverberate for centuries to come. This is a first in the Hebrew Bible for a number of reasons, not least because it is the earliest reference to Israel as a nation whose new association to God is described in filial terms as God's *son*. It signals, moreover, a shift in the purposes of God, for this was *the* moment that salvation-history was taking a new turn – a new order was about to begin. Out of all the surrounding nations of the then known world God had singled out one nation more than any other, not because it was more powerful or numerous but simply because it was God's sovereign choice to do so. The author of Deuteronomy looking back on this event makes it abundantly clear:

[1] John J. Schmitt, 'Israel as Son of God in Torah', *BTB* 24 (2004), pp. 69–79.
[2] Walter Brueggemann, *Exodus*, NIBC (Nashville: Abingdon Press, 1994), p. 717.
[3] N. T. Wright, *Justification: God's Plan and Paul's Vision* (Nottingham: IVP, 2009), p. 130.

The LORD did not set his affection on you and choose you because you were more numerous than other peoples, for you were the fewest of all peoples. But it was because the LORD loved you and kept the oath he swore to your forefathers that he brought you out with a mighty hand and redeemed you from the land of slavery, from the power of Pharaoh king of Egypt.[4]

Of course, we should not overlook the fact that all this was in fulfilment of the earlier promise made to the patriarch Abraham when God told him: 'I will make you into a great nation and I will bless you . . . and all peoples on earth will be blessed through you.'[5]

It is a well recognized fact that the book of Exodus has as its major storyline the deliverance of the people of God from the oppression of Pharaoh; it is seldom noted, however, that this event was essentially a titanic tussle between two main protagonists which centred primarily on the notion of 'sonship'. For this is not only the moment when God would inaugurate a filial relationship with the nascent nation of Israel but there is here another 'son' with which Yahweh must contend, namely, Pharaoh's *firstborn son* (23). Thus, the statement *Israel is my firstborn son* was nothing less than

> a direct assault on the royal succession in Egypt. In all likelihood the first-born male was directly in line to follow his father on the throne: the new Pharaoh would be a god, the incarnation of Ra, eternal, omniscient, omnipotent and worthy of worship.[6]

What unfolds is a showdown between Yahweh and Pharaoh, 'the then world's first super-power',[7] as they lock horns and do battle over these respective sons, which would ultimately demonstrate who is sovereign (i.e., king) and who is really in control.

The passage itself where the filial pronouncement is located may be brief and comprise only a couple of verses, but there is a lot of theological weight that betrays their conciseness. Several points should be noted: first, the literary structure of the passage is in the form of a chiasm (so-called after the Greek letter 'chi' which is the shape of our English letter X) where a number of striking features are in evidence:

---

[4] Deut. 7:7–8.
[5] Gen. 12:2–3.
[6] John Currid, *Exodus*, vol.1 (Darlington: Evangelical Press, 2000), p. 114.
[7] J. A. Motyer, *The Message of Exodus*, BST (Leicester/Downers Grove: IVP, 2005), p. 114.

A *say to Pharaoh . . . Israel is my firstborn son* (22)
   B *And I told you, let my son go* (23)
      C *so he may worship me*
   B[1] *But you refused to let him go*
A[1] *so I will kill your firstborn son*

Second, the chiasm is concentrically structured and is framed by twin references and a play on words between the firstborn son of Israel and the putting to death of the firstborn son in Egypt (AA[1]). The theme of sonship, therefore, functions as bookends or as a literary *inclusio* in the whole passage and is 'the central factor in the liberation of Israel'.[8] This is immediately followed by two parallel statements in the inner part of the chiasm (BB[1]) which describe the redemption or emancipation of Israel from slavery. Also peppered throughout the structure is a proliferation of first and second person pronouns ('I' and 'you'): *my firstborn son; I told you; Let my son go, so that he may worship me;* and *I will kill your firstborn son*, all of which accentuates the personal nature of the clash between Yahweh and Pharaoh. The statement situated at the centre, however, is the climax of the chiasm and provides the reason for Yahweh's spectacular intervention to save his son – *so he may worship/serve me* (C).

We need to look further at what it all means. As we do so, we should note that the statement *Israel is my firstborn* is an important one, and the first in the chiasm, which raises a number of matters that we will spend some time considering prior to looking at God's promise of a dramatic deliverance.

1. The birth of a nation: Israel, God's firstborn son (4:22)

Contextually, the declaration *Israel is my firstborn son* (22) is immediately prefaced by a specific command given to Moses by Yahweh: *Then say to Pharaoh, 'This is what the LORD says'*. Moses is the person charged with the responsibility of speaking on behalf of God, which in one sense is not surprising because there are important parallels in his life experience and that of Israel's. Both, for example, are rescued from a water ordeal (cf. Exod. 2:3–10; 14 – 15); escape to Midian (cf. Exod. 2:11–22; 16 – 18); and experience a theophany (cf. Exod. 3; 19). More important, both know what it means to live in slavery and oppression (cf. Exod 2:1–2; 3:7), which is significant, for the announcement that Yahweh's firstborn

---

[8] Matthew Vellanickal, *The Divine Sonship of Christians in the Johannine Writings*, AnBib. 72 (Rome: Biblical Institute Press, 1977), p. 10.

son is called 'Israel' comes at a strategic moment for the people of God – they are currently languishing in bondage and oppression, subject to cringing fear and the ruthless control of their Egyptian taskmasters (Exod. 1:11). Earlier in the book we learn that part of Pharaoh's brutal regime was to introduce birth control measures in an effort to curtail the male population of the Hebrews (Exod. 1:22). Thus, at this time God's people are helpless and utterly hopeless, a point made clear by the author's repeated description of them as a household of slaves (e.g., Exod. 13:3, 14; 20:2, LXX). Yahweh, however, is about to intervene in spectacular fashion by taking the necessary action in order to emancipate this slave and does so with an unforgettable opening salvo: *This is what the LORD says: Israel is my firstborn son* (22). Yahweh's decisive action on behalf of this people is paramount in the relationship, for the pronouncement is a reminder that the nation's filial relationship is solely and directly a result of the divine initiative and underscores the sovereignty of God as well as the immense privilege of belonging to his household.

It is also an act of divine favour, as James D. G. Dunn notes: 'The story of Israel's salvation is to be found in nothing in themselves and in nothing in what they were doing or could do as a slave people. *But solely in the grace of God*'.[9] Previously known as a slave to a tyrant and as 'my people' in relation to God, this people have now been singled out to become a nation with the distinctively intimate and familial expression of *my . . . son*.[10]

To be called a *firstborn son* also underscores the fact that Israel was in a position of prominence and pre-eminence and had the right of headship over the family after the father, the head of the household, died. A firstborn son received double the inheritance (Deut. 21:17) that is unless, as in the case of Esau, he sold his birthright to his younger brother and so instead of Esau exercising his right as the head of the family, Jacob assumed this role and the privileges that went with it (Gen. 25:29–34). A firstborn son enjoyed an elevated status within the household as a person of honour, which brought accompanying responsibilities and privileges to ensure the family name was not brought into disrepute. Such a son was in turn consecrated to the Lord, a point made clear later in the book of Exodus in respect of the physical family, when Yahweh himself affirms: 'the first offspring of every womb among the Israelites belongs to me, whether human or animal' (Exod.

[9] James D. G. Dunn, *New Testament Theology: An Introduction*, LBT (Louisville: Abingdon Press, 2009), p. 76 (emphasis added).

[10] Brueggemann, *Exodus*, p. 717.

13:2, TNIV; Num. 3:12; 8:16). Israel as son is therefore attached to the Lord, an association which is not transient or fleeting but a lasting reality, because no matter what would happen a firstborn son could not finally be cast out (Jer. 31:9). Indeed, as the firstborn son continued the family line into the next generation, so this filial identification for the nation of Israel was symbolic of Yahweh's relationship and divine ownership of the nation in the succeeding generations.

But there is irony in this pronouncement as well, for the name by which God's son is to be called will be 'Israel', meaning 'struggles with God', which not only points back in time but also forward to the future. Regarding the former, the name is traced to Jacob and his encounter with God at Peniel (Gen. 32:28) where he 'struggled' with Yahweh and was renamed 'Israel'. In respect of the latter, the name 'Israel' points prospectively, for while this 'son' will soon be delivered from Egyptian bondage, the nation's filial struggles are by no means over. Rather, the path ahead for this new son will be one strewn with adversity and hardships, difficulties it has to be said that were often of Israel's own making. Thus, bound up with the nation's new name 'Israel' and the new designation 'son' is the *important subtheme of suffering*. This note is already evident in the current turmoil and bondage which Israel was experiencing and accentuates the ensuing actions of Yahweh on behalf of the nation, making it a poignant and pivotal moment in the salvific purposes of God. But, significantly, the place of suffering is *also* the place of provision (and deliverance) in which this new relationship as 'son' is born. In other words, the place of suffering becomes a *theo*phanic place, the place where *God* manifests himself to his people in a way that we do not expect. This close nexus of sonship *and* suffering, moreover, is one that runs the gamut of the Scriptures, for these twin realities are not only worked out here in the life of the nation of Israel and the Israelites in the Old Testament (e.g., Deut. 14:1–2), but continue, as we shall see, into the New Testament, specifically in the life of Jesus as the suffering Son of God (e.g., Rom. 8:17) as well as in the lives of believers as the sons and daughters of God as they groan their way to glory (e.g., Rom. 8:18–25).

a. Israel: God's adopted or firstborn son?

One of the key debates that surrounds the declaration *Israel is my firstborn (běkôr) son* (22) has to do with how to understand the nature of Israel's filial relationship to Yahweh. Some scholars like James I. Cook regard Israel as being in an 'adoptive relationship to

Yahweh . . . [which is] foundational to the Old Testament'.[11] Cook is partly swayed by Paul's remarks in Romans 9:4 where he reminds the Roman house churches of the many privileges the Israelites possessed: 'Theirs [the Israelites] is the adoption as sons; theirs the divine glory, the covenants, the receiving of the law, the temple worship and the promises.' Paul certainly understood Israel as an adopted son and it is often assumed that the relationship described in Exodus 4:22 is an adoptive one; however, when we look for the term which Paul uses to refer to adoption (i.e., *huiothesia*), it is not found in the Greek translation of the Old Testament scriptures (LXX) or any other literature contemporary with the apostle for that matter (e.g., Philo the Jewish exegete or Josephus the historian). We would have expected the above Greek term for adoption which Paul uses for the Israelites (Rom. 9:4) to have been employed in the Old Testament (LXX), but it is nowhere be found.

There are at least two reasons why it is unlikely that Israel's relationship to God is an adoptive one. First, the Jews did not practise adoption and there is no mention of or provision made for such a practice in biblical law. Second, there were other procedures in place in Israelite society that obviated the need for adoption, as Leon Morris[12] helpfully points out:

> Provisions such as polygamy, the giving of a concubine to provide children and the levirate marriage took care of most situations. This probably accounts for the fact that there are no laws on adoption in the Old Testament and that even the word is lacking.

The language used in Exodus 4:22 to describe God's relationship to Israel as son is different to the apostle Paul's language in his letters (i.e. Rom. 8:15, 23; 9:4; Gal. 4:5; Eph. 1:5). When the nation is described as *Israel is my firstborn son* in Exodus, the author is drawing from a different conceptual field, that of biological or natural birth. Of course, there is no notion of a physical relationship between God and Israel as there was in other religions between their deities and the people. The same language of 'birth', moreover, is used later in Deuteronomy 32:6, 18 where we read, 'Is he not your Father . . . the God who gave you birth' (cf. Hos. 11:1; John

---

[11] James I. Cook, 'The Concept of Adoption in the Theology of Paul', in James I. Cook (ed.), *Saved by Hope: Essays in Honor Richard C. Oudersluys* (Grand Rapids: Eerdmans, 1978), p. 131; see also George A. F. Knight, *A Christian Theology of the Old Testament*, BTCL 21 (Carlisle: Paternoster, 1998), p. 160.

[12] Leon Morris, *The Epistle to the Romans* (Leicester: IVP, 1988), p. 314. See Trevor J. Burke, *Adopted into God's Family: Exploring a Pauline Metaphor*, NSBT 22 (Nottingham: IVP, 2006), ch. 3 and Appendix.

1:12–13). Indeed, in Jeremiah 31:20 the prophet describes Yahweh's consuming affection for the nation of Israel as follows

> is not Ephraim my dear son,
> the child in whom I delight?
> . . . my heart yearns for him;
> I have great compassion for him

where the word 'compassion' in the Hebrew means 'womb' (*raḥămîm*). The language of *birth* means that Israel owed its national existence as son to the creative or 'procreative action of Yahweh'.[13] In Exodus 4:22–23 then, God's son is brought into the world and onto the world stage, a true *birth*day moment, signalling the beginning of a long and lasting relationship and 'privileged position'[14] for the nation of Israel. Just as in the ancient Near East, where sons were educated and trained for the outside world, so now Israel will undergo a period of instruction and preparation by Yahweh for its filial role in the cosmos.[15]

The language of biological birth used in Exodus therefore stands in contrast to Paul's adoption term, which is a *legal* expression rooted in the Roman socio-legal context of the first century and describes the legal transaction or transfer of a son, usually an adult, out of one family and the placement of him in another family with all the attending privileges and responsibilities. Commenting on the Exodus text Old Testament scholar Walter C. Kaiser[16] rightly observes that the Hebrew word *bēn* 'son' connotes

> a familial relationship: a people who made up the family of God. *Israel was not a family in an adopted sense* or a mere ethnic, political, or social unity. Rather, it was a family formed, saved, and guarded by God the 'Father' of this family.

'God gave birth to the nation through his saving act, thereby establishing the father-son relationship with Israel.'[17] Brendan Byrne, who, in seeking to situate the term 'son' against its Jewish background comes to the same conclusion. God's association with

[13] Christopher J. H. Wright, *God's People in God's Land: Family, Land, and Property in the Old Testament*, BTCL 14 (Carlisle: Paternoster, 1990), p. 16.

[14] *TDOT* II, 'Bekôr', pp. 121.

[15] Schmitt, 'Israel as Son of God', p. 79.

[16] Walter C. Kaiser, *The Promise-Plan of God: A Biblical Theology of the Old and New Testaments* (Grand Rapids: Zondervan, 2008), pp. 70–71 (emphasis added).

[17] R. Alan Culpepper, 'Children of God', NIDB vol. 1, A-C, p. 590.

the nation of Israel was not one of adoption; rather he states 'Israel was . . . in a relationship of *sonship* with respect to God'.[18]

b. Sonship as an expression of the covenant

Another significant issue which the pronouncement *Israel is my firstborn son* (22) raises is whether Yahweh's relationship to the nation can be understood as an expression of the covenant. J. A. Motyer makes the point that 'the whole story of Exodus is a covenant narrative';[19] moreover, the connection between the covenant and household terminology, used here to describe the nation of Israel, is a close one. As William Dumbrell points out, 'when delineating the Sinai relationship we cannot overlook the very important use of kinship terminology and family terms'.[20] The two ideas (sonship and covenant) are related in the sense that both demonstrate a number of similar aspects: for example, just as the notion of covenant is a statement of God's intent, so too the initiatory declaration *Israel is my firstborn son* carries with it the objective of Yahweh for this nascent nation. God is intentionally entering into a new relationship with Israel. Further still, when God enters into a covenant in Old Testament terms it is also a claim of ownership and expectation, two aspects which undergird God's relationship with Israel his son – the nation comes under the sovereign protection of Yahweh which carries with it an accompanying responsibility to live in accordance with the Father's demands. That there is a relationship between the two notions cannot be doubted, as Denis McCarthy points out, 'the concept of Israel's divine sonship in the Old Testament is very like the concept of . . . the covenant'.[21]

There are important differences between them, however, for it is clear that one can break a covenant, but one cannot stop being a son to one's father.[22] Also, the relationship between Yahweh and

---

[18] Brendan Byrne, *'Sons of God' – 'Seed of Abraham': A Study of the Idea of the Sonship of God of All Christians in Paul Against the Jewish Background*, AnBib. 83 (Rome: Rome Biblical Institute, 1979), p. 81. I have argued this view in fuller detail in Burke, *Adopted into God's Family*, pp. 48–54.

[19] Motyer, *Exodus*, p. 20.

[20] William J. Dumbrell, *Covenant and Creation: A Theology of the Old Testament Covenants*, BTCL 12 (Carlisle: Paternoster Press, 1984), p. 99. Paul R. House, *Old Testament Theology* (Downers Grove: IVP, 1998), p. 95, also writes in relation to Exod. 4:22: 'Both Israel and David have a covenant with the Lord that amounts to a family relationship'.

[21] Denis McCarthy, 'Israel, My Firstborn Son', *The Way* 5 (1965), pp. 186.

[22] Christopher J. H. Wright, *Knowing God the Father Through the Old Testament* (Oxford: Monarch, 2007), p. 84.

Israel is not a natural one[23] but one which is new and which God has chosen to initiate and enter into with Israel. This is the very essence of any covenantal relationship, for a covenant essentially forges relationships between two parties or people that are not 'natural' as are those between *real* parents and their children. Real parents, for example, do not have to commit to looking after their offspring – it is inherent in the relationship and comes with the turf of real family relationships. A covenant however, as John Goldingay points out,

> comes to be involved when people extend a commitment *beyond such natural groupings*, as happens when two people get married, or when a kinship group extends its membership to a people not born within it, or when two nations enter into a covenant or treaty relationship.[24]

This suitably describes what is happening between Yahweh and the nation in the declaration *Israel is my firstborn son* – Yahweh enters into an association with Israel, previously unknown to him as a nation, a relationship that is not 'natural'.[25] But what is remarkable about this declaration is that although it is not a natural familial relationship, the nation's connection with Yahweh is nevertheless couched in the language of the household. In summary, while the language in Exodus 4:22 may not be as overtly covenantal as the more explicit royal statement between Yahweh and King David in 2 Samuel 7:8–16 which we will consider later,[26] it comes close to the language of the covenant in the Old Testament. In fact, the declaration *Israel is my firstborn son* in Exodus 4:22 describing Yahweh's relationship with Israel as son may even be a circumlocution, a roundabout way of articulating the covenant. As one commentator has remarked, sonship is 'another way of expressing the covenantal relationship and added a more personal and relationally durable dimension to it'.[27]

---

[23] A much debated point is the origin of the term 'covenant' itself and whether it stems from the physical family or from the very nature of 'family' within the Godhead; see Jeffrey J. Niehaus, 'Covenant: An Idea in the Mind of God', *JETS* 52.2 (2009), pp. 225–246.

[24] John Goldingay, *Old Testament Theology*, vol. 2, *Israel's Faith* (Downers Grove: IVP and Milton Keynes: Paternoster, 2006), p. 183.

[25] Perhaps more than a metaphor is at work in the relationship between Yahweh and Israel – it is literal and real; see David R. Tasker, *Ancient Near Eastern Literature and the Hebrew Scriptures about the Fatherhood of God*, St.BL 69 (New York: Peter Lang, 2004), p. 191.

[26] See ch. 3.

[27] Christopher J. H. Wright, *Deuteronomy*, NIBC (Peabody: Hendrickson Publishers and Carlisle: Paternoster Press, 1996), p. 32.

2. A Sovereign Father who intervenes on behalf of his son (4:23)

a. 'Let my son go . . .'

No sooner has Yahweh informed Pharaoh of Israel's new filial identity than he is told via Moses: *And I told you, let my son go* (23b). Since the book of 'Exodus is the story of the son of God who stands in need of salvation'[28] it is not surprising that Yahweh will want to jealously guard this special relationship with the nation, and he is about to take the necessary steps to ensure this will happen. The reason for this is clear: Yahweh as father has rights and so speaks authoritatively in those terms. Also bound up with the notion of the firstborn is the fact that a

> father has the right to expect that his firstborn son will work with him and for him, and eventually accept responsibility for the house and the fields or flocks, and if necessary responsibility for his father and mother and other family members who cannot look after themselves.[29]

Israel belonged to God and God expected that his son would serve him loyally in the years that lie ahead. Israel was the one in whom Yahweh's (and the world's) hopes and intentions to bless the world depended. Presently, however, the nation in its current infancy status is vulnerable and easily preyed upon, and in need of rescue and protection. But as one commentator has asked in relation to Yahweh's responsibility and in regard to this text: 'what parent would not go to the end of the world to protect his or her child? Especially a child that has been imprisoned, beaten, enslaved or worse?'[30] Indeed, if Yahweh is to be known by any name it is surely as a protector of the weak, the vulnerable and the ill-treated, and in Old Testament times children (not to mention widows, the poor and the orphan) all fell into that category. But as things are, Pharaoh is standing in the way of Israel as the firstborn son receiving the inheritance to which it is rightly due.

Pharaoh's heart was so hardened and encrusted that in order for him to release Yahweh's son Israel it would require a judgment

---

[28] Motyer, *Exodus,* p. 23.

[29] John Goldingay, *Old Testament Theology,* vol. 1, *Israel's Gospel* (Downers Grove: IVP and Milton Keynes: Paternoster, 2003), p. 320.

[30] Brent A. Strawn, 'Israel, My Child: The Ethics of a Biblical Metaphor', in Marcia J. Bunge, (ed.) *The Child in the Bible* (Grand Rapids/Cambridge: Eerdmans, 2008), p. 115.

commensurate with the action of which Pharaoh himself was guilty, killing the male Israelite babies (Exod. 1:22). Pharaoh was going to pay by losing his firstborn son, as the text makes clear: *Let my son go . . . But if you refuse to let him go I will kill your firstborn son* (23). In other words, the punishment will fit the crime, or as one author has rather graphically and succinctly put it: 'Israel is *my* family. You mess with *my* family, I'll kill *your* kid.'[31] Yahweh's action to remove Pharaoh's firstborn son was therefore a direct assault on royal succession, for in Egyptian thought the firstborn male stood in line to the father's throne and the new Pharaoh would be a god and regarded as an incarnation of Ra.[32] This tit-for-tat sonship, which is essentially a simple principle of Hebrew law, the so-called '*lex talionis*' (Exod. 21:23), is for real and Yahweh is now 'playing for keeps, the only way a treasuring, concerned parent can'.[33] The upshot of this head-to-head encounter and Yahweh's actions have been put well by one commentator:

> In the dispute about the question to whom Israel belongs and who is her legitimate ruler, Pharaoh or Yahweh, Yahweh at last will show that he has intimate emotional ties with Israel. Pharaoh had better know that to Yahweh Israel is not just his own people, they are also dear to him . . . *Pharaoh is going to be hit at his most sensitive spot*, the spot where he has touched Yahweh himself, in the love for the firstborn son.[34]

The next section provides the outcome of this head-to-head encounter.

b. '. . . so that he may serve me' (ESV)

Yahweh finally provides the reason why Israel should be released, which is purposely stated and sits at the centre of the chiasm: *so that he may serve me* (23). Yahweh's actions will have massive repercussions never before seen on such a scale. Uncertain times call for the certain actions of a sovereign God to intervene in the affairs of this emerging nation – Yahweh will not tolerate anyone getting in the

---

[31] Burton L. Visotzky, *The Road to Redemption: Lessons from Exodus on Leadership and Community* (New York: Crown Pub. 1998), p. 74 (emphasis added).

[32] Jeffrey J. Niehaus, *Ancient Near Eastern Themes in Biblical Theology* (Grand Rapids: Kregel, 2008), pp. 37ff.

[33] Brueggemann, *Exodus*, p. 720 (emphasis added).

[34] Cornelius Houtman, *Exodus*, transl. Johan Rebel and Sierd Woudstra, 3 vols., HCOT (Kampen: Kok, 1993), 1:430 (emphasis added).

way, least of all a Pharaoh who thinks he can decide the destiny of God's special son. Where family relationships are concerned the well of divine passion runs very deep in a narrative like this, where sonship, sovereignty and salvation all join hands.

The central question in the encounter is this: who really is in control and to whom does Israel really belong? And who was this son going to really serve? At its most fundamental level this struggle, as Brevard Childs observes, is a 'conflict . . . over *paternal power*'[35] and Yahweh's decisive action is nothing less than the taking of a slave from 'under the *patria potestas* of Pharaoh'[36] by establishing another household in which God is the new *paterfamilias* (head of a household)[37] of the nation, Israel, his firstborn son. The earlier command to *let my son go* points up the fact that the long period of serfdom to the Egyptians is about to be fully and finally eclipsed by a new and lasting relationship of sonship to God. Put another way, the whips of slavery and oppression are to be discarded and replaced with the filial cords of God's paternal love for his new son, Israel. Yahweh's intervention is timely and the events that are about to ensue are nothing short of a manifestation of 'the grace of *salvation* . . . [which] bestows the grace of *sonship*'.[38]

This question of who Israel as son will serve in the future will be a recurring one – not only for the nation but also later for Christ as Son of God (e.g., Matt. 4:1–11) as well as for believers as the sons and daughters of God (e.g., Rom 8:13–14) – that strikes at the very heart of the nation's filial relationship with God. Indeed, who we serve and who is in control of our lives are important questions, for no-one is entirely free. Here, it should be noted, Israel is really exchanging one kind of servitude for another. There is not and cannot ever be a *via media* or halfway house as far as serving God is concerned. Jesus makes this same point in the Sermon on the Mount when he challenges his disciples as to where their allegiance lies and whether or not they are storing up earthly or heavenly riches: 'No one can *serve* [Gk be a 'slave' of] two masters. Either he will hate the one and love the other, or he will be devoted to the one and despise the other. You cannot *serve* [Gk be a 'slave' of] both God

[35] Bervard S. Childs, *The Book of Exodus* (Philadelphia: Fortress Press, 1974), p. 102.

[36] Mark Stibbe, *From Orphans to Heirs: Celebrating our Spiritual Adoption* (Oxford: Bible Reading Fellowship, 1999), p. 42.

[37] Leo G. Perdue, 'The Household : Old Testament Theology and Contemporary Hermeneutics', in Leo G. Perdue *et al.* (eds.), *Families in Ancient Israel* (Louisville: Westminster John Knox Press, 1997), p. 229.

[38] Motyer, *Exodus,* p. 91.

and Money'.[39] Paul in Romans 6:15–23 makes a similar point by reminding the Romans Christians that they too have moral choices to make which demonstrate whether they are still 'slaves to sin' (v. 20) or 'slaves to God' (v. 22).

Certainly for Israel as son there was none of the crippling or cringing fear associated with being under the domination and tyranny of Pharaoh. But Israel is about to move from one form of servitude to another, as Leviticus 25:55 looking back on this event makes clear: 'For the Israelites belong to me as servants [or 'slaves']. They are my servants [or 'slaves'], whom I brought out of Egypt. I am the LORD your God.' Such is the paradox for this child of God, a paradox captured in the hymn of George Matheson, the remarkable blind Scottish preacher, when he wrote:

> Make me a captive, Lord,
>   *and then* I shall be free;
> Force me to render up my sword,
>   and I shall conqueror be.
> I sink in life's alarms,
>   when by myself I stand;
> Imprison me within thine arms,
>   and strong shall be my hand.[40]

c. A young son who needs to grow

The imagery of God birthing Israel his *firstborn son* (22) into being in order to be brought under his sovereignty is also a reminder that this nation is a fledgling youngster who needs to develop and mature. Eugene Peterson rightly makes the connections when he states that 'Exodus is birth *and* infancy'.[41] The prophet Hosea looking back on this event describes the nation's infancy status as follows: 'When Israel was a child, I loved him, and out of Egypt I called my son'[42] where the filial term 'highlights *the childlike status of Israel*,'[43] and therefore greatly accentuates the hard-hearted actions of Pharaoh in failing to release God's son. The giving birth to a child in the natural realm, moreover, is a more instantaneous (though very painful act, I am reliably informed by my wife!) action than growing up into maturity, which is often an arduous and longer path that lasts

---

[39] Matt. 6:24.
[40] Emphasis added.
[41] Eugene G. Peterson, *The Message* (Colorado Springs: NavPress, 2005), p. 16 (emphasis added).
[42] Hos. 11:1.
[43] Strawn, 'Israel, My Child', p. 115.

throughout life. This new filial association with God is therefore not to be understood as a static relationship; rather, it is a developing one where the need for growth is important. 'Sonship', moreover, is a dynamic relationship and 'it has to be a conscious sonship expressed in actions according to the wishes of the father's heart'.[44] In other words, functionality lies at the heart of the relationship, for just as this is a 'Father in terms of not what he is, but of what he *does*, so the son is son precisely in the continued *action* of his life as son'.[45] Thus, the emphasis on sonship suggests the need for responsibility and maturation for Israel, as another writer concludes:

> In need (*immature*) and growing up (*maturing*), Israel's self-presentation as a child and the self-understanding that comes by means of this metaphor constitutes a profound confession of immaturity, need for further growth, and dependent status.[46]

The inauguration of a new filial relationship with Israel in Exodus 4:22 is a reminder to us that God's young offspring stands on the threshold of life, with all the prospects and potential that lie ahead. As we read this text, the sense of privilege wrapped up with all the possibilities of a bright future that could ensue cause the heart to beat faster and the pulse to quicken. For what will become of this young son? How will this child turn out? In the natural realm, there is nothing more disappointing than for a parent to see a young infant who fails or refuses to make progress through all the many stages of development – from infancy into childhood and the teenage years, culminating in a well-rounded and mature adult. Imagine, if you will, a mother with a thirty-year-old son dressed in a suit who instead of having grown up into adulthood is still sitting on her knee – it is preposterous! So also in the spiritual realm Israel needs to grow up.

Important too from a divine perspective is that the emancipation of the people of God from slavery and the establishing of a new relationship of sonship is not a *carte blanche* for the nation to do as it pleases. It is not God's will for this youngster to remain in an infantile status but to grow and mature. For this to actually happen will mean coming under the tutelage and training of Yahweh as Father in order to learn how to progress into adulthood. Thus, bound up with the relationship is the expectation for this son to make good moral choices and to behave honourably in the eyes of other surrounding

---

[44] Vellanickal, *Divine Sonship*, p. 17.
[45] Ibid.
[46] Strawn, 'Israel, My Child', p. 127 (author's own emphasis).

nations. As we read this text, we left to wonder about this young child; the problem with growth is that it takes time and brings with it much uncertainty and, as is often the case, we will only find out later how this son really turns out.

d. A son saved from slavery into community

We noted in our introductory chapter how sonship proved for Israel to be a significant saving event, emancipation from the slavery and domination of the Egyptians. When we put Exodus 4:22–23 alongside the later text of Exodus 6:7 we see this salvific aspect more clearly. In the former, the Lord stated *Israel is my firstborn son . . . let my son go, so that he may worship me* and the full implications of the nation's liberation are described as follows: 'I am the Lord, and I will bring you out from under the yoke of the Egyptians. I will free you from being slaves to them and I will redeem you with an outstretched arm.'[47] Israel, God's son, is spectacularly rescued *from* the oppression and captivity of the Egyptians. But the story does not end there for salvation is not something that is merely 'or quintessentially deliverance *from Egyptian bondage*' but is to be more positively understood also as 'deliverance *into* community'.[48] This point is made clearer in Deuteronomy 4:20 where the writer reflects on events in the past: 'But as for you, the Lord took you and brought you out of the iron-smelting furnace, out of Egypt, to be the people of his inheritance, as you now are.' The upshot of all this, as Joseph Hellerman has helpfully pointed out, 'is that salvation in the Old Testament is a community-creating event. God saved the Israelites not just so they could relate to him as individuals but, most importantly, "to be the *people* of his inheritance".'[49]

This communal aspect in the Old Testament is one which is picked up in the New Testament, as is evident by the plural descriptions 'sons of God' (e.g. Matt. 5:9; Gal. 3:26). It is so important as we read the Scriptures that we grasp just how fundamentally important the sense of community was to the ancient way of life where *the group always trumps and is prized above the individual*. In light of the seismic events in life of the nation of Israel, God's son and their spectacular rescue from Egyptian slavery, God has called them from bondage into a lifetime of community, a new family no less, where

---

[47] Exod. 6:7.
[48] Joseph H. Hellerman, *When the Church was a Family: Recapturing Jesus' Vision for Authentic Christian Community* (Nashville: Broadman and Holman Academic, 2008), p. 128.
[49] Ibid. (emphasis added).

they are to know the joys and sorrows, the blessings and the struggles, as they walk, serve and fellowship *with each other* as sons and daughters (e.g. Deut. 14:1–2) of the living God.

Summary

We began our journey in the Old Testament by considering a key biblical text in the story of sonship (Exod. 4:22–23) and of salvation-history, when God intervenes in the life and dealings of a people by making them into a nation, a nation whom he called Israel, his firstborn son. In language akin to the covenant, this son is saved from the bondage and slavery of the Egyptian Pharaoh who himself paid for his own tyrannical actions by the killing of his firstborn son. In giving birth to the nation Israel, this child now comes under the sovereignty and tutelage of God as Father in order to be trained and taught and with the accompanying expectation to grow and obey. This calling, moreover, was also a call to community so that these sons and daughters of God may walk together on the long journey that lies ahead. Thus, as this young child sets out with the potential of a bright future and the whole of life stretching ahead, there is a palpable sense of optimism as we ponder how this filial relationship will turn out.

Deuteronomy 1:31; 8:5; 14:1–2; 32:1–43
2. A son heading home

Walter Brueggemann in the preface of his insightful book *The Land: Place as Gift, Promise, and Challenge in Biblical Faith* begins with an appraisal of contemporary society and what it means for many in our world to feel lost, isolated and to have no place or sense of belonging. He describes what life is like for the many millions of people who have fallen on difficult times and who live in 'cardboard city' with no settled abode, alienated from others in our increasingly fractured society. In downtown Chicago and only a few blocks from where I am writing these words, shops with luxury goods in their windows sit in uneasy juxtaposition alongside the many homeless people who daily wander the streets of this metropolis looking for another quarter to help them find something to eat and a place to stay for the night. Brueggemann, in his usual perceptive way, captures the sense of alienation when he writes that 'this sense of being lost, displaced and homeless is pervasive in contemporary culture. The yearning to belong somewhere, to have a home, to be in a safe place, is a deep and moving pursuit. Loss of place and yearning for place are dominant images.'[1]

Brueggemann's comments would have suitably resonated with the nation of Israel, who having been released from slavery in Egypt by an act of son-making had been living a nomadic existence – a sojourning son no less – by wandering for forty long years in the wilderness. As the curtain lifts on the book of Deuteronomy, the nation is poised on the borders of Canaan, the promised land, which it is about to enter. The nation of Israel may be God's son, but this is a son who is currently destitute and without any fixed abode. All

---

[1] Walter Brueggemann, *The Land: Place as Gift, Promise, and Challenge in Biblical Faith* (Minneapolis: Augsburg Fortress, 2002), p. 1.

this is about to change, however, for in accordance with Mosaic law, the firstborn son was the one who would inherit, and God had already promised the nation of Israel a piece of real-estate, the land, as Exodus 15:17 makes clear: 'You will bring them in and plant them on the mountain of your inheritance – the place, O LORD, you made for your dwelling, the sanctuary, O LORD, your hands established.' These twin notions of sonship (i.e., Israel) and the land, moreover, are not only deeply emotive topics for some believers today but are so closely interwoven together in Deuteronomy that they have prompted one commentator to ask vis-à-vis Israel's predicament: 'What was the LORD's *firstborn son* doing languishing in a foreign country when his *inheritance* awaited him?'[2] What indeed?, we might add, but it is precisely this question which the book of Deuteronomy answers, for if Deuteronomy is about anything it is most certainly about a son heading 'home'.[3]

1. A firstborn son's inheritance: the land (1:31)

a. Remember what you are: no longer a slave but a son

This verse is situated in the first section of the book of Deuteronmy, which comprises three main speeches made by Moses the prophet[4] with the remainder of the book taking the form of three 'appendices': 'The Song of Moses' (Deut. 32); 'The Blessing of Moses' (Deut. 33); and 'The Death of Moses' (Deut. 34). The main purpose of this first speech (1:6 – 4:49), is essentially didactic as well as being a warning to Israel of the seductions which await their entry into the Promised Land. Appropriately, then, the command to 'Remember' (e.g., Deut. 4:10; 8:2; 9:7; 11:2; 32:7) is a key word repeatedly sounded both as a reminder to Israel of what God had accomplished on their behalf, but also as an order for them to reflect on what they had been (i.e. slaves): 'Remember that you were slaves in Egypt and that the LORD your God brought you out of there with a mighty hand and an outstretched arm.'[5] Israel should not forget their previous relationship to their taskmasters in Egypt but the command 'remember'

---

[2] Christopher J. H. Wright, *Old Testament Ethics for the People of God* (Downers Grove: IVP, 2004), p. 88 (emphasis added).
[3] Having said this, it is also true that Israel and the Israelites were a people constantly on the move and the author or editor of the book of Deuteronomy knows full well that this is not the final destination because the nation will be ejected from the land, before finally being returned (cf. Deut. 32).
[4] Deut 1:6 – 4:49; 5:1 – 28:68; 29:1 – 31:29.
[5] Deut. 5:15.

was also a memory aid to reflect on God's gracious dealings with them and to help shape their life together as a community.

Against what they once were, Deuteronomy 1:31 sounds the note of how God has intervened in saving power by bringing his people out of the bondage of Egypt into an intimate, familial relationship and establishing Israel the nation as son. Thus, they are not to be afraid as they go forward for *the LORD your God carried you, as a father carries his son, all the way you went until you reached this place*. The filial note struck early on is a particularly important one as far as an understanding of this key Old Testament book is concerned. Although there may only be a handful of references to Israel's relationship to God as son (cf. 1:31; 8:5; 14:1–2; 32:6), 'Deuteronomy stand[s] at the heart of Biblical theology'[6] where 'the sonship of Israel . . . has a . . . central place in the theology of this book'.[7] Another author concurs when he states: 'Deuteronomy . . . proclaim[s] with remarkable explicitness the Bible's view of Israel as the son of God'[8] and is an indispensible piece of the larger meta-narrative of this theme. The word *son* in 1:31, moreover, is in the singular and collectively describes the nation as a whole. It is a clear reminder of privilege and of what God had done for Israel. In other words, the nation is called to continually reflect on *whose they were and the one to whom they now belonged*, especially in this period of transition as they move forward and when they could easily become distracted and neglectful of their filial relationship to God.

b. A young son in need of a father's provision and protection

Israel is specifically told to remember *how the LORD your God carried you as a father carries his son* (31). The verb 'carried'[9] connotes the idea that there were periods during Israel's nomadic existence in the desert when God's young son easily grew tired and weary from all the travelling. The years of wilderness wandering alluded to here proved to be difficult and uncertain times for the nation of Israel. But, as is often the case, God's child must go through those desert times if they ever want to finally reach home. Indeed, Israel's period in the desert was not only symbolic of its

---

[6] Edesio Sanchez, 'Family in the Non-Narrative Sections of the Pentateuch', in Richard S. Hess and M. Daniel Carroll (eds.), *Family in the Bible: Exploring Customs, Culture, and Context* (Grand Rapids: Baker Academic, 2003), p. 42.

[7] Christopher J. H. Wright, *God's People in God's Land: Family, Land, and Property in the Old Testament*, BTCL 14 (Carlisle: Paternoster, 1990), p. 19.

[8] John J. Schmitt, 'Israel as Son of God in Torah', *BTB* 24 (2004), p. 76.

[9] Duane L. Christensen, *Deuteronomy*, rev. ed., Word 6A (Nashville: Nelson Publishers, 2001), p. 32.

own spiritual condition but also an indication of its youthfulness and inexperience, a time for God's son to learn many lessons in order to mature. God had not only birthed this nation into being, but this son, this nascent nation, must continue to grow and develop into adulthood.[10] Certainly, the filial metaphor, as we noted earlier, bespeaks vulnerability and the need for protection, but it also necessitates maturity and every parent knows that the latter does not happen overnight. Thus, whereas Israel's training as son in the book of Exodus could be likened to a schooling period,[11] now that the nation is about to enter its inheritance, the land of Canaan, there is the expectation on the part of Yahweh that there should be a ripening and developing in character. In the book of Deuteronomy, 'the son imagery . . . grows to a fullness and roundedness',[12] and, adds the same writer,

> with the proper instruction, encouragement, protection (both from bullies and from diseases), and with the proper fostering of selfworth . . . the son can grow into a responsible adult, capable of making mature judgments and trustworthy choices. Israel is expected to live, to chose, to behave himself well.[13]

In other words, time has moved on for Israel and circumstances have changed to the extent that

> the murmuring narratives witness an Israel that realizes (after a fact) that things were different prior to Sinai. It could get away with more back then. Following Sinai, its murmurings are not acceptable. A new stage has been reached. *It is time to grow up*, take more responsibility, especially given the repeated parental provision of food and drink, deliverance and care.[14]

Deuternomy 1:31 is also particularly noteworthy for the tenderness of the language used, since there were periods in the desert when the nation was unable to go any further because of a lack of strength. It was at such moments of vulnerability that Yahweh picked up his son and carried him in his arms. God fulfils his paternal obligations throughout this time when, as a loving father, he

---

[10] Schmitt, 'Israel as God's Son', p. 79.
[11] A. D. H. Mayes, *Deuteronomy* NCBC (London: Oliphants, 1979), p. 191.
[12] Schmitt, 'Israel as God's Son', p. 79.
[13] Ibid.
[14] Brent A. Strawn, 'Israel, My Child: The Ethics of a Biblical Metaphor', in Marcia J. Bunge (ed.), *The Child in the Bible* (Grand Rapids/Cambridge: Eerdmans, 2008), p. 127 (emphasis added).

provided sustenance and bestowed all manner of blessings on Israel, nurturing and providing for his son all the way through the wilderness to the present time. The picture portrayed is one of intimacy, constancy and care. Yahweh is not like some absent landlord who merely dropped by from time to time in order to make his presence felt. No, unlike the British politician and one-time leader of the Liberal Party David Steel, who when his own son hit troubled times admitted publicly 'I was the classic absentee father. I've always felt guilty about that',[15] God's covenant loyalty, presence and attentiveness to his fledgling child Israel never failed nor was it ever in doubt. God was in this for the long haul. He had cared for this child during the most difficult period in the nation's young existence, as a later text in Deuteronomy makes clear: 'The LORD your God has blessed you in all the work of your hands. He has watched over your journey through the vast wilderness. These forty years the LORD your God has been with you, and you have not lacked anything.'[16]

c. The firstborn son's inheritance, the land

The destination towards which this son was headed is stated at the end of verse 31: *how the LORD your God carried you, as a father carries his son, all the way until you reached this place.* The *place* in question, of course, was the Promised Land, the inheritance of the firstborn son which was 'something unconditional and simply "given"',[17] a point repeatedly stressed throughout the book of Deuteronomy. There is a close nexus, moreover, between the themes of sonship and inheritance, the latter being frequently referred to throughout the book (e.g. 4:21, 38; 12:9; 15:4; 19:10; 26:1). In fact, no less than 'sixty-nine times the writer of Deuteronomy repeated the pledge that Israel would one day "possess" and "inherit" the land promised to her'.[18] Furthermore, both 'sonship' and 'inheritance' are familial expressions where the latter enriches the former to the extent that to speak of the land as the inheritance of Israel is a metaphorical way of describing Israel's filial relationship to God as Father. The two ideas are used interchangeably, where some passages describe Israel as God's son or spiritual offspring while other texts use the term inheritance. The linkage of the two ideas is robust to the extent

---

[15] 'Sins of the Sons (and Daughters)', *Guardian*, 8 April 1999.
[16] 2:7; cf. 8:3–4; 29:5–6.
[17] Christopher J. H. Wright, *Knowing Jesus Through the Old Testament* (Downers Grove: IVP, 1995), p. 123.
[18] Walter C. Kaiser, *The Promise-Plan of God: A Biblical Theology of the Old and New Testaments* (Grand Rapids: Zondervan, 2008), p. 93.

that the gift of the land, as a historical indicative which owes nothing to the action or merit of Israel, is directly related to the same unconditional feature of Israel's sonship; it is because Israel is Yahweh's firstborn son that the land is given as an inheritance.[19]

In other words, the former underlies the description of the land as Israel's inheritance. Of course, chronologically speaking sonship has priority for one is 'only an heir, *if first a son*; but if a son, then assuredly an heir also'[20] and so 'in describing the land as Israel's *inheritance*, Deuteronomy must regard Israel as *Yahweh's* son'.[21]

Though the term 'inheritance' does not occur in Deuteronomy 1:31, the close relationship between these two ideas is readily apparent where the writer reminds the nation of *how the LORD your God carried you, as a father carries his son, all the way you went until you reached this place*. The *place* is the land, the inheritance of God's firstborn son, Israel. The expression *all the way* is a further reminder that even though God had promised the land to the nation of Israel, God's son had gone on a rather circuitous route of wandering in the wilderness for forty years, thereby demonstrating even as early as the outset of the filial relationship a measure of waywardness and prodigality. But the relationship was primarily founded on a covenant Yahweh had made with Israel and was therefore a guarantee they would indeed reach *this place*, the land he had promised to give them. God would keep his word and covenant even if his son would break it, a sure sign of his faithfulness in the face of the increasing filial faithlessness of the nation, which has already occurred and will continue to unfold.

2. A father's actions and a son's obedient response (8:5)

Deuteronomy 8:5 once again finds the author looking backwards and forwards to the possession of the land by Israel. The undergirding notion of Israel as a son in need of learning and training is the main point, highlighting the educational dimension of the father-

---

[19] Wright, *God's People in God's Land*, p. 20.

[20] Thomas A. Smail, *The Forgotten Father: Rediscovering the Heart of the Christian Gospel* (London: Hodder and Stoughton, 1980), p. 46. Smail's comments are made in the context of the New Testament but his point is also true for the Old Testament context here. As we shall see later, what has changed between the Old and New Testament eras is the *nature* of the inheritance. For example, there is no mention of the land in the New Testament as the believer's inheritance.

[21] Wright, *God's People in God's Land*, pp. 18–19 (author's own emphasis).

son relationship: *Know then in your heart that as a man disciplines his son, so the LORD your God disciplines you.*

As noted, Israel's period in the wilderness represented a time of immaturity and adolescence when a son must be taught and learn important lessons.[22] This is not surprising, given that a father's primary role within the family, certainly a Jewish household, was to teach his children the Torah, a point repeatedly mentioned in the book in regard to the physical family (e.g., 4:10; 6:7; 11:19).[23] Moses therefore portrays God as doing for the nation of Israel what every father was expected to do for his own children, to instruct and guide his offspring.

The invitation to reflect on the past is given in Deuteronomy 8:2: 'Remember how the LORD your God led you all the way in the wilderness these forty years.' It is a truism that history is a good teacher but history itself is no guarantee that Israel (or we!) will not make the same mistakes again, for if the lessons from the past are to do us any good they must be heeded so as not to be repeated. Thus, Israel is called to reflect on God's actions on the nation's behalf, described here as 'leading', 'humbling', 'testing' and 'causing you to hunger', tests which were *purposely* set by this Father for his son: 'in order to know what was in your heart'.[24] In addition to these paternal responsibilities was the painful necessity for God to administer discipline when his son disobeyed. As we shall see later the hard lessons of disciplining a stubborn and wayward son are also to the fore in the prophets (e.g., Isa. 1:2, 4; Jer. 4:22) and here in Deuteronomy 8:5 God exercises this very responsibility toward Israel: *Know then in your heart that as a man disciplines his son, so the LORD your God disciplines you.* The verb 'discipline' (*yāsar*) connotes at times the negative side to a father's actions where a son must be reproved and rebuked so that he may learn from wrong actions and conduct that has taken place. Certainly, Israel, as God's son, had at times in the past made poor choices: for example, no sooner had the last chisel mark been made on the tablet of the Ten Words (i.e., the Decalogue, Exod. 20) than the nation was found grovelling and bowing down in worship to a man-made image, the golden calf (Exod. 32). As a result, God's people had been

---

[22] Peter C. Craigie, *Deuteronomy*, NICOT (Grand Rapids: Eerdmans, 1995), p. 186; S. R. Driver, *Deuteronomy* ICC (Edinburgh: T&T Clark, 1896), p. 108.

[23] Family relations, especially in the area of the training and education of one's offspring, play an important part in the story-line of Deuteronomy; see Raymond Brown, *The Message of Deuteronomy: Not by Bread Alone* (Leicester: IVP, 1997), pp. 56, 64, 141.

[24] Deut. 8:2–3.

languishing in a kind of no-man's land ever since. Instead of demonstrating obedience the nation behaved in a recalcitrant manner, often acting like their New Testament counterpart, the prodigal son (Luke 15:11–32).

But the verb 'discipline' also has a positive side and describes the nurturing *and affective* aspect of the relationship – God's disciplinary actions were always carried out in love and were for the building and strengthening of the character of his son. Proverbs 3:11–12 makes clear that the Lord's actions towards his people were undergirded by affection and are always in the best interests of his spiritual offspring: 'My son, do not despise the LORD's discipline and do not resent his rebuke, because the LORD disciplines those he loves, as a father the son he delights in.' If God's son, Israel, ever needed proof of God's covenant love for them it need look no further than this one fact – he cared enough to correct and discipline them. The writer to the Hebrews makes a similar point when he points out that a son who is never disciplined evidences his bastard status and not belonging – such a person is not a true descendant: 'For what son is not disciplined by his father? If you are not disciplined (and everyone undergoes discipline), then you are illegitimate children and not true sons'.[25] In the ancient world, moreover, there was nothing worse than a father who allowed a son to become reckless, dishonouring his name and the reputation of the household. A son was not supposed to bring his father's name into disrepute and if he did the latter would exercise his parental right by disciplining him. And if, as we noted earlier, Deuteronomy is about a son on the move (literally), then there must also be spiritual advancement commensurate to this on the part of Israel. God's loving yet admonishing actions were an integral part of the educational and growing process to help bring this about.

3. Children who are (to be) holy (14:1–2)

As we move from the two previous texts to consider Deuteronomy 14:1–2, one significant difference to note is the shift from the use of the term 'son' in the singular to 'sons' in the plural. This is an important change; in the former the emphasis is upon the sense of privilege and status of being God's son (individual) whereas in the latter the focus is on the Israelites as 'children' (plural) and the required *response* to God as their Father. Chapter 14, therefore, is the first occasion in the book of Deuteronomy where 'sons/children' is

[25] Heb. 12:7–8.

used in the plural and sets out what God expects from the Israelites. Chris Wright notes in this regard:

> When Israel is described in the singular as God's child, or God is spoken of as father, the emphasis is on what God has done, or should do for the nation as a whole . . . When the Israelites are described in the plural as God's children . . . the emphasis tends to be what is expected of children, namely, obedience and loyalty.[26]

This chapter opens with a bold emphatic indicative statement which is meant to contrast with the previous chapter where apostasy and judgment prevailed. It reads: *You are the children of the LORD your God* where in the original language the filial language is to the fore and is therefore a deliberate contrast and reminder to steer clear of worshipping other gods (cf. Deut. 12:30). The verse literally reads: *Sons you are to Yahweh your God* (1a). If an indicative statement is a pronouncement of fact then it is because the Israelites *are* the children of God that the imperative is issued in the next phrase: *Do not cut yourselves or shave the front of your heads for the dead* (1b). In other words, the privilege of being in a filial relationship to God carries with it the responsibility for the way the Israelites as God's sons and daughters are to live.

As we read this command and what follows it might seem to us to be a meaningless ritual for the children of Israel to follow. But this is to misconstrue the command because the behaviour required is part and parcel of what makes the Israelites distinct and set apart as belonging to Yahweh. The order entails not cutting the body or shaving of the head, which were common rites in the ancient Near East and were especially prevalent in Canaanite cultic practices in relation to Baal. The Old Testament refers to such practices in Jeremiah 16:6, Ezekiel 7:18 and Amos 8:10; they were forbidden in Israel because of their association and conformity to pagan rituals. The body, moreover, was to be respected (Lev. 19:27–28) and not to be degraded. In these and other ways (not least having to conquer the nations inhabiting the land) the Israelites would face formidable challenges when entering the land; living among other pagan nations the temptation of assimilating to their practices and ways was an ever-present one.

It is true that God initiated the filial relationship between himself and the Israelites and had already set them apart when he brought his people out of Egypt, but as David Peterson suggests there is the

---

[26] Christopher J. H. Wright, *Deuteronomy*, NIBC (Peabody: Hendrickson Publishers and Carlisle: Paternoster Press, 1996), p. 185.

moral responsibility on the latter to now walk worthily of the Lord and to make 'sanctification as a way of life'.[27] In the Old Testament the term sanctification was a technical term of cult ritual – it connotes cleansing and consecration (e.g., Exod. 19:10, 22). Now Israel was expected to avoid anything that would pollute, which included breaking from every form of idolatry and false religion. The reason why the Israelites are not to live in conformity to the surrounding pagan practices is given in the next phrase which parallels the opening indicative statement: *for you are a people holy to the LORD your God* (2a). As God is the Holy One he cannot be associated with anything 'unholy'. 'As children of Yahweh their divine Father, they were to set aside customs unworthy of their relationship.'[28] The Israelites as God's children were obligated to become like God, to be a holy people and live according to his directions. For the Israelites, holiness was only to be found in a relationship with the Holy One.

God himself had sanctified Israel by rescuing them from Egypt, now they are commanded to keep the laws (ritual, social and moral) by not profaning them among the nations. Sanctification was to be a way of life for the sons and daughters of God. Growing in his likeness means becoming like him. But more than mere association is involved here, for this is a deep family relationship and the maxim 'Like father like son' would have resonated with the hearers of this text – God (the Father) is holy and so his children were to be no different, they were to be like him in imitating who he was and how he conducted himself in relation to them. In the same way that Israel as a result of its relationship to Yahweh must be holy and is a holy nation, so these sons of Yahweh must be holy.

Systematic theologians distinguish between positional (set apart as holy) and progressive (an ongoing process) holiness, and here the latter is clearly in view for the Israelites. Holiness is not a short sprint but a long marathon, or to change the analogy, sanctification is not the momentary flourish of a firework, more the slow burn of a candle. Progressively becoming more like God the Father is not a static notion but a dynamic, ongoing process of maturation because 'to know God is to know him as a holy God and to grow in him is to grow in holiness'.[29] In other words, if the witness of God's children is to be legitimized in the eyes of a watching world they

---

[27] David Peterson, *Possessed by God: A New Testament Theology of Holiness and Sanctification*, NSBT 1 (Leicester: Apollos, 1995), p. 21.
[28] J. A. Thompson, *Deuteronomy: An Introduction and Commentary* TOTC (London: IVP, 1976), p. 177.
[29] Derek Tidball, *The Message of Holiness*, BST (Nottingham: IVP, 2010), p. 39.

must see to it that they live distinctly different to the nations around them.

4. Sing a song of sonship (32:1–43)

We fast forward towards the end of the book to Deuteronomy 32, regarded by many to be the oldest reference to Israel's filial relationship to God (6).[30] Here the author's thoughts are projected towards the future where it is 'not just the immediate future' which is in view 'but the long-distance history of Israel is surveyed'.[31] What is anticipated is the future disobedience of Israel and the Israelites, their eventual removal from the land, before they are finally brought back and resettled in it.

It has been said that the nation of Israel was born in song (cf. Exod. 15) and this coupled with the filial imagery makes this chapter in many ways a song of sonship, though clearly it is a song tinged with poignancy and sadness – more like a dirge at times – which eventually gives way to joy as God vindicates his people in the midst of the nations when Israel, as son, is restored (32:27–43). The sublime poetry of the passage is immediately striking, together with repeated descriptions of the Israelites mostly in the plural as *children* (5, 20), *sons* (8) and *sons and daughters* (19). God, moreover, is described as a father no less than three times (vv. 5, 6, 18, 19) and the imagery of *birth* (18) is also included.

Andrew Dearman has helpfully drawn attention to the similarities between Deuteronomy 32 and the prophecy of Hosea, in particular chapter 11,[32] a chapter we shall consider later.[33] He regards Deuteronomy as 'an independent pre-exilic composition'[34] and so even though the Israelites are on the verge of entering into the land there have already been some ominous signs and warnings (e.g., Deut. 8:5) of how events will unfold. Despite the fact that God had clearly set out how the Israelites as the children of God are to conduct themselves in accordance with the covenant, there is the expectation that they will not listen and will in fact fail to do so. Thus, as the book comes to a close in chapter 32, Moses is entrusted with one final act before handing over to Joshua, namely to teach

[30] Wright, *God's People in God's Land*, p. 16.
[31] Wright, *Deuteronomy*, p. 294.
[32] See J. Andrew Dearman, *The Book of Hosea*, NICOT (Grand Rapids/Cambridge: Eerdmans, 2010), p. 353. Dearman considers the more likely reason for the similarity of language is that both are drawing from common traditions.
[33] See ch. 4.
[34] Ibid., p. 353.

the Israelites this filial song so that it will be a 'witness . . . against' them in the future.[35]

a. The corruption of the children (5–6)

Deuteronomy 32 itself takes the form of a covenant lawsuit where God brings a number of charges against the Israelites. In the opening verses God summons his people by calling on the heavens as a witness (1). Most of the filial descriptions of the Israelites are in the plural (*children*, 5, 20; *sons*, 8; *sons and daughters*, 19) where more negative comments in regard to the Israelites are in view, a reminder that God's people are not behaving as they ought. These descriptions are therefore a warning of the need for obedience on the part of all individual members of the nation. In fact, the waywardness of the Israelites, God's children, is an issue which the prophets later address (e.g., Isa. 1:2–4; Hos. 11:1–7) as they repeatedly call God's people back to the covenant. Indeed, in the prophetic literature, as here, the language of sonship is not used to provide assurance but accusation and in a peculiarly perverse way becomes the disciplinary rod or stick in the hand of God as parent as he seeks to bring the recalcitrant Israelites back into line. They are therefore chastised as offspring who have acted *corruptly* (5), *crooked* (5), even *deserted* (18), and have become *unfaithful* children (20). God's family is not living as he had intended them and the accusations against them are all the more threatening as they are couched in the first person singular ('I', 1, 3) and in paternal terms (6). God particularly charges them with having acted *corruptly* or more precisely having *acted corruptly towards* him (5), where the language is personally oriented since what is primarily perverted is their relationship of kinship to God.

In addition, and to their greater chagrin, God's children had become a 'twisted' (i.e., *warped*, 5) and 'tortuous' (i.e., *crooked*, 5) generation which was nothing less than 'a grotesque mockery of what God had created them to be'.[36] Such behaviour was irrational and was no way to respond to the beneficence of the God who had chosen the Israelites only for them to turn around and willingly forsake their 'sonship in favour of their own selfish ends'.[37] The Israelites are even described as *no longer his children* (5), a serious accusation as they appear to have renounced their true parentage,

---

[35] Deut. 31:19.

[36] Eugene H. Merrill, *Deuteronomy*, NAC 4 (Nashville: Broadman and Holman, 1994), p. 411.

[37] Ibid.

a charge that required death by stoning (Deut. 21:18–21). These children had walked out on God and it was because of this, as one commentator points out, that the Israelites find themselves 'in the dock'.[38] The above description may seem over exaggerated and hyperbolic but given that the filial language here is in the plural it underscores the responsibility on the part of the Israelites to obey their parent. Thus, the author here is looking at the relationship from the 'children's' perspective and not vice-versa and while on the one hand, *they* may have renounced God as parent, God on the other as we shall see, cannot ever let them go.

b. The pathos of a parent (6, 18–36)

The parent-child relationship is not a one-way road but a two-way street with reciprocity sitting at its very core. Thus, the Israelites' conduct draws from God the following response: *Is this the way you repay the LORD . . . ? Is he not your Father, your Creator, who made and formed you?* (6) The verb 'repay' can mean 'treat' (TEV), and who among us as we were growing up has not at some time or other heard the parental rebuke: 'What way is that to treat your mother or father'? The verb 'create' does not here convey the notion of creation *ex nihilo* as in Genesis 1:1; rather the emphasis is on the relationship to God and of his having brought the nation into one of sonship.[39] Maternal and paternal imagery are mixed together, for the Israelites we are told, had *deserted the Rock, who fathered you; you forgot the God who gave you birth* (18). *The LORD saw this*, the text continues, and as a consequence *rejected them because he was angered* (19), a rejection which for the moment might look permanent but as our story continues is not.

There is also anger on the part of God mingled with pain and sorrow. These verses depict a real theodicy: if God is to be true to his holy character, he knows Israel must face judgment; equally he is their parent and has every right to sever the filial relationship, yet he has no desire to do so. The tension between these two notions has stretched God's forbearance to the limit and the Israelites as God's children have caused him heartache. As a consequence of their conduct and disobedient conduct, God is seen to suffer. They have proved to be *children who are unfaithful* (20). We earlier noted how suffering is an important subtheme of the larger meta-narrative of sonship – sons and daughters of God will

---

[38] Anthony Phillips, *Deuteronomy* (Cambridge: Cambridge University Press, 1973), p. 216.

[39] Craigie, *Deuteronomy*, p. 379.

suffer adversity of one kind or another – but in this instance we are faced with how suffering might also be an integral part of the parental side of the relationship, an aspect we had not perhaps reckoned on. The question of whether God suffers (the impassibility of God), moreover, is not only a philosophical one to discuss but also impacts all people, especially those Christians who have been tragically torpedoed into grief. But God as parent is also caught up in the drama of adversity. God here is not impassible, unmoved or untouched by the actions and defection of the Israelites; rather, he is deeply stirred and involved in regard to their behaviour towards him.

Terence Fretheim, in his book *The Suffering of God: An Old Testament Perspective*,[40] discusses this question and provides three reasons for divine suffering: God suffers *because, with* and *for* his people. The former is clearly to the fore in this text on Deuteronomy for God suffers *because* of the reckless behaviour of his spiritual progeny, the Israelites. Indeed the prophetic literature provides several examples of the passibility of God: we read in Hosea 11: 8–9: 'How can I give you up, Ephraim? How can I hand you over, O Israel? . . . My heart recoils within me; my compassion grows warm and tender. I will not execute my fierce anger; I will not again destroy Ephraim' (ESV). Jeremiah 31:20 also records the deep mourning of God: 'Is not Ephraim my dear son, the child in whom I delight? Through I often speak against him, I still remember him. Therefore my heart yearns for him.' God is like a long-suffering parent where, says Fretheim, 'the parental pathos is the heart of God.'[41]

Nicholas Wolterstorff, a Christian theologian and philosopher, in his book *Lament for a Son*, also grapples with this issue in the heart-wrenching story of his twenty-five-year-old son who died while he was skiing on a mountainside. In the book and speaking as a parent he reasons that not only does everyone suffer but it is those who love most who suffer most:

> We are one in suffering. Some are wealthy, some are bright; some athletic, some admired. But we all suffer. For we all prize and love; and in this present existence of ours, prizing and loving yield suffering. Love in our world is suffering love. Some do not suffer much, though, for they do not love much. Suffering is for the loving; If I hadn't loved him, there wouldn't be this agony.

[40] Terence E. Fretheim, *The Suffering of God: An Old Testament Perspective* OBT (Philadelphia: Fortress, 1984), p 120.

[41] Ibid., p. 120.

Later, where he reflects further on the parental love of God, Wolterstorff goes on to say: '*God is love. That is why he suffers...* God is not only the God of the sufferers but the God who suffers. The pain and fallenness of humanity have entered into his heart.'[42] God is not immune from suffering but also suffers and laments *because of* the Israelites, his children whom he greatly loves (Deut. 7:7), and he does so here chiefly in spite of their prodigality. The heart of God is laid bare in Deuteronomy 32 and when we consider the hurt and pain which the Israelites have brought to this divine parent, we begin to understand how much his spiritual offspring have grieved him. Certainly, the Israelites must be judged and punished and eventually go into exile but God cannot give them up, and in verse 27, the turning-point in the song, he has every right to *blot out their memory from mankind*. If that was to happen, we might ask what then would become of Israel, his chosen inheritance?

In response there is hope signalled in verse 27 as well as earlier in verse 21 in language which the apostle Paul uses in Romans 9 – 11 and in chapters where he also addresses the seemingly hopeless situation of the nation in his own day and how God will one day turn things around. Now the song of sonship has a more hopeful melody, for God will use ways to make his people envious by *those who are not a people* (21), a point picked up by Paul in Romans 9:24–29. In the mysterious providences of God, Israel will be made jealous by a bunch of no hopers, the Gentiles, who will play a role in the greater ingathering of the Israelites. God too will be seen to be vindicated in his character as one who is faithful to his promises (Rom. 3:3) and whose word has not failed (Rom. 9:6). But for the moment, God *will judge his people* (36), and the Israelites will be ejected from the land, though they will rise from the embers of the exile and eventually return to it (cf. Isa. 43:6–7; 63:15–16; 64:7–9; Jer. 31:9–10, 20; Hos. 11:10–11).

The theme of sonship is therefore infused with hope and as we shall see in a later chapter the filial relationship is strong enough to survive the long exile to come, for God knows full well that 'you can break a covenant, but you cannot stop being a son to your father'.[43]

---

[42] Nicholas Wolterstorff, *Lament for a Son* (Grand Rapids: Eerdmans, 1987), pp. 81 and 89 (emphasis added).

[43] Christopher J. H. Wright, *Knowing God the Father Through the Old Testament* (Oxford: Monarch, 2007), p. 84.

Summary

Israel's relationship to God as a firstborn son is a very special one and, in accordance with the culture of the times, such a son could expect to become the head of the family as well as being the one who inherited a double portion. For Israel, this birthright took the form of the land as God had earlier promised, and so the nation is instructed to move forward and claim it by entering the Promised Land. It would take a while to get there, however, as this young child goes walkabout on a rather circuitous route via the wilderness, which proved to be a schooling period, a time for this child to grow in maturity and in preparation for the next stage of the journey.

Once they reach the land, God's son Israel must be obedient and live as a distinct and different people from the other nations around. When they go wrong, God's child can expect to be corrected and disciplined. The Israelites as sons and daughters of God are especially reminded to imitate God and to be holy just as their Father is holy. Significantly, prior to taking up residency in the land – and even before (e.g. Exod. 32) – Deuteronomy warns us that this filial relationship will be characterized by disobedience; in fact, in the future God's son will not only go astray but will eventually be taken into exile (with the prospect of a return) thereby causing the heart of the divine to grieve *because* of Israel's sinful conduct.

2 Samuel 7
3. A son sworn in: the king

In 2007–8 the Democratic Party's race to choose a candidate to run for president of the United States of America was a bruising and very public affair between the eventual winner Barack Obama and the runner up Hillary Clinton. It was a closely followed contest for a number of reasons, not least for the fact that whichever candidate won it would mean that the United States for the first time in its history would either have a female or an African-American president. Of particular interest to the American people was the fact that if Hillary Clinton could pull it off she would be exchanging roles with her husband, Bill Clinton, who himself had earlier served as the 42nd president of the United States. In the end it seemed the American electorate was looking for a fresh start, a change from the old ways of governing which Clinton's rival, Barack Obama, was promising he could deliver. Hillary Clinton was eventually forced to concede defeat and the *Economist* magazine, seizing the moment as well as the shift in mood of the American people, used a telling headline, 'The Fall of the House of Clinton',[1] which not only described the termination of Hillary Clinton's personal presidential ambitions but ushered in the end of an era in American politics.

Having considered Israel's filial relationship to God as 'son', another piece of the jigsaw puzzle of sonship is that of 2 Samuel 7:11–16[2] where we read of another *house*, a house that stands in complete contrast to the aspirations of the earthly dynasty of would-be US

[1] 'The Fall of the House of Clinton', *The Economist*, 7–13 June 2008, pp. 38–42.
[2] Some literary and historical critics have concluded that the author of 2 Sam. 7 was confused and that this chapter represents a late fourth-century *midrash* (interpretation) based on Ps. 89, that in short it has little historical worth; see Walter C. Kaiser, *The Promise-Plan of God: A Biblical Theology of the Old and New Testaments* (Grand Rapids: Zondervan, 2007), pp. 117–118, for a strong rebuttal of these views.

president, Hillary Clinton, precisely for the fact that behind it was not the personal ambition of an individual but the selfless, sovereign initiative of a covenantal God who had it in mind to bring blessing to the world. This time sonship is focused not on the nation of Israel or individual Israelites, but a king, though these are related, as N. T. Wright points out: 'The two ideas of Israel as son and David as son belong together, since in some Jewish thought the Davidic king represents Israel, so that what is true of him is true of the people.'[3]

The importance of 2 Samuel 7 in Scripture cannot be overestimated. Such a statement might seem clichéd but in the case of this chapter it is true, for not only is 2 Samuel 7 'one of the most important chapters of the Bible'[4] it is also the biblical equivalent 'to the Magna Carta or the United States Declaration of Independence, texts that have also inspired a whole people and engender national identity'.[5] 2 Samuel 7 is also significant for the fact that it is a long literary unit in the form of a narrative where the reader is invited to pause and take a deep breath in view of the magnitude of the events that are about to unfold.[6] This passage, as Walter Bruggemann has noted, is 'the dramatic and theological centre of the entire Samuel corpus. Indeed, this is one of the most crucial texts in the Old Testament for evangelical faith'.[7] Theologically it is important because the theme of sonship sits dead centre in the chapter (v. 14). Moreover, this relationship of father to son, as we shall see in later chapters, has crucially important messianic associations, for the notion of sonship is not only played out in the life of David and his immediate progeny but also in the New Testament in relation to King David's greater Son, Jesus Christ, and with God's sons and daughters who are in solidarity with him (cf. Luke 1:31–33; Rom. 1:3–4; 8:3, 12–17; Heb. 1:5).[8]

1. God himself will build a 'house' (7:1–16)

Immediately prior to this chapter David, king of all Israel, had defeated his enemies and had brought a measure of peace and secu-

---

[3] N. T. Wright, 'Romans', in NIB 10 (Nashville: Abingdon Press, 2002), p. 416.
[4] Bill T. Arnold, *1 & 2 Samuel*, NIVAC (Grand Rapids: Zondervan, 2000), p. 473.
[5] Ibid., p. 472.
[6] Ibid., p. 471.
[7] W. Brueggemann, *First and Second Samuel*, IBC (Louisville: John Knox, 1990), p. 253.
[8] See Robert D. Bergen, *1, 2 Samuel*, NAC (Nashville: Broad and Holman, 1996), pp. 337–338.

rity so that the nation had finally begun to flourish in the land. The ark too has been returned to Jerusalem (2 Sam. 6) and with his enemies conquered David has begun to settle into the luxury of the palace (7:1). Bethlehem, where David had begun as a humble shepherd boy, may be only six miles from Jerusalem but it had taken him twenty years to get there.

It is often said that it is in periods of inactivity we get itchy feet and want to do something – anything! – for God. For David it seems this was so, and who could blame him, since God had done so much for him? But David for all his weaknesses is uneasy in his mind and identifies a discrepancy between his own lavish surroundings and the temporary tent which currently houses the ark. He laments: *Here I am, living in a palace of cedar, while the ark of God remains in a tent* (2).[9] David was not overhasty, as his next move shows, because he has the foresight to know that whenever you have an inkling for a building project it is always wise to go and ask God or his representative before you go buying the bricks! Thus, he seeks counsel and advice from the prophet Nathan regarding what he should do, an action which immediately underscores his humility and is noteworthy for the fact that it sets him apart from his predecessor Saul who rarely, if ever, 'enquired of God' and whose rule had proved such a monarchical disaster.

David's initial inquiry about building a *house*, it should be noted, is the first of eight usages of this word in the chapter (Heb. *bayît*, vv. 5, 6, 7, 13, 16, 19, 25, 26, 27, 29), which as the narrative proceeds turns out to be a clever play on words. Along with this word is another term that dominates the landscape in this chapter, namely, *forever*, which occurs more often here than any other chapter in the books of Samuel and Kings. It is used on three occasions by God (13, 16 [twice]) and five times by David in his prayer (24, 25, 26, 29 [twice]).[10] In other words, the *house* God has in mind here is for keeps. Turning to the former, David's desire to construct a *house* prompts Nathan to initially give him the green light, only to be told that same night that Yahweh had never commanded any of his servants to erect a physical building, a *house* (4–5).[11]

God responds with a 'Thanks, but no thanks' answer by swiftly

[9] The Hebrew states that the ark is sitting in a temporary structure made of 'mere curtains'.

[10] Victor Hamilton, *Historical Books of OT: Joshua - Esther* (Grand Rapids: Baker, 2001), p. 317.

[11] In v. 5c, which is a question, there is an emphasis on the word 'you', the thrust of which is to condemn the very notion that David could do *anything* for Yahweh.

withdrawing the building permit because God cannot be controlled by a prophet nor can 'the royal apparatus ... make Yahweh its patron'.[12] This is not the time for David to be engaged in construction of a physical edifice, and timing – in accordance with the divine timescale – is everything in the kingdom of God. Moreover, rather than king David building a house for Yahweh, *God* tells David via the prophet Nathan that *he*, Yahweh, will erect a house, but it will not be any temporary, physical structure; rather, this *house* will be something much more far-reaching and grand – a dynasty no less – that will come from David's *own body* (12)! In the conversation that ensues (5–16), God proceeds to give David a history lesson where divine sovereignty is to the fore, evident by the fact that God is the first person subject in twenty-three verbs in this passage, and these verbs carry all the action: *God's* action. Furthermore, whereas David is fixated with the construction of a physical building, God is only interested in creating a people, a family of sons and daughters no less, in which people and relationships are always of greatest importance. This carries the plotline of our theme a little further. Robert Bergen captures the contrast well when he comments on the two 'houses':

> David did not need to construct an impressive but lifeless building in which the Lord could dwell; the Lord had already constructed an impressive living building in which to dwell and that edifice was the life of David. Though the ark resided in a lifeless tent of skin, in a very real sense the Lord resided in the living tent of David.[13]

Though the narrative does not explain why David is precluded from building a temple, 1 Chronicles 28:3 gives us an important clue: 'You are not to build a house for my Name, because you are a warrior and have shed blood.' Nevertheless, David's motive for seeking to erect a permanent structure, a temple, in which the ark of the covenant could be housed was a good one since (in his eyes) this was more fitting for God. But ultimately he needed to know that both these were mere symbols and could themselves if not handled properly lead to the veneration of a building. More to the point, David needed to understand that temple-building is not a human initiative but a divinely appointed one and must only be undertaken at God's behest and through his choice of nominee (i.e., Solomon). It is also possible that bound up with David's desire to

[12] Brueggemann, *Samuel*, p. 254.
[13] Bergen, *1, 2 Samuel*, p. 339.

build the temple and God's preclusion for him to do so may have been the myopic tendency on his part that God could somehow be confined or localized to one place (the temple). David needed to know (as we do too) that God is present wherever his people meet in his name, be it a barn, an attic, a forest, house or the grandeur of a cathedral. Nathan's intervention was therefore a timely reminder to David, if ever he needed one, that the temple 'was a place where they could meet God, *but not the only place where God could be found*'.[14]

2. David, the son of the house (7:8–17)

In the midst of the household language of this chapter God tells David how he is going to make his name great by first reminding him of his humble beginnings (8–11). An important literary feature of the biblical writings is how an author immediately prior to outlining a new departure in the redemptive purposes of God describes the past in order to accentuate what he, God, has done and accomplished on behalf of those involved (cf. 1 Sam. 1 – 2). As believers under the new covenant it too is a salutary lesson for us to reflect every so often on our own spiritual journey and to draw encouragement and strength from where we once were to where God wants to take us. God reminds David how he had taken him as a young shepherd pasturing sheep (8) and raised him to a position of leadership over all Israel. One of the great repeated themes of Scripture is how God reverses the fortunes of people (e.g. Hannah, Mary) by raising the humble and bringing low those who are conceited and puffed up. David, the author tells us, had also known God as 'an ever-present help in time of trouble' (9, cf. Ps. 46:1). *Now*, God tells David, *I will make your name great, like the names of the greatest men of the earth* (9b). How this is going to come about is explained further in verses 11 and following where God promises that the *house* he will establish will be not in David's day but after his days are completed on earth, when God *will raise up your offspring*[15] *to succeed you, who will come from your own body* (12). The language and the promise here is 'rich in Abrahamic allusions, especially language concerning "seed" to come from David's own body'. From

[14] Mary J. Evans, *The Message of Samuel*, BST (Leicester/Downers Grove: IVP, 2004), p.197 (emphasis added).

[15] Joyce G. Baldwin, *1 and 2 Samuel: An Introduction and Commentary* (Leicester/Downers Grove: IVP, 1988), p. 215, makes the important observation here that 'the original word implies not only one generation but many. In God's perspective, history is seen whole, its purpose clear and certain to be achieved'.

the narrative elsewhere we know that David has had no problem fathering physical progeny and so the previous comment may appear 'technically redundant' but it is included precisely 'because of the contact it makes with Genesis 17 in pointing to an unborn son. As Yahweh establishes a house for David, it will not be through sons he has, rejecting primogeniture, but through a son who is to come'.[16]

Then in verse 14, a capstone verse, the author explains what this means more fully – we see an advance on the language used. David earlier in the chapter had been described as a *servant* (5) but now the special relationship is described much more intimately where the covenant[17] is couched clearly and unmistakably in filial terms: *I will be a father to him, and he will be my son*. This formula has a striking resemblance to the text in Exodus 4:22, 'Israel is my firstborn son', reminding us that what God had done for the nation of Israel he was now going to do for the king and his descendents. Filially speaking, verse 14 of 2 Samuel 7 is not only the 'most significant'[18] verse in the passage but is the Old Testament equivalent to verse 15 of Romans 8 in the New Testament: both sit at the nuclear point in the chapter. It is true that the promise is not made explicitly with David, but to David's descendant, the bearer of the Davidic covenant. However, in Psalm 2:7, regarded by many as a Davidic psalm, the king is addressed directly, 'You are my Son; today I have become your Father' (cf. Ps. 89:26–27), making clear that David can be understood as being in a filial relationship with God. In other words, David is the crucial conduit or channel through whom God has ordained to work and through whom the blessings for the nations will take place.

In terms of the filial language used, we noted earlier how the term 'son' originally applied to the nation of Israel under the covenantal terms of the Sinai accord which here is now widened and specifically given a royal dimension – the king and his descendants are also regarded as having a special relationship with Yahweh as son. 'As the covenant promises and demands were central constituents of the Israel-Yahweh son-father relationship, they are central also in the conception of the relationship between Yahweh

[16] David G. Firth, *1 and 2 Samuel* AOTC (Nottingham: Apollos; Downers Grove: IVP, 2009), p. 385.

[17] Though the Hebrew word for covenant is not used here as a designation for the Lord's promise to David, it is used in 2 Sam. 23:5 and occurs with reference to numerous other Old Testament passages as well (e.g. Ps. 89:3). Furthermore, most commentators are agreed that the passage is replete with covenantal language; see Firth, *Samuel*, p. 387.

[18] G. Cooke, 'The Israelite King as Son of God', *ZAW* vol. 73 (1961), p. 206.

and David in his line.'[19] But while there are similarities between the Sinai and the Davidic covenants in that both are couched in family terms,[20] there are also differences. For example, this is the first time in Scripture that a *king* is spoken of in terms of having a filial relationship with God and so what had earlier applied nationally (i.e., Israel) and corporately (i.e., Israelites) is now applied individually (i.e., a king) to David as monarch. David, of course, in his role as king will also represent his people, for the two ideas of Israel as son and David as son 'belong together, since in some Jewish thought the Davidic king represents Israel, so what is true of him is true of the people'.[21] Still, this relationship represents 'an extraordinary declaration, a genuine *novum* in Israel's faith' for 'in one sweeping assurance, the conditional "if" of the Mosaic Torah is overridden, and David is made a vehicle and carrier of Yahweh's unqualified grace in Israel'.[22] In short, this is nothing less than a new departure in God's gracious unqualified dealings with the king.

a. A son who can expect to be disciplined (14)

But what exactly is required of this son, for do not filial privileges also bring filial responsibilities? The following verses answer that question and causes us to remember an earlier point that sonship is essentially a functional category in which a number of expectations sit at the heart of the relationship between God as Father and David and his descendants as 'son(s)'.

No sooner has the ink on the covenantal pact dried (14a) than God immediately sounds the caveat: *When he does wrong, I will punish him with the rod of men, with floggings inflicted by men* (14b). What is to be noted here is that the same kind of discipline and ethical sanctions in regard to Israel as son are also in place in the inaugural promise made to Israel's king as son. Implicit in this warning in verse 14b is the presupposition that sons were supposed to obey their parents, an expectation attested by other Old Testament Scriptures: 'My son, keep your father's commands'.[23] Obedience, therefore, sits at the heart of this father-son relationship and the use of the word *when* (14b, not 'if'), reflected in a number

[19] Ibid., p. 225.
[20] William J. Dumbrell, *Covenant and Creation: A Theology of the Old Testament Covenants* BTCL 12 (Carlisle: Paternoster Press), p. 151.
[21] N. T. Wright, 'Romans', p. 146.
[22] Walter Brueggemann, *Theology of Old Testament: Testimony, Dispute, Advocacy* (Minneapolis: Augsberg Fortress, 1997), p. 605.
[23] Prov. 6:20.

of English translations (e.g., NIV), is a hint of the realism involved: namely, that there will be future times of filial waywardness and of failure to keep the commands of the covenant. When that happens, David and his progeny can expect to be corrected and disciplined. But this is not the discipline or the heavy-handedness of a cold, unattached figure, rather the manifestation of affection which a loving Father has for his child, a point echoed later in the New Testament in Hebrews 12:5–6: 'My son, do not make light of the Lord's discipline, and do not lose heart when he rebukes you, because the Lord disciplines those he loves, and he punishes everyone he accepts as a son.'

It is also important for the king to comply with God's will since his obedience as 'son' will have important repercussions both at the national and familial levels: as regards the former, just as the people of Israel are God's son, so too is the king as the inclusive representative of the people.[24] Ancient Near East society and culture, moreover, was undergirded by the principle of corporate solidarity, where the individual actions of a person invariably affected and infected everyone else in the group and had profound and far-reaching consequences – the honour of the entire nation was involved and at stake. Thus, 'Israel's king was not to be a *super-Israelite*, lording it over his subjects, but a *model Israelite*, setting them an example of what it means to be an obedient son of Yahweh'.[25] Regarding the latter, David is not only the representative head of the nation, he is also apex or head of his own physical household and is also expected to be a model example for his own sons to imitate. This was a commonly held expectation in the ancient Near East. As the narrative in the book of Samuel unfolds, however, David's relationship with Bathsheba (2 Sam. 11) and the trail of moral devastation left behind as a result of his sins of adultery and subsequent murder of Uriah, shows us he categorically failed in these areas. Indeed, the principle of 'like father like son' functions in a negative way in the storyline for it shows how for David the chickens finally come home to roost in that his own sinful actions are replicated in the lives of his sons: Amnon's raping of his sister Tamar (2 Sam. 13:1–21) and Absalom's subsequent murder of his brother Amnon (2 Sam.13:23–39). Though God would forgive David his sin (cf. Pss. 32; 51) he still had to live with the *consequences* of his actions. And so must we.

---

[24] Charles H. H. Scobie, *The Ways of our God: An Approach to Biblical Theology* (Grand Rapids, Eerdmans, 2003), p. 377.

[25] Christopher J. H. Wright, *Knowing the Father through the Old Testament* (Oxford: Monarch Books, 2007), p. 92.

b. A son who will be forever loved (15–16)

Despite the fact that David and his progeny would fail at times, God was committed to the covenant, as verse 15 makes clear: *but my love will never be taken away from him*. The Davidic covenant above everything else is grounded in Yahweh's covenantal love (*hesed*) and commitment to it and to his progeny, a love which will know no end. The pact, moreover, was personal (*from him*) and also poignant, for while God's love would never be taken from David this stands in contrast to the phrase that follows: *as I took it from Saul, whom I removed from before you* (15). Compared to the events associated with the first king of Israel, Saul, a new era has dawned, since the second king of Israel and his descendants will be eternally loved by and bound to Yahweh, a love which must not be construed in terms of the soppy, dripping sentimentality often associated with the glitz and glamour of Hollywood and make-belief of Tinsel-Town. Rather, it is a covenantal love, a deep and abiding commitment by Yahweh to the enduring dynasty he has promised to establish and which extends beyond the initial son and his relationship to him. God promises that his covenant commitment would never be taken away from David's descendants, which stands in stark contrast to Saul. Whereas 'Saul forfeited it . . . this is not to be the experience of David's line'.[26] Rather, the unconditional nature of the Davidic covenant is clearly stated in verses 15–16 in that though David may be disciplined, he will not be set aside but his *house* will last *forever*, a point underscored by the double usage of the adverb 'forever' in verse 16.

These promises were meaningful to David and Solomon as well as for later generations to come but their ultimate fulfilment is found in Jesus of Nazareth, the Son of God. Though there are only two texts in the New Testament which directly cite 2 Samuel 7:14,[27] there are many allusions to it, as we shall see in later chapters: for example, repeatedly Jesus is called 'Son of David' (Matt. 1:1; Mark 10:47; Rom. 1:3–4), the one who builds the true temple (John 2:19–22), and the one who ultimately inherits David's throne, which is an eternal kingdom (Heb. 1:8). God's reign is expressed in the New Testament primarily and fundamentally through King Jesus, the Son of God, whose kingship and kingdom will know no end.

So, what was King David's response? We turn to the next part of the chapter for the answer.

[26] Firth, *Samuel*, p. 386.
[27] 2 Cor. 6:18; Heb. 1:5.

3. A son who submits to the sovereign rights of the Father (7:18–29)

Subdued by God's sovereign and timely intervention of what he, God, and not David is going to do, the king can only make one possible response – he *sits* (18),[28] which 'effectively puts him out of the action'[29] and keeps God dead centre. 'This may be the single most critical act David ever did, the action that put him out of the action.'[30] David is taken out of the driver's seat and is instead *sat before the LORD* (18), his submissive posture being the only appropriate one for the prayerful response he is about to make in light of all that God has told him. But David is far from passive, for the prayer he offers demonstrates that he has listened to God's word delivered by Nathan the prophet and has close connections with the dynastic promise uttered in the earlier section (7: 5–17). The continuity and frequency of certain key words tie both passages together, including *house* (8 times in 1–17; 7 times in 18–29), *forever* (twice in 1–17; 4 times in 18–29) and *servant* (twice in 1–17; 10 times in 18–29).[31] This prayer uttered by David 'is a sequence of deference, doxology and demand'.[32]

a. Deference

David's servile position is clearly evident in a number of ways: first, it is seen in the way that prayer is framed by his understanding of himself as a *servant* (18, 29 [twice]; cf. 25–26 [twice]), which occurs, as we have just noted, no less than ten times in 7:18–29. David's servanthood is also set in contrast with the greatness of God (22) who does great things, including *great and awesome wonders* (23). The majesty of God and David's insignificance is particularly well illustrated in the 'the grammar of his prayer',[33] and in the elevated

---

[28] Henry Preserved Smith, *The Books of Samuel*, ICC (Edinburgh: T&T Clark, 1969), p, 302, points out that '*Sitting* is not the usual attitude of prayer in the Old Testament' (italics original).

[29] Eugene H. Peterson, *First and Second Samuel*, Westminster Bible Companion (Louisville: Westminster John Knox Press, 1999), p. 168.

[30] Eugene H. Peterson, *Leap Over a Wall: Earthy Spirituality for Every Day Christians* (San Francisco: Harper Row, 1997), p. 162.

[31] I owe these statistics to Firth, *Samuel*, p. 389, who also makes the valid point that even though some have argued that as there is no mention of the temple in 7:18–29 these verses belong more properly to 6:1–19 and the ark narrative, there is good reason for David not to mention the temple since he has just been told by God that he will not be the one to build it.

[32] Brueggemann, *Samuel*, p. 259.

[33] Peterson, *Samuel*, p. 169.

language used to describe God. Earlier he had referred to God as an impersonal object (7:2) but now the language he employs is pervaded with the personal. On seventeen occasions David describes God by name, first as *God* (25, 28) as well as with other more eminent terminology: the *Sovereign LORD* (e.g., 18 [twice], 19, 20), and the 'Lord of Hosts' (26–27, ESV). In addition, he uses the personal pronoun for God forty times,[34] which if taken cumulatively underscores the fact that David in light of what God revealed to him via the prophet Nathan finally recognizes and acknowledges his lowly position and God's highly exalted status. Little wonder then that he exclaims: *What more can David say to you?* (20).

b. Doxology

In light of David's understanding of who God is and what he has done for him David cannot remain silent but is driven to thanks and praise. The 'thanks' takes the form of three rhetorical questions in verses 18, 20 and 23. The first focuses on David's astonishment about what God has accomplished for his family as well as recognizing where he once was compared to where he has now been brought, and asks: *Who am I, O Sovereign LORD, and what is my family, that you have brought me this far?* The second almost leaves him speechless when he asks *What more can David say to you?* (20) but which leads to an outburst of praise and doxology concerning the greatness of God who does great and awesome things. The third thanksgiving is found in verse 23, which reflects back to the time when God had singled out Israel as special and unique, where phrases like *one nation* and *redeem* call to mind the time when God made Israel his son (Exod. 4:22). David gives thanks in light of the fact that 'Israel is distinctive because Yahweh is distinctive. In Israel, but more specifically in David, Yahweh has enacted a *novum* in world history'.[35]

c. Demand

Though David is deferential he is no less determined for all that, because he wants more than anything for God to both establish the promise (25) and also bless his house (29). David's desire is to see that God keeps his word. Brueggemann paraphrases some of verses 25–29 and imagines a conversation taking place between David and God in the following terms: 'You really should not have made this

[34] Ibid.
[35] Brueggemann, *Samuel*, p. 260.

offer' but 'since you did, I expect the promise to be kept'.[36] David, of course, expects to play an important role in God bringing about his promises for he is aware that his own position and the future of his dynasty are both inextricably connected to who God is and what God has done and will yet do. The prayer fittingly ends in verse 29 with the assurance on the part of David to ask God to act in accordance with his word:

> Now be pleased to bless the house of your servant, that it may continue forever in your sight; for you, O Sovereign LORD, have spoken, and with your blessing the house of your servant will be blessed forever.

Summary

The nation of Israel is not the only one in Scripture described as being in a filial relationship to God, the king is as well (7:14). In clear covenantal terms the king is referred to as a son of God and as a consequence is representative of Israel. King David and his descendants' role in the story of sonship is strategic, but his desire to build a house for God is met with the response that God will build a different kind of house, a dynasty, one which would not be a physical edifice but which would come from his own body. He (and his descendants) is immediately reminded, like the earlier son Israel, of the importance of obedience and of the expectation of being disciplined in love, but he too fails to walk in the ways of the Lord. Such is the nature of the Davidic covenant, however, that God will bless the progeny of the king and fulfil the filial promises made concerning another Son, Jesus Messiah.

[36] Ibid.

Hosea 11:1–11; Isaiah 1:2–4
4. A prodigal son returns home

'Home is where you start from,' T. S. Eliot the poet and literary critic once said, and we could add, it is the place where we return again and again. Homecoming is a deep and emotive experience within the heart of us all. Our home, particularly if it is a stable, childhood home, is such a sacred space, a place filled with memories, familiar smells, sights, sounds and items, including furniture, books, sports equipment, and maybe some animals, but most important of all the people and the familial relationships we hold so dear. The memories of our family and all the above things linger long in the mind and we rightly refuse to let them go. Throughout history, however, people have had their families torn apart because of displacement from their habitual abode: one thinks immediately of the people of Darfur where thousands exist in refugee camps waiting for the time when they can return home to their villages. Or we could cite the removal of thousands of Tutsis from Rwanda or we might think of the ethnic cleansing in the former Yugoslavia where hundreds were displaced from their families and homeland. I cannot claim to have experienced anything like this nor hope to fully appreciate what it must feel like for these people to be unable to be reunited with family or go back to their homes. I do, however, know what it is like to live outside my own native land and have done so for a number of years now. Every time I fly into the George Best Belfast City Airport from Nigeria, Wales, Fiji or Chicago where I now live, it is always a home-coming experience like no other, for all of the above memories described at the beginning of this chapter converge in a most emotive moment: 'I'm returning home!'

We return to our story of sonship again, this time in respect of the nation of Israel and the prophetic literature; primarily the book of Hosea, but also Isaiah and Jeremiah. Hosea, as we shall see, also portrays a future home-coming like no other where Israel, after having been in exile, is a prodigal son now ready to return home (11:10–11). We will look at these verses in a moment, but before we do we must turn to the beginning of chapter 11 because the author offers us here a vista of Israel's entire filial relationship to God. As one commentator has pointed out: 'the son/Israel embarks on a three-part historical journey in chapter 11':[1] the past (11:1–4), present (11:5–9) and the future (11:10–11). As we focus on these three phases God is giving his son Israel a history lesson.

1. The past (Hosea 11:1–11)

a. What God has done for Israel (11:1–4)

Hosea prophesied during the middle of the eighth century immediately prior to the nation being taken into exile. With the mighty Assyrian army now breathing down the neck of God's people, they are in a state of moral confusion and sin and living far away from their God. The author graphically portrays the ensuing events soon to take place by the use of many metaphors[2] in the portrayal of his message. God is portrayed as a 'great lion' (5:14) and Israel to a 'wild donkey' (8:9) and the latter is also described as a 'vine' (10:1) and a trained, stubborn 'heifer' (10:11). In Hosea 11, however the more intimate language of the family (in the singular) takes over, where God is likened to a parent and Israel to a *child* and *son* (1), language which is in keeping with the general thrust of the book, for 'the primary institution . . . [and] . . . root metaphor employed by Hosea is to portray Israel and Judah as YHWH's household'.[3] This 'familial imagery for Israel is central in Hosea'[4] even though as we shall soon see Israel is 'a distracted family'[5] and in grave danger because if the people of God do not change their ways the irony is that they will return to the state from which God had rescued them all those centuries ago, slavery.

It has often been said that in order to move on in the future a necessary prerequisite is to first understand what has happened in the

---

[1] Gale A. Yee, *The Book of Hosea: Introduction, Commentary, and Reflections*, NIB (Nashville: Abingdon, 1996), p. 278. I have slightly amended the verses which Yee uses.

[2] See J. Andrew Dearman, *The Book of Hosea*, NICOT (Grand Rapids: Eerdmans, 2010), pp. 9–16.

[3] Ibid., p. 45.

[4] Ibid., p. 278.

[5] Derek Kidner, *The Message of Hosea: Love to the Loveless* (Leicester: IVP, 1981), p. 17.

past. So, in verses 1–3 the prophet is looking back over his shoulder as he reminds God's people, Israel, of how much had been done for the nation. The repeated use of the past tense is an obvious feature of this section as God recounts how he had *loved* (1), *called* (1, 2), *taught* (3) and *healed* (3) his people. Unfortunately, Israel did not respond in kind and God's people is described as a nation that *went from me, sacrificed to the Baals* and *burned incense to images* (2). The pathos of the passage is patently obvious too as God is seen to repeatedly address the community in the first person singular, *I*, and this coupled with the past tenses accentuates the prophet's message and the pain which Yahweh felt. We shall now look at the four verbs above which, as far as God is concerned, describe a history of parental goodness.

(i) God loved his child (1, 4)

There is an unmistakable poetic quality about the opening verses of this chapter as God directly addresses the nation in the first person and in what we might call the lyrics of love: *I loved him* (1, cf. 4). The past is clearly in view as the prophet recounts Israel's infancy status when God set his love upon the nation (Exod. 4:22–23). Divine passion runs deep in this passage and throughout Hosea as a whole for 'no one before', as David Hubbard has noted, 'had spoken so repeatedly of God's love for his people'[6] as much as this prophet. The Hebrew root 'love' (*'āhab*) recurs no less than on eighteen occasions in the book, with the most likely reason for the repetition of this affectionate language being the historical situation of Hosea's own family, especially his relationship with his wife, Gomer, which becomes a conduit for understanding God's love for Israel. God's love for Israel was the very bedrock of the father-son relationship at the beginning, as Deuteronomy 7:7–8 records: 'It was not because you were more numerous than any other people that the LORD set his heart on you . . . for you were the fewest of all peoples. It was because the LORD loved you' (NRSV). Divine love, moreover, continued to be the glue as well as the means by which God continued to guide his son, as verse 4 makes clear: *I led them with cords of human kindness, and with ties of love.*[7]

---

[6] David Allan Hubbard, *Hosea: An Introduction and Commentary* (Leicester/ Downers Grove: IVP, 1989), p. 29.

[7] Some commentators think that the author here returns to the earlier animal imagery (i.e., 10:11) and its master and the need for the former to be controlled and managed (e.g., 4:16). But given the close proximity with the earlier familial metaphors (11:1) and the highly affective terminology ('loved' and 'called') it is more likely that the father-son metaphor is continued.

(ii) God called his Son (2)

God had also *called* (*qārā'*) his *son*, where the verb can mean the naming of someone, and indeed *Israel* was how this nascent nation came to be known at the inauguration of (and throughout) its relationship to God (Exod. 4:22). *Israel* was also the name which would distinguish this nation from all the surrounding customs at the time. But the verb 'call' is one among many others which the prophet Hosea employs to demonstrate God's conviction that Israel was his own (e.g., 1:2; 2:14–15; 13:5). Often the terms 'love' and 'call' are related, especially when describing God's choice of his people. So, the replay button is pushed as a reminder to Israel to reflect on the time when God called or 'chose you' (Deut. 7:7). 'Love' (*'āhab*) and 'call' (*qārā'*) not only denote *choice* but are also the language of the covenant, signifying how God had set his affection on this small, insignificant nation and elected it to be his very own. It specifically recalls the moment in Exodus 4:22–23 when God rescued Israel out of the slavery and bondage of Egypt and brought the nation to live in the Promised Land.[8]

(iii) God taught this child to walk (3–4)

God not only *loved* and *called* his son but like any responsible parent he endeavoured to ensure the nation kept on the right path. If the earlier imagery of father and son denotes the deliverance or salvation of Israel out of Egyptian slavery (1–2, the exodus), the language in verse 3 goes further by elucidating the next natural stage in the relationship, the walking or guidance God provided for youthful Israel during the period of the wilderness.[9] At such a time when Israel was still young and wearied easily with the journey from Egypt to the Promised Land, God tenderly and attentively cared for his people. As we noted in chapter 1, Israel was a very young child at the Exodus, but here in verse 3 where the period of the desert or wilderness is in view, 'Ephraim (that is *Israel*) *is a child no longer* . . . [but] like some aloof and scornful adolescent he has forgotten or never realized – or simply does not want to know – what he owes to this relationship'.[10] Indeed, Israel by this time ought to have demonstrated a measure of growth and maturity but God bore with his

---

[8] Dearman, *Hosea*, p. 277.

[9] Walter Brueggemann, *Tradition for Crisis: A Study in Hosea* (Richmond: John Knox, 1968), pp. 27 and 33, views 11:1–2 as describing the Exodus and v. 3 the wilderness journey. He comments on v. 3 as follows: 'In chapter 11, the wilderness motif follows immediately upon the Exodus motif we have already considered.'

[10] Kidner, *Hosea*, p. 102 (emphasis added).

undeveloped child; in language which is rich and emotive in content God *was to them like those who lift infants to their cheeks* (4, NRSV). God is like a parent crooning over his kid, 'as a father absorbed in coaxing and supporting the child's staggering steps; picking him up when he tires or tumbles "making the place better" when he hurts himself'.[11] Filial Israel should have shown more signs of growth and progress, but at times the nation's relationship to God was stunted and stationary and in need of a kick-start in order to move forward.

(iv) God healed his Son (3)

Children are full of the vigour and vitality of youthfulness but they are often vulnerable and prone to periods of illness. The verb 'heal' (*rāpā'*) is used in verse 3 and could describe the physical healing necessary when someone is ill (e.g. 5:13; 6:1). Here there is probably another allusion to the wilderness narrative in the sense that if Israel heeded the instruction and advice of God, he would heal them:

> If you listen carefully to the voice of the LORD your God, and do what is right in his sight, if you pay attention to his commands and keep all his decrees, I will not bring upon you any of the diseases that I brought upon the Egyptians, for I am the LORD who heals you.[12]

Another nuance associated with the verb 'to heal' found in the book of Hosea is in describing forgiveness and the restoration of relationships (e.g., 7:1; 14:4) and this may also be a second meaning, the healing of the alienation between God and Israel. If this is so, it further describes another appropriate and necessary parental responsibility in this context, namely, forgiveness.[13]

Loved, called, taught and *healed*: what more could child-Israel want or need? In giving an answer to this question, we will consider some verses in Hosea 11 but also writings from another prophet (Isaiah) who prophesied during part of the eighth century, in which the Israelites are also described in the plural as 'children' or 'sons and daughters' and where the past is also in view, the period prior to Israel and the Israelites being taken into captivity by the Assyrians.

---

[11] Ibid.
[12] Exod. 15:26.
[13] Dearman, *Hosea*, p. 282.

b. How Israel and the Israelites had responded (Hos.11:2; Isa. 1:2–4)

(i) They went from me (Hos.11:2; Isa. 1:2–4)

The bright prospects of Israel's youth faded quickly and rapidly but it was nothing to do with the provision that God had made for them and everything to do with the poor choices which the nation and the Israelites had made. Israel did a runner, like the prophet Jonah, for we are told that the more God called the more these recalcitrant children ran in the opposite direction – *they went from me* (11:2). Children are often easily distracted and have short memories, prone to forget the past and what their parents have done for them. Certainly, Israel did not deserve anything which had been provided for them but the nation's response was less than what was expected. In fact, Israel's apostasy when considered against the parental goodness of God is less than ingratitude, a point noted by Derek Kidner:

> More than once we have been reminded of the bright promise of Israel's youth, so quickly to fade. *The promise arose out of God's grace rather than their good qualities,* and the fading of it out of sheer perversity – for it is one of Hosea's emphases that *Israel's sin,* so far from springing from hardship or ignorance, *was their reply to heaven's kindness and concern.*[14]

When we turn to the prophet Isaiah and in particular a lawsuit passage, we find that like Hosea, he also accuses the Israelites of similar desertion. In Isaiah the heart of the divine is laid bare as the heavens and the earth are called upon as witnesses against the Israelites' unfaithfulness. Sometimes sin is trivialized and we only see it in piecemeal form and not from a divinely, panoramic perspective. But God sees our all our transgressions and here a number of accusations are brought against his people. Again, before God accuses, he first reminds his people of how he had raised them. *I reared children and brought them up* (1:2), declares the Lord, where the emphasis is upon God's spiritual offspring (lit. 'children have I reared') and the time when God gave birth to the nation (Exod. 4:22). God not only reared these spiritual progeny, he also *brought them up* which describes his patient, providential care during the wilderness, including up to the time of Isaiah.[15] *But they* [i.e. they of

---

[14] Kidner, *Hosea*, p. 101 (emphasis added).
[15] J. Alec Motyer, *The Prophecy of Isaiah: An Introduction and Commentary* (Leicester/Downers Grove: IVP, 1993), p. 43.

all people] *have rebelled against me* (1:2), declares the Lord. God's children, the Israelites, have deliberately and willingly refused to accept the nature of the parent-child relationship and have sought to go their own stubborn way. In fact, they even make animals look smart, for while some beasts of the field can be stubborn, for example the *ox* (1:3) and the *donkey* (1:3), they are also renowned for being dense and dim. But even *they* learn and remember their *master* (1:3), the one to whom they belong. In contrast, *Israel*, pines the Lord, *does not know, my people do not understand* (1:3). What an indictment!

The Lord's accusations through the prophet Isaiah continue as the Israelites are further described as *children given to corruption* (1:4) where instead of living a distinctively different lifestyle, their sin had spoiled and ruined their reputation. In light of God's parental goodness, how on earth could all of this possibly happen? At the heart of the Israelites' sinfulness was how they stood in relation to the Lord and their commitment to search after and follow him. Instead of seeking the Lord, the exact opposite proved to be the case, for the Israelites *have spurned the Holy One of Israel*. More than that, they *turned their backs on him* (1:4).[16] Thus, instead of endeavouring to draw ever closer to God their parent, these children were becoming more and more estranged and alienated from him. Instead of acting like God's family, they were behaving like foreigners or aliens (like a '*non*-Israelite'[17]), outsiders who did not belong to the household.

(ii) They sacrificed to the Baals, and they burned incense to images (Hos. 11:2)

Israel was not only guilty of divine defection, the nation also engaged in offering sacrifices to the Baals, an action also attributed to Gomer, the prophet's wife (Hos. 2:13). While some have concluded that such actions are anachronistic because such worship was not a part of Israelite society, this is not an unreasonable charge, for no sooner had God given the Ten Commandments to Moses than the Israelites were engaging in the worship of the golden calf, 'a *cultic item* that Hosea could easily identify with the fertility cults of his generation'.[18] For Israel, this act soon led to the worship of other cults, such as Baal of Peor (Num. 25) and so we see that the fruits of the nation's apostasy of which Hosea speaks were sown as

---

[16] Ibid.
[17] Ibid., p. 44 (emphasis added).
[18] Duane A. Garret, *Hosea, Joel*, NAC 19A (Nashville: Broadman and Holman, 1997), p. 222.

early as the exodus event when God entered into a filial relationship with the nation. It is a reminder that if bad habits are not nipped in the bud early in life they can later on in adulthood become straggly weeds with deep roots that are resistant and hard to dig up. The tense of the verb 'to sacrifice' (2) moreover denotes a continuous action in the past rather than a one-off event, which effectively puts Israel's conduct into the category of being a 'serial offender'[19] a violator and denier of the nation's relationship as son to God.

That was the past; we now move to the present.

2. The present (Hos. 11:5–9)

The tender tone of Hosea 11:1–4 changes to threat in verses 5–9 where the reality of exile stares God's people straight in the face. Verse 5 is probably not a question but a simple negative statement that Israel is going to return to exile and the exodus will be undone by the return to slavery from which the nation had been rescued all those years ago. Then Israel will be under a different lord, no longer a Pharaoh but the king of Assyria. The play on words in verse 5 is that Israel would not *return* to Egypt but would instead go to Assyria because they refused to return to the Lord. Israel's past rebellion and waywardness continues in the present and God is faced with squaring the circle of, on the one hand, his fierce love for his people and, on the other, exacting the necessary punishment and discipline, thereby remaining true to his holy character.

The present tenses are particularly apparent in verses 8–9 and in what are arguably the most poignant words in Scripture where God's heart is laid bare in the threefold questions: *How can I give you up, Ephraim? How can I hand you over, Israel? How can I make you like Zeboiim?* With regard to the insight this chapter gives us into the character of God, Derek Kidner rightly comments that it is 'one of the boldest in the Old Testament – indeed the whole Bible – in exposing to us the mind and heart of God in human terms'.[20] God had borne with the sins of his people and had exercised divine forbearance to the nth degree, but he knows that Israel must be punished (if he is true to his holy character) and be handed over to their oppressors. Judgment must come first if repentance is ever to occur. The twin aspects of parental beneficence and childish rebellion are thrown together with the reality that Israel is going *to return*

[19] Dearman, *Hosea*, p. 281.
[20] Kidner, *Hosea*, p. 100.

to Egypt (5) and to be ruled by Assyria (5), where *swords will flash in their cities* (6). It is an agonizing action that must be taken and we are once again confronted with the pathos of a God who loved his son Israel so much.

It is a truism that those who love much get hurt most. And it is often the case that we are hurt most by those we love most. Love hurts, and God is heard to exclaim in great anguish: *all my compassion is aroused* (8). The decision to judge his children was not a cold, calculated or detached action and as their parent God has tried everything, but to no avail. God struggles with the impending decision he has to make and laments having to punish his children. This text, as the earlier one in Deuteronomy 32, also raises the issue of the (im)passibility of God, of whether or not God suffers. In chapter 2, we noted that God is not apathetic and suffers alongside and *because* of his people; here in Hosea 11:8–9 we can go further to say that God identifies even more and actually suffers *with* his people. Although God is going to punish, he is concerned deeply for them. After all wasn't this the same God who immediately prior to forming Israel into a nation and making them his son, promised to deliver them from Egyptian bondage, thereby also identifying with their experience: 'I have indeed seen the misery of my people in Egypt. I have heard them crying out because of their slave drivers, and I am concerned about their suffering'?[21] Why shouldn't God feel so again? Now, some centuries later in Hosea, with the prospect of exile staring God's people in the face, God mourns and laments over the actions that will ensue. As one Old Testament commentator notes: 'Although God punishes his people for their sins, he empathizes *with* their suffering . . . God immediately turns from the role of judge to that of *fellow-sufferer*'.[22]

If heartache could be placed on a scale of suffering, we might put the rebuff of a stranger at the bottom followed next by the upset of a clash between friends, but at the very top must surely be the stinging, jilting pain of a parent-child estrangement alongside the deep wound of a betrayal in marriage. In this prophecy, God is portrayed as experiencing both, as the heart of the divine aches for his people Israel and the actions about to take place. The deeper the love, the deeper the pain, and the unfolding of these events and the God who is at the centre of it all has been well described by David Hubbard:

---

[21] Exod. 3:7.
[22] Terence E. Fretheim, *The Suffering of God: An Old Testament Perspective*, OBT (Philadelphia: Fortress, 1984), p. 136.

The depth of what God feels, as Hosea understands those feelings, can never be separated from the height of who he is. The sharpness of the pain that registers in the divine complaints is directly related to the majesty of the Person who is suffering. And that language of suffering takes on its pathos from the familial relationship which controls Hosea's prophecy.[23]

Nowhere else in the Old Testament, certainly not until Jesus, do we find 'a clearer passage of *wounded majesty*'. God, the provider of every good thing for his people, has everything thrown back in his face and thus 'the story of God's son Israel is the story of a defection of unnatural proportions'.[24] Israel has lived a profligate lifestyle, a prodigal son no less, far away from God, and it is deeply felt. Wounded majesty, wounded love!

Prodigal sons, of course, come in many shapes and sizes. At the most recent Lausanne Conference, 2010 in Cape Town, South Africa, Stefan Gustavsson of the Swedish Alliance, addressed the question of the shifting spiritual landscape in Europe by reminding the delegates of an earlier talk given by Francis Schaeffer to the Lausanne conference in 1974 who emphasized the need for 'sound doctrine' and being able to give 'honest answers to honest questions'. Gustavvson provided a telling illustration of how truth has been eroded in Europe over the last one hundred years by reminding delegates of how on 1 April, 2010 an online store was selling the product Game Station. Before the product could be purchased, shoppers had to sign up to the necessary terms and conditions, which read as follows:

By placing your order . . . you agree to grant Us a non-transferable option to claim, for now and for ever more, your immortal soul. Should We wish to exercise this option, you agree to surrender your immortal soul, and any claim you may have on it, within 5 (five) working days of receiving written notification from game-station.co.uk.

What's more, the company included an option for shoppers immediately prior to making their purchase to click on a button in order 'to nullify your soul transfer' where they would be rewarded with a five pound coupon. Only 12% of shoppers for that day noticed this and at the end of trading on that first day of April 2010, the other

[23] Hubbard, *Hosea*, p. 45.
[24] Sinclair B. Ferguson, *Children of the Living God* (Edinburgh: Banner of Truth, 1989), pp. 11–12.

88% of the transactions totalled 7,700 human souls! Gustavsson went on to apply this illustration to the spiritual condition of the Christianity in Europe:

> We Europeans, it seems to me, have in a similar, careless way sold our souls and dispersed our rich inheritance. *Europe has become the prodigal son* ... Europe has denied the gospel and replaced it with other convictions, pre-eminently secularist.[25]

Truth decay, secularization and pluralism, have all been endemic in European society and culture for decades now and there is a desperate need to return to the gospel and the word of God. In all these ways, Europe has sold its soul and spiritually speaking is a continent in crisis.

Israel too was in crisis and on the verge of being swallowed up by the great powers of history, shattered by the ravages of invasion. The period of exile which was about to ensue would last for seventy long years where an entire generation would die. When that happened imagine for a moment what it may have been like for some of that dying generation living in exile. In my mind's eye I can see some of them asking the questions: 'Is there a future for Israel and the Israelites as God's children?', 'Will we ever be able to return home?', 'Has God forgotten us forever?' Interestingly during a later period of exile in Babylon the Israelites were commanded by their tormentors to 'sing one of the songs of Zion',[26] and one wonders if the song of sonship (Deut. 32) that Moses had earlier taught them prior to his death was among their repertoire? 'Will we ever be able to sing *this* song again?' As we turn to our next section this is not the end, for while the Israelites may have repeatedly broken the covenant, the relationship of sonship, though twisted, had never been entirely broken.

3. The future: sonship the ground for hope (Hos. 11:10–11)

Bill Bryson, the popular travel writer, in his book *I'm a Stranger Here Myself*[27] describes the period in his family life when it was time for the couple's children to go off to university. It is a moment many parents can look back to as it effectively closes one chapter in

[25] See the link <http://soundcloud.com/ian-buchanan/ws-10007–1>.
[26] Ps. 137:3.
[27] Bill Bryson, *I'm a Stranger Here Myself* (New York: Broadway Books, 2000), p. 132.

the life of a family and also opens up a new one, an experience which my wife and I are slowly coming to grips with as parents. One thing was for sure for Bryson, family life would never be the same again. Reflecting on his feelings during that time when his children left home, he desperately wished he could turn back the hands of time. It was he pines, 'like losing a son' and he poignantly concludes: 'I would give anything to have them both back.' Bryson's sentiments resonate with many parents.

Now certainly, God as parent does not need Israel or the Israelites any more than he needs us. Israel as a nation had been sent into exile, a punishment for her sins and waywardness. The grace which God had shown to Israel was thrown back in his face and met with disgrace. If the nation is ever going to rise from the embers of the exile it will not be due to anything which this son can do but is wholly dependent again on renewed grace and on God. Could things really change? Was there really hope for this son? Israel did not deserve grace but change is in the air here, for the arrogance and the open flaunting of her sinful ways are things of the past. We read that *when God roars* (10) the response is met twice by *children* [who] *will come trembling from the west* (10–11), an indication that the period of discipline has come to an end.[28] God takes the initiative, for he had in mind not to cast Israel off forever, and this in addition to the clear change of heart of his children which results in a change in their behaviour, as is evident by the fact that the nation no longer runs after other lovers to bed (2:5) but now wishes to *follow the LORD* (10). God cannot give them up (11:8); his love remains, and this together with the future tenses and the repeated use of the third person plural 'they' remind us that these 'sons will come back, shaken and ashamed, home to me again'.[29] Judgment *and* mercy converge here in God's dealings with his people, Israel. Israel had come a long way, which in retrospect was 'a saw-toothed history' and a saw-toothed journey, as Eugene Peterson pointed out:

> Israel was up one day and down the next. One day marching through the Red Sea, singing songs of victory, the next day they were grumbling in the desert because they missed having Egyptian steak and potatoes for supper. One day they were marching around Jericho blowing trumpets and raising hearty hymns, and the next day they were plunged into an orgy at some fertility shrine.

[28] Dearman, *Hosea*, p. 293, n. 62.
[29] Kidner, *Hosea*, p. 141.

'But all the time', concludes Peterson, 'we realize something solid and steady; they are always God's people. God is steadfastly with them, in mercy and judgment, insistently gracious.'[30]

As we read these verses and the depths to which Israel plummeted in sinning against God by breaking the covenant, it is a reminder that God still loves his people, though he certainly expects repentance from sin. Today, God can also choose, should he so wish, to break down the most hard-hearted of people and manifest his love to those we least expect to receive grace, including the person living next door to us, those in our family circle, or a spouse for whom we have been praying for many years. And God is still in the business of saving the most heinous of sinners and make them his sons and daughters.

A similar story of restoration is also told by other Old Testament prophets when Israel – described clearly in the language of sonship – will be brought back into the land. Jeremiah, for example, looks forward to the dawning of a new day and a brighter more hopeful era:

> They will come with weeping;
>   they will pray as I bring them back.
> I will lead them beside streams of water
>   on a level path where they will not stumble,
> because *I am Israel's father*
>   and *Ephraim is my firstborn son*.
> 'Hear the word of the LORD, O nations;
>   proclaim it in distant coastlands:
> 'He who scattered Israel *will gather them*
>   and will watch over his flock like a Shepherd.'[31]

He later echoes the same sentiments where the future for Israel is couched in filial terms:

> Is not Ephraim my dear son,
>   the *child* in whom I delight?
> Though I often speak against him,
>   *I still remember him*.
> Therefore my heart yearns for him;
>   I have great compassion for him,
>   declares the LORD.[32]

[30] Eugene H. Peterson, *A Long Obedience in the Same Direction: Discipleship in an Instant Society* (Downers Grove: IVP, 2000), p. 87.
[31] Jer. 31:9–10 (emphasis added).
[32] Jer. 31:20 (emphasis added).

And the same hope which God's children celebrated in anticipation of being repatriated in the land, is told by the prophet Isaiah:

> I will say to the north, 'Give them up!'
>   and to the south, 'Do not hold them back.'
> *Bring my sons from afar*
>   *and my daughters from the ends of the earth* –
> everyone who is called by my name,
>   whom I created for my glory,
>   whom I formed and made.[33]

In all of these texts what is noteworthy is that there is a sense of permanence within the father-son relationship between God and Israel, so although the relationship had been tarnished, bruised, and battered it was not entirely severed. Indeed the original language of sonship which inaugurated the filial relationship between God and Israel in the first instance (Exod. 4:22–23) is appealed to once again in the post-exilic era. The God who brought his firstborn son out of the slavery of Egypt would once again, with a fresh enactment of grace, bring his son back home from exile. Ultimately the father could not disown his son and a new exodus is ushered in where the impetus for this restoration finds its spring and origin in the purposes of God and not in those who committed the offence. Thus, there is a measure of durability about the relationship as Chris Wright notes:

> in the prophetic texts, the relationship of sonship not only survived even *after* the judgment of exile had fallen on the nation, but could be appealed to as the basis for a fresh act of redemption and a restored relationship.[34]

In all this, the impetus for the restoration comes not from those who have committed the offence but from God who cannot let them go. When this Father calls, son-Israel will come running home.[35]

---

[33] Isa. 43:6–7 (emphasis added).

[34] Christopher J. H. Wright, *Knowing Jesus Through the Old Testament* (Downers Grove: IVP, 1995), p. 126 (italics original).

[35] This return from exile is portrayed in the books of Haggai, Ezra, and Nehemiah, though N. T. Wright is of the view that Israel was still (theologically speaking) in exile and it was not until the coming of Jesus, God's Son that this is brought to an end; see *The New Testament and the People of God*, 4th ed. (London: SPCK, 1997), p. 269.

Summary

The prophet Hosea picks up the story of Israel's relationship as son – past, present, and future – where the nation is reminded of all that God has done in terms of saving them at the time of the exodus and bringing them through the desert until the present time. The filial relationship deteriorates further in the present and God is confronted with a moral dilemma: he deeply loves this reckless child who still shows no sign of the growth that was expected, but the situation demands that he must punish Israel if he is to remain true to his holy character. God feels the hurt, this time empathizing *with* this recalcitrant child who ironically returns to the state from which God had rescued it, slavery.

But that is not the end, for the same language of sonship with which God had entered into covenant with the nation of Israel is brought into service again with a fresh enactment of grace as God calls his prodigal son back home.

Part Two
Sonship in the New Testament

Luke 2:6–7; 1:32–36; Matthew 2:13–18; 3:13–17; 4:1–11; Luke 9:28–36; Matthew 27:33–54; Romans 1:3–4

5. Jesus *the* Son of God

With the Old Testament part of our storyline of sonship complete,[1] we now turn our attention to the New Testament where the filial plot thickens. We firstly consider Jesus' relationship to God as Son, which is important since he stands in line with the Adam-Israel-David trajectory, the rich, storied background that provides the context to properly understand his filial relationship to the Father. In fact we ignore this earlier Old Testament context to our peril, for 'the imagery of Jesus as Son is best viewed against this backdrop. Jesus is the son born from the womb of Israel and the Davidic line, both of which carry the legacy of divine sonship'.[2]

This background is also crucial for a number of other reasons: first, the New Testament authors of the books we will consider demonstrate an awareness of this rich Old Testament heritage. Secondly, the failures and disappointment of earlier sons (i.e. Adam, Israel, the Israelites and David) heighten our expectations of how Jesus' filial relationship will pan out – will his sonship be any different to his forebears? Third, it is important for us to have an understanding of Jesus' relationship to God at this point of our narrative

---

[1] Space does not permit us to look at the importance of 'son' in the era between the Old and New Testaments. For a brief discussion see, Matthew Vellanickal, *The Divine Sonship of Christians in the Johannine Writings*, AnBib. 72 (Rome: Biblical Institute Press, 1977), pp. 45–52.

[2] 'Jesus, Images of', in *DBI*, pp. 437–451. Of course, Jesus as the Second Adam (Rom. 5:12–21) undoes the devastation which Adam, the son of God, wrecked in the Garden.

of sonship for there 'are approximately 150 New Testament references to Christ as "Son" '[3] most of which occur in the Gospels, and most importantly they pave the way for what follows. Only when we have first understood Jesus' filial relationship to his Father will we ever be able to grasp the significance this might have for the Christian's relation to God as his sons and daughters.

So, what sort of son was Jesus and how does he compare to those other sons of God who preceded him? To whom did Jesus give his allegiance and loyalty? And, do the New Testament authors present Jesus' sonship as a model for Christians as the children of God to emulate and follow? To help us answer these questions we will mainly focus on the critical points in Jesus' life, namely, his *birth* (Luke 2:6–7; 2:13–18), *baptism* (Matt. 3:13–17), *temptation* (Matt. 4:1–11), *transfiguration* (Matt. 17:5), *death* (Matt. 27:43, 54) and *resurrection* (Rom. 1:2–4). Each of these scenes is a cameo of the life of Jesus and should help us glean important insights into his sonship. So, in terms of his historical career, who on earth was Jesus? We begin with the synoptic Gospels before turning to Paul's writings, though the latter of course were written earlier.

1. Birth and infancy narratives

a. Mary's 'firstborn, a Son' (Luke 2:6–7)

Luke 2:6–7 is a familiar text at Christmas time but these are also very important verses for our theme because it has been rightly said that Christmas is about a son, a Son away from 'home'. The infancy narratives are told with a brevity and simplicity of language. The evangelist tells us that Joseph and Mary were required to travel to Bethlehem to register because Joseph 'belonged to the house and line of David' (Luke 2:4). He goes on to say that *while they were there, the time came for the baby to be born, and she gave birth to her firstborn, a son* (6–7). Mary, often neglected in Protestant theology, is important for she is the God-bearer, the one through whom the Son of God would be born. Jesus was in a very real sense Mary's son – her firstborn – which resonates with the language used earlier of Israel in Exodus 4:22–23, and so Jesus is an integral part of the rich and many-layered tradition of sonship which flows directly out of the Old Testament. This firstborn son is not only first by reason of being the first child and therefore special, but is also thereby the leader of a new spiritual family.

[3] 'Son', in *DBI*, p. 805.

Though this is a very human story of a young teenage peasant girl, God's fingerprints are all over the text as he is the one super-intending the proceedings that are unfolding as verse 6 makes clear: *While they were there, the time came for the baby to be born*. The *time* of which Luke speaks refers not only to the fact that Mary's period of gestation was coming to an end (cf. Luke 1:57), but that 'events are progressing according to *the divine plan*'.[4] Joel Green further stresses that we have 'to a degree not fully appreciated ... in the Third Gospel [that] Luke's narrative is *theo*logical in substance and focus: that is, it is centered on *God*'.[5] In other words, God is the one who moves the hands of the clock of salvation-history as the countdown for Mary's firstborn son enters the world.

The apostle Paul strikes a similar note when he writes: 'But when the time had fully come, God sent his Son, born of a woman, born under law, to redeem those under law, that we might receive the adoption as sons.'[6] For Paul too, time does not ripen of its own accord nor is it the mere passing of time to which he refers; rather this is the climactic moment when God sovereignly intervened in salvation-history by sending his only Son into the world in order to redeem us. As we shall see later, according to Paul, Jesus' sonship is also the basis for our becoming the sons and daughters of God (e.g. Gal. 4:4–7).

(i) Jesus, God's Son (Luke 1:32–36)

Luke 2:6–7, however, is not the first time that the evangelist mentions sonship in his Gospel for earlier the angel Gabriel appeared to Mary to disclose how the birth of this promised son would come about: *The Holy Spirit will come upon you, and the power of the Most High will overshadow you. So the holy one to be born will be called the Son of God* (35–36). In other words, Mary's son is also God's Son, the latter being the first direct reference to the sonship of Jesus in the Gospel of Luke. This mention of Jesus' sonship resonates with and is the fulfilment of the earlier Old Testament uses in 2 Samuel 7:14, Psalms 2:7 and 89:26–27, by not only showing that Jesus has a special relationship with God but that he is also God's representative on earth.[7] What is also important to note here in verse

[4] Joel B. Green, *The Gospel of Luke*, NICNT (Grand Rapids: Eerdmans, 1997), p. 128.
[5] Ibid., p. 22 (emphasis original).
[6] Gal. 4:4–5.
[7] Green, *Luke*, p. 90. See also Brendan Byrne, *The Hospitality of God: A Reading of Luke's Gospel* (Collegeville: Liturgical Press, 2000), p. 24.

35 is the way in which the author brings together the twin notions of sonship and the Holy Spirit. The angel declares to Mary: *The Holy Spirit will come upon you . . . so the holy one to be born will be called the Son of God.* 'Luke insists on the links between the Son and the Spirit.'[8] Here Jesus, as a direct consequence of God's creative power via the Holy Spirit, comes as the Son of God, as Green again notes: 'Jesus is the "Son of God" . . . as a result of his conception, itself the result of the miraculous work of the Spirit.'[9]

This interlocking of the twin themes of sonship and the Spirit, moreover, is not only important at Jesus' conception but also occurs later in the Gospel (see below) at the inauguration of his public ministry on earth, at his baptism and temptation (Luke 3:21–22; 4:1, 3, 9, 14, 18). The combining of the two ideas of Jesus' Sonship and the Spirit is also a significant one for Paul (see below) when, for example, he says that 'God sent *the Spirit of his Son* into our hearts, the Spirit who calls out "Abba, Father"' (Gal. 4:6). And both are brought together by Paul at the crucial moment of assurance for the Christian when 'the Spirit himself testifies with our spirit that we are God's children' (Rom. 8:16).

(ii) There's a new kid in town

Two other points are worthy of note in this early infancy narrative in Luke. First, the phrase 'Son of God' (1:35) is one of the many important titles for Jesus in the New Testament, but this is a designation that had other resonances at the time: emperors, for example, such as Caesar Augustus (Luke 2:1), took on such a title for themselves.[10] Roman rulers after their death and even during their lifetime were often deified and given the title 'son of God'. Thus by identifying Jesus chiefly as *the Son of God* (and not '*a* son of God') Luke is not only subtly subverting the ruling powers and authorities of his day, he is also in the words of the American rock band, the Eagles, telling his readers 'there's a new *kid* in town'! There was only one show in town on that epoch-making night outside Bethlehem over 2,000 years ago and it did not take place in a comfortable palace but in a borrowed guest-room and it was (and still is) all about Jesus. In other words, Luke wants his audience (and us) to know that the first Christmas and Christianity is not about

---

[8] François Bovon, *Luke the Theologian* (Waco: Baylor University Press, 2006), p. 211.

[9] Green, *Luke*, p. 91.

[10] Other terms in the gospel narrative in addition to 'Son of God' which had an imperial edge to them, and which make the coming of Christ so subversive, include 'gospel' (2:10), 'Saviour' (1:47; 2:11) and 'peace' (2:14).

any earthly potentate, in this case the emperor, but only and always about Jesus, Mary's firstborn son, Jesus *the Son of God.*

(iii) A son clothed in humility (Luke 2:6–7)

Second, we should not overlook the manner in which this Son of God came. After Mary had given birth to her firstborn son we are told *she wrapped him in cloths and placed him in a manger* (7). Today, when a child is born into a family a mother (and father) may spend months carefully planning the purchase of baby clothes, making sure the colour is right (blue for a boy, pink for a girl!) as well as taking care that they have enough changes of clothing for those 'accidents' that can happen from time to time. A firstborn child, moreover, is always special, since it signifies the beginning of a new phase in family life, when two adults become parents for the first time. The sometimes excessive amounts of money spent preparing for parenthood today stands in complete contrast to Luke's account of this peasant family, for we are told Mary's firstborn son was simply wrapped in strips of cloth. James Resseguie,[11] in a fascinating study of Luke's Gospel, has shown how clothing maps the contours of spiritual life, where the garments a person wore and their colour were indicative of social status. For example, in Luke 16:20 the colour purple and the fine linen worn by the rich man are indicative of wealth and prosperity, garments 'so costly that normally only kings would afford them'.[12] Certainly there was nothing unusual for a child born in the ancient world to be wrapped in swaddling-cloths, but Jesus, Mary's firstborn son, is dressed in strips of cloth and then laid in a feeding trough for animals (7) which upsets ancient and modern sensibilities! To the Jewish mind this is hardly the way for the Messiah to appear. But this is exactly the point the evangelist is making and it is in keeping with God's new agenda, for though Jesus is a unique son, he comes into the world in humility and meekness. The quietness of Jesus' coming as the Son of God, the one who steps out of eternity into history is in the 'everyday ... strips of rags not the regal arabesque garments,'[13] – the extraordinary dressed in the ordinary – and by so doing he identifies with those he had come to save.

[11] James L. Resseguie, *Spiritual Landscape: Images of the Spiritual Life in the Gospel of Luke* (Peabody: Hendrickson, 2004), p. 91.
[12] Gildas Hamel, *Poverty and Charity in Roman Palestine: First Three Centuries C. E.* (Berkley: University of California Press, 1990), p. 64.
[13] Resseguie, *Spiritual Landscape*, pp. 91–92.

b. 'Out of Egypt I called my Son' (Matt. 2:13–18)

Our second infancy narrative is in Matthew's account and the visit of the magi who, when they found Jesus with Mary and Joseph, presented their gifts to him. Dreams have an important role to play in what immediately follows, first in the way that the magi are warned not to return to Herod but to go back home by a different route (2:12); and second, the medium by which Joseph is told to *get up . . . take the child and his mother and escape to Egypt* (13). Once there, the new family was to stay in Egypt until the death of Herod, events which the evangelist, in the first of a number of references, views as the completion of prophecy: '*And so was fulfilled*[14] *what the Lord had said through the prophet:* '*Out of Egypt I called my son*' (14).

It is the last phrase, *out of Egypt I called my Son*, which is of particular significance to us, where Old Testament resonances are not hard to find, for this is the language of Hosea 11:1, used originally to describe the nation of Israel as son. Indeed, there are similarities in the events which happened to Israel in the Old Testament and in the life of Jesus here in this passage: for example, just as God delivered Israel his son from the hands of the tyrant Pharaoh so now Jesus as God's Son is rescued from the hands of another oppressor, king Herod. But there are also differences here in that Israel escaped *from* Egypt whereas Jesus escapes *to* Egypt, which has caused some to question whether there is any typology involved here. It could be argued, moreover, that in Hosea 11:1 the author is reflecting on Israel's *past*, the time when God called the nation as his son out of Egypt. In Matthew 2:13–15, however, the evangelist is describing events that are to take place in the *future*, Jesus' subsequent sojourn in Egypt, and actions which centre on an individual and not a nation. Thus, it might appear we have an example of illegitimate transfer. How do we reconcile these differences?

First, there does not need to be an exact correspondence between antitype (Israel as God's son) and the type (Jesus as God's Son) for typology to work. There is typology here, but as R. T. France makes clear:

> Matthew's typology is decidedly loose . . . but typology depends on meaningful associations rather than exact correspondences, and in each of these quite different ways the mention of Egypt is sufficient to provide food for thought . . . between the events God directed in Egypt . . . and what the same God is now accomplish-

---

[14] Cf. 1:22; 2:15, 17, 23; 8:17; 12:17; 13:35; 21:4; 27:9.

ing through the new deliverer . . . identified by the prophetic text as his Son.[15]

A 'type' is basically a pattern and it is clear there are similarities and commonalities between the two texts which the author does not want his readers to miss. Essentially what Matthew is doing here is using the exodus, the forming of a new people of God as God's son, which was a 'potent symbol' pointing to a much greater work and deliverance which God was to bring about. He takes this up and applies it to the 'new exodus' that has been ushered in by Jesus. In other words, Matthew is recapitulating salvation history, the exodus story, by taking a well-known metaphor of Israel as God's son in the Old Testament which he uses to describe another exodus in the New Testament, one associated with his unique and only Son, Jesus. Matthew is thus keenly aware that Jesus' filial role over against Israel's is new and superior, for unlike the latter he never failed as son nor did he repeatedly disobey God or his word (see next section). In light of this and in response to the criticism to do with typology France concludes:

> Thus far from Matthew's having seized on a convenient use of the word 'son' . . . in relation to Egypt and illegitimately transferred it to a quite different kind of son, this quotation in fact expresses in the most economical form a wide-ranging theology of the new exodus and Jesus as the true Israel which will play a significant role throughout Matthew's gospel.[16]

In conclusion, in this the most Jewish of gospels, Jesus is the true Son of God Israel never proved to be. Jesus as Son is the new Israel of God, the one who rights all the wrongs of all the previous sons of God who had failed so miserably. By using the phrase *out of Egypt have I called my Son* the author signals a new exodus when Jesus would enact the role not only of God's present deliverer but also of God's 'son' Israel himself.

2. Baptism: the beloved son (Matt. 3:13–17)

We move away from the infancy narratives to consider the first of several stories which have to do with Jesus' sonship as an adult. Here

[15] R. T. France, *The Gospel of Matthew*, NICNT (Grand Rapids: Eerdmans, 2007), p. 80.
[16] Ibid.

Jesus' identity as divine Son is clearly seen at his baptism. One of the questions which students of this passage often raise, however, is why Jesus was prepared to undergo baptism. After all baptism is for sinners and Scripture elsewhere tells us Jesus never committed any sin (Heb. 4:15). In response to this, Matthew 3:13–17 does not address the question of Jesus' sinlessness, nor does it seek to. In fact, it is not the baptism itself that is central to the events that are happening here; rather the climax lies in the declaration of Jesus' identity, who he is, namely, God's unique Son.[17] Thus, whereas in the earlier infancy narratives where Jesus' sonship is assumed (Matt. 2:15), here his *filial identity* is explicitly and overtly brought out into the open.

Also important to what is taking place here is how the evangelist has carefully arranged his material: the baptism sits in immediate juxtaposition to the temptation narrative (Matt. 4:1–11). This is no accident but is deliberate and theologically very important to Matthew, for both have to do with Jesus' filial relationship to his Father (cf. 3:17 and 4:3, 5), a point observed by Donald Guthrie who writes:

> The close connection . . . between the baptism and the temptation narratives means that each must be interpreted in terms of the other and since *both focus on relationship* it must be intended that at the commencement of the mission, *the declaration of Jesus as Son of God* and its consequences should be clearly understood.[18]

As we turn to the text, we note that after John's initial demurring about whether or not he should baptize Jesus, he is told by Jesus that what is about to happen is *to fulfil all righteousness* (15), an echo of Isaiah 53:11 which speaks of the servant as the 'righteous' one who will make people righteous by 'bearing their iniquities'. John acquiesces and the baptism proceeds, but rather than the actual baptism itself being described the emphasis falls on the events that immediately follow when Jesus comes up out of the water. Nevertheless, the baptism of Jesus is an echo of the past, pointing back to the Old Testament (as well as pointing ahead to the next passage, 4:1–11). Thus, just as Israel emerged from the Red Sea to go into the wilderness so Jesus here comes up out of the waters of baptism to be led into the wilderness. These similarities (as well as obvious differences) have prompted Gordon Fee to write: 'Jesus [is] stepping into the role of Israel as God's Son, going through the waters, followed by forty days in the wilderness, but succeeding

[17] Ibid., p. 118.
[18] Donald Guthrie, *New Testament Theology* (Leicester: IVP, 1991), p. 309.

precisely at the points where Israel failed when they were tested forty years in the wilderness'.[19] At every point and in every way Jesus was the true son that Israel never proved to be.

It is only as Jesus is coming up out of the water, the evangelist tells us, that Jesus *saw* the Holy Spirit in the shape of *a dove* descending on him (16). The Spirit by whom Jesus was conceived is the same Spirit who anoints God's Son Jesus for the messianic office. It is then that the silence is finally broken with the Father's voice of approval *This is my Son, whom I love*. As we earlier noted in Luke's infancy narrative of Jesus' conception, so here at his baptism the two ideas of Jesus' Sonship and the Spirit are intertwined. The baptism of Jesus is a defining moment – a truly Trinitarian event where Father, Son and Holy Spirit collaborate in unison – and of immense significance, for it demonstrates 'Jesus' experience of God . . . and . . . his understanding of his mission, was his sense of sonship and his consciousness of Spirit'.[20] Moreover, it was not only at his baptism that Jesus was conscious of the relationship between the Spirit and his sonship but his understanding of these things proves crucial for the whole of the future ministry upon which he is soon to embark, as James Dunn concludes: 'In short, Spirit and sonship, sonship and Spirit, are but two aspects of the experience of God out of which Jesus *lived and ministered*',[21] an important linkage used to describe believers in Paul's writings (e.g. Rom. 8:14), as we shall see later.

After coming out of the water, as noted above, the only one who is heard to speak in the narrative is the Father uttering divine approval: *This is my Son, whom I love, with him I am well pleased* (17). The affective declaration of 'my beloved son' is noteworthy and immediately causes a number of important Old Testament texts to spring to mind. There is an echo of Psalm 2:7 (cf. 2 Sam. 7:12–14) where King David was addressed, 'You are my Son; today I have become your Father'. Genesis 22:2 also comes into view. Here Abraham is told to offer his son Isaac as a sacrifice. God's instruction to the patriarch is couched in emotive language and with great pathos, evident in the original language by the piling up of phrases for maximum rhetorical effect: 'Take your son, your only son, Isaac, whom you love.' And, Isaiah 42:1 is also in mind where in the messianic servant song we read: 'Here is my servant, whom I uphold, my chosen one in whom I delight.' These texts fuse together

[19] Gordon D. Fee, *Pauline Christology: An Exegetical-Theological Study* (Peabody: Hendrickson, 2007), p. 542.

[20] James D. G. Dunn, *Jesus and the Spirit* (Philadelphia: The Westminster Press, 1975), p. 62.

[21] Ibid., p. 67.

and bring out the fuller meaning of Jesus' sonship, showing that he clearly stands in line with the rich Old Testament heritage above. The accounts of Jesus' birth and baptism, moreover, present Jesus as Son of God to his Father as well as his standing in line as the Davidic Messiah.

Finally, what is also interesting about the audible words spoken here is how Jesus is the Son the Father loves or, better, is described as the 'beloved' Son. It should be noted that of the eight occasions where the adjective 'beloved' (*agapētos*) is used in the Synoptic Gospels (Matt., Mark and Luke) all of them apply exclusively to Jesus as Son of God (e.g., Mark 1:11; Luke 3:22). In light of this, the affection of the Father, coupled with Jesus' filial identification at his baptism, has prompted C. Spicq, the renowned Greek scholar, to insightfully remark of Matthew 3:17: 'Only Christ is perfectly beloved. He is unique in the order of love just as he is in the order of sonship.'[22]

3. Temptation: the obedient son (Matt. 4:1–11)

In Matthew's ordering of events, Jesus' baptism is situated immediately prior to his temptation for at least one important reason: Jesus must first be *attested* by the Father before he is *tested* by the devil. The temptation account itself reveals a number of important parallels with the Old Testament. While it is possible that the allusion here is to Moses' forty-day fast on Mount Sinai immediately prior to receiving the law (Exod. 24:18), the more prominent biblical echo is rooted in God's son Israel's forty years of wilderness wanderings when the nation experienced an absence of water and food (Exod. 15:23; 16:3). The evangelist recapitulates a number of ideas in connection with the nation of Israel's relationship to God which are worth noting.[23] For example, just as Israel was led (Deut. 8:2) so Jesus was *led*[24] *by the Spirit* (1); again, the arena for both is the same, a dry and desolate wasteland (Deut. 8:2; Matt. 4:1). More importantly another parallel that is often overlooked is the filial identity of both (Deut. 8:5; Matt. 4:3, 6); indeed, sonship is central to the temptation narrative for *the taunts by Satan strike at the very heart of Jesus' filial relation to his Father.* Two out of the three

[22] Ceslaus Spicq, *Agape in the New Testament: Synoptic Gospels*, vol. 1 (St. Louis: B. Herder Book Co., 1963), p. 50, n.2.

[23] Though another son, Adam, who was tempted in the garden, also springs to mind.

[24] 'Being led by the Spirit' is one of the distinguishing marks of believers as the sons of God for Paul (e.g. Rom. 8:14). See ch. 7.

temptations test Jesus' obedience as son to his heavenly Father. In verse 3 the tempter invites Jesus to publicly demonstrate his power – 'apparently, the devil was from Missouri (the 'Show Me' state)'[25]: *If you are the Son of God, tell these stones to become bread* (3). In verse 6 Satan comes again to inquire: *If you are the Son of God ... throw yourself down*. For Jesus as God's son, obedience sits at the heart of the temptation narrative and so his response, as we shall see, is not so much related to what he would or could do but rather to his identity, who he *was*.

Jesus is tempted at a point when he was most vulnerable and at a time of greatest physical need. Matthew tells us that it was *after*[26] *fasting forty days and nights, he was hungry* when *the tempter came* (2–3) to him. This is the strategy of the evil one, who comes at a point of weakness and extremity, testing which for the nation of Israel as God's son in the Old Testament also took place in a feral and challenging environment:

> Remember how the LORD your God led you all the way in the desert these forty years, to humble you and test you in order to know what was in your heart, whether or not you would keep his commands. He humbled you, causing you to hunger and then feeding you with manna, which neither you nor your fathers had known, to teach that a man does not live on bread alone but on every word that comes from the mouth of the LORD. Your clothes did not wear out and your feet did not swell during these forty years. Know then in your heart that as a man disciplines his son, so the LORD your God disciplines you.[27]

This text, spoken of the nation of Israel, God's son, now presents itself before Jesus, only this time the words did not come from Yahweh but from his greatest adversary, the evil one. Would Jesus, like Israel as son, cave in to satisfy his own need by filling his stomach with food, or would he listen and depend on God and his promises by being obedient to him? Would Jesus see through the externals of food to the deeper realities of what was at stake here – obedience to his heavenly Father? As we consider these questions, there is little doubt Jesus would have been familiar with the above Old Testament text and Israel's failure to heed God's word. In

---

[25] Daniel B. Wallace, *Greek Grammar Beyond the Basics: An Exegetical Syntax of the New Testament* (Grand Rapids: Zondervan, 1996), p. 693.

[26] The participle ('fasting') is in the past tense (aorist) and here denotes action prior to the main verb ('he hungered'). Thus, Jesus' testing took place *after* not during his forty-day fast.

[27] Deut. 8:2–5.

responding to the tempter, Jesus provides us with a paradigmatic pattern of sonship; he did what we as God's sons and daughters should always do namely, he quoted Scripture back to Satan by repeatedly referring to Deuteronomy: *People do not live on bread alone but on every word that comes from the mouth of God* (4, TNIV; Deut. 8:3). In so doing, Jesus saw through the evil one's temptation to satisfy his own more immediate and transient needs over against the greater, eternal purpose of following and doing the will of his Father.

Manifold are the methods of the evil one, and so if the devil cannot force Jesus to satisfy his own basic needs over against his Father wishes, he will tempt him into a spectacular display of his own power and authority so that everyone can see his Father's care and protection. If Jesus would comply, that, according to Satan, would really capture the popular imagination, for then everyone down below would witness this grand spectacle! Thus, Jesus is taken to the highest point in the temple and ordered: *If you are the Son of God . . . throw yourself down* (6). Satan cites and twists Scripture in an effort to remind Jesus of the protection he can expect, *the angels . . . will lift you up in their hands, so that you will not strike your foot against a stone.* The implication is clear, that if God protected Israel as his sons, he will certainly protect *the* Son of God. Jesus responds: *It is also written: 'Do not put the Lord your God to the test'* (7; Deut. 6:16).

In one last-ditch effort, Jesus is taken to the highest mountain and promised in a mock show of power by Satan: *All this I will give you, if you will bow down and worship me.* The allusion to the Old Testament here is clear: Israel arrived at Mount Sinai (Exod. 19) where immediately after they turned from God to worship an idol (Exod. 32:1–6) – what one commentator calls 'Israel's calf-hearted response'.[28] Jesus by contrast is looking out on all the kingdoms of the world from a *very high mountain* (8) and insists that God is the only one who should be worshipped. Jesus again quotes Scripture: *Away from me, Satan! For it is written: 'Worship the Lord your God, and serve him only'* (10; Deut. 6:13). The score at the end of this satanic onslaught is a resounding victory for Jesus: the Son of God 3 – Satan 0, and it leaves us in no doubt that Jesus will not be deflected from the higher goal of listening to and obeying his Father.

In this text Jesus is in a very real sense caught between listening to the evil one or obeying God his Father who helped him overcome,

---

[28] Scott Hahn, *A Father who Keeps his Promises: God's Covenant Love in Scripture* (Cincinnati: St. Anthony Messenger Press, 1998), p. 145.

an experience Mario Sepulveda, one of the thirty-three Chilean miners trapped underground for two months in 2010, also identified with when he was brought to safety: 'I was with God, and I was with the devil,' he confessed. 'They fought and God won.'[29] As a consequence of this encounter, Jesus' sonship (acknowledged earlier in his baptism) is authenticated; he is suitably 'qualified' and now ready to embark on his public mission by being God's emissary to a needy world. This text also shows that Jesus' obedience comes from deep reflection of filial identity: from start to finish, the overriding emphasis in the passage is Christological and is further endorsement of Jesus' Sonship by the Father.

4. Transfiguration: the suffering son (Luke 9:28–36)

The importance of the transfiguration in the New Testament is borne out by the fact that all three synoptic Gospel writers include it. Immediately prior to this incident is what most scholars and commentators agree is a crucial turning point in Jesus' earthly ministry: Jesus has just disclosed to the disciples that he would suffer and die but after three days he would rise again. Judging by the disciples' response this was earth-shattering (cf. Matt. 16:22), but Jesus is disclosing the type of Messiah he is – not the popular, warrior-like figure who in accordance with Jewish belief must come in great power and might in order to scatter his enemies but rather a suffering servant, symbolized by his choice of animal, a donkey as opposed to a horse, when riding into Jerusalem on Palm Sunday.

In this passage Jesus' ensuing death is very much on his mind and this is the context which we need to keep in mind, since what is about to be revealed is for the benefit and encouragement of his disciples as the Saviour proceeds towards Calvary. In light of unfolding events, it is now that his disciples needed to trust him as they have never done before. Jesus takes his inner core of disciples, Peter, James and John, with him on to a mountaintop. Interestingly, we have already seen how mountains played a part in an earlier narrative, the account of Jesus' temptation by the evil one (Matt. 4:8). In regard to this, Bonnie Thurston in an insightful little book entitled *The Spiritual Landscape of Mark* looks at what she calls 'the geography of Jesus',[30] the different terrains and shifting scenes

---

[29] *Newsweek*, 25 October 2010, p. 18.
[30] Bonnie B. Thurston, *The Spiritual Landscape of Mark* (Collegeville: Liturgical Press, 2008), p. 37.

in which Jesus finds himself (lake, desert, mountain, city, etc.) in the Gospel. Thus, for example, the desert is synonymous with a place of uninhabitability where God led the children of Israel through a difficult experience. Mountains too, those mysterious and majestic landscapes which beckon all serious climbers to scale their dizzy heights, are in Scripture often places of encounter with God. Moses, for example, meets God on Mount Sinai (Exod. 19) and is given the law (Exod. 20); Elijah meets God in prayer on Mount Carmel when the false prophets of Baal are defeated by God (1 Kgs 18); and Isaiah the prophet encounters God via a vision in the temple situated on Mount Zion in Jerusalem (Isa. 6).

Now Jesus is on another mountaintop[31] where he encounters God and where we are told *the appearance of his face changed, and his clothes became as bright as a flash of lightening* (29). We noted earlier how important clothing is in Luke's Gospel and here again the manner of clothing is important to note as the word for 'bright' is *leukos*, the word from which we get the English term leucocytes (white blood cells), meaning 'white'. This is 'a "white" garment . . . one that is thoroughly washed and "fulled," i.e., bleached in special clay to make it as white as possible . . . [these are] costly and take a long time to process'.[32] This transfiguring of Jesus' outer garments, more importantly, 'provides a glimpse into his inner character: his transcendent glory, his Otherness', as well as his identity, which is disclosed in verse 35 as *my Son*. Jesus' true character (divine) and true identity (*Son*) are both revealed to the disciples so that they might trust him as he goes to the cross to die. In addition, and as we noted, earlier Jesus has been talking to the disciples about his death, his *departure*, a highly significant word in that Luke, unlike Matthew or Mark, here chooses the word 'exodus' (*exodos*) to describe it. Once again we should not miss the linkage between Jesus' 'exodus' (31) and his Sonship (35), echoing Israel's filial identity in Exodus 4:22–23 and exodus from Egypt. Especially significant is the way in which the stories of Israel and Jesus are bound up with the two ideas of *sonship* and *salvation*. Israel as son of God who failed so miserably was in need of salvation, but Jesus who is perfect and obedient in every way is now on his way to the cross and by his death will provide salvation for us.

---

[31] Scholars debate whether the mountain is Mount Tabor in Galilee or Mount Hermon, further north on the border of modern-day Lebanon.

[32] Resseguie, *Spiritual Landscape*, p. 92.

5. Death: the Son of God on the cross (Matt. 27:33–54)

The first part of this passage, leading up to the climax in verse 54 is 'thick with mockery';[33] three times Jesus is taunted, by bystanders (39–40), the Jewish leaders (41–43), and the *robbers* (44) and on three occasions and within the space of seventeen verses he is described as *the Son of God* (40, 43, 54). This triple declaration of sonship corresponds with the earlier temptations where Jesus was mocked three times by the devil and where his filial relation to his father was tested (Matt. 4:3, 6). Thus, immediately prior to the beginning of his public ministry Jesus was tempted to take a shortcut to glory and now at the end of his earthly ministry he faces a similar test to *save* himself rather than remain on the cross. The first taunt comes from the bystanders, who mock Jesus with the jibe: *You who are going to destroy the temple and build it in three days, save yourself! Come down from the cross, if you are the Son of God!* (40).The reference to the destruction and the rebuilding of the temple constitutes a messianic claim where the test is that if Jesus is a messianic pretender he should prove it. Jesus is tempted to exercise the supernatural power with which the Messiah was endowed (Isa. 11:4), thereby proving his identity. But Jesus had many times demonstrated God's power at work throughout his ministry and he refuses to comply with their demands because the cross is the way to glory not for himself but for God and for what would be accomplished for those who will later come and trust in him.

The second jeer comes from the Jewish leaders, *the chief priests, the teachers of the law and the elders*: '*He saved others,' they said, 'but he can't save himself! He's the King of Israel! Let him come down now from the cross, and we will believe in him. He trusts in God. Let God rescue him now if he wants him, for he said, "I am the Son of God"'* (41–43). The mockery here takes the form of a command. The first part of the challenge emphasizes Jesus' healing miracles (*he saved others*, 42), while the second part accuses that Jesus is nothing more than a faith healer and not the Messiah, the Son of God. If Jesus could do miracles it would not be too much for him to perform one final spectacular show now. The irony is that these leaders are in for a shock, because God is about to do something miraculous and deliver or 'save' Jesus, not immediately nor in the way they expect, but by his staying and dying on the cross, which we know is not the end. These leaders are therefore in for a real surprise!

Between these two instances and the last reference to Jesus' filial relationship (54), Jesus goes the way his Father had intended and

---

[33] David L. Turner, *Matthew*, BECNT (Grand Rapids: Eerdmanns, 2008), p. 663.

that he himself had chosen: he suffers and dies on the cross. Jesus the Son, as Paul puts it, 'became *obedient* to death – even death on a cross'.[34] His death is accompanied with many miraculous events – the curtain in the temple is torn in two, tombs are opened – but it is the confession by the Gentile soldiers and not by any Jew (in this *the* most Jewish of Gospels) who seem to begin to grasp the significance of who Jesus really is: *When the centurion and those with him who were guarding Jesus saw the earthquake and all that had happened, they were terrified, and exclaimed, 'Surely he was the Son of God!'* (54). But this is not only a confession, it is much more, for it is also a confirmation *and* a condemnation of those who earlier had taunted Jesus concerning his filial identity. Jesus is vindicated as these Roman soldiers indict the Jewish leaders by the way in which they acknowledge what the others refused or failed to see, that even in death (and throughout his life) Jesus really *is* the Son of God. 'The title *Son of God*, which had been used in mockery in vv. 40, 43, is thus restored to its proper place.'[35] How ironic it is in this confession by the Gentiles that Jesus' death opens up the way for them to become God's sons and daughters while 'the *sons* of the kingdom' (Gk *huioi*, Matt. 8:12, ESV), the Jews, Matthew tells us, will be on the outside. In other words, membership in the kingdom of God is not based on race but on grace and it takes place through faith in what God's Son had accomplished by his death on the cross.

6. Resurrection (Rom. 1:2–4)

a. Jesus: Son of David and Son of God (1:2–4)

Finally, we turn to consider Jesus' resurrection in Paul. Although Paul does not speak very frequently about Jesus as 'God's Son' or 'his Son',[36] he does so at strategic points in his letters. Romans 1:2–4[37] is a very good example, verses which have too 'often been allowed to fall off the front of the letter'[38] but which function as a

---

[34] Phil. 2:8.

[35] R. T. France, *The Gospel according to Matthew: An Introduction and Commentary*, TNTC (Leicester: IVP, 1985), p. 402.

[36] See L. W. Hurtado, 'Son of God', in *DPL*, pp. 900–906.

[37] Many scholars think that Paul has taken these verses from elsewhere and incorporated them into his letter. For a recent robust defense of Pauline authorship see James M. Scott, *Adoption as Sons of God: An Investigation into the Background of HUIOTHESIA* (Tübingen: Mohr, 1992), pp. 223–236.

[38] N. T. Wright, *The Resurrection of the Son of God* (Minneapolis: Fortress Press, 2003), p. 242.

preface to everything Paul is about to say in this letter, regarded by many to be the nearest thing to a Christian manifesto. Fundamental to understanding these verses is of course the theme of sonship, but closely allied with this is the foundation upon which the Christian faith stands or falls and which for us is the next stage in Jesus' earthly life, his resurrection. In fact, Romans has not been noted for its emphasis on the resurrection of Christ but as Tom Wright help-fully observes, 'Romans is suffused with resurrection. Squeeze this letter at any point, and resurrection spills out; hold it up to the light and Easter sparkles all the way through.'[39]

Romans 1:2–4 comprises and compresses a lot of theology, verses which are every bit as important as the thesis statement the apostle makes a little later in 1:16–17, for they tell us much about the content of Paul's gospel. The repetition of the noun *son* (*huios*) in verses 3 and 4 makes it clear that what Paul is discussing in these verses is nothing less than 'Son-Christology'[40] where Jesus' filial relationship as God's Son is the sum and substance of his gospel.[41] In fact, Jesus' filial relationship to God is important to Paul, which in itself is not so surprising for this was the apostle's message immediately after he had met the risen Lord and was converted on the road to Damascus. Luke informs us how Paul 'immediately began to preach in the synagogues that Jesus is the Son of God'.[42] In order to see verses 3–4 in context, we will cite the opening verses of the letter:

> *Paul, a servant of Jesus Christ, called to be an apostle and set apart for the gospel of God – the gospel he promised beforehand through the prophets in the Holy Scriptures regarding his Son, who as to his earthly life was a descendant of David, and who through the Spirit of holiness was appointed the Son of God in power by his resurrection from the dead: Jesus Christ our Lord* (TNIV).

b. Jesus as Davidic Messiah (1:2)

Paul, like the Gospel authors we noted earlier, also places both Jesus' appearance on the world-stage *and* his gospel in their Jewish context, which is not too surprising given that Paul himself was a

---

[39] Ibid., p. 241. This theme has been recently developed by J. R. Daniel Kirk, *Unlocking Romans: Resurrection and the Justification of God* (Grand Rapids: Eerdmans, 2008).

[40] S. Kim, *The Origin of Paul's Gospel* (Tübingen: Siebeck, 1981), p. 111.

[41] For further treatment of this passage see Trevor J. Burke, *Adopted into God's Family: Exploring a Pauline Metaphor*, NSBT 22 (Nottingham: IVP, 2006), pp. 102–107.

[42] Acts 9:20.

Jewish-Christian. Regarding the latter, Paul states he was set apart for *the gospel he [God] promised beforehand through his prophets and the Holy Scriptures* (2), a clear reminder that the good news finds its historical roots in the soil of the Old Testament. Although Paul here mentions the prophets he is probably thinking more generally of the Old Testament Scriptures as a whole. The 'prophets' he has in view included Moses (Acts 3:21–22) and David (Acts 2:29–30) as well as prophets whom we normally associate with that role, including, for example, Isaiah, who promised through the gospel a brighter future for the nation of Israel.[43]

Jesus, too, stands in line with the Old Testament promises, for Paul continues *regarding his Son, who as to his earthy life was a descendant of David*. Paul's mention of Jesus as *Son* recalls Israel's filial status but here the apostle especially connects Jesus with the sonship of king David, something which the New Testament authors repeatedly do.[44] For Paul, 'Jesus' Davidic sonship is a necessary qualification for the Messiah'.[45] Of course there were many sons of God who could claim Jewish descent, some of whom as we saw earlier include the Israelites and King David. Thus, these verses are particularly rooted in key texts we have already looked at, including Exodus 4:22–23, 2 Samuel 7:12–14 and Psalms 2:7, 89:26–29. The language used of Israel's as God's firstborn son in Exodus 4:22–23 is transferred to the Davidic king in 2 Samuel 12:14–16 as the kingly 'son of God'. Moreover, the promise to David that God would raise up a 'house' from David's own body who would rule 'forever' finds fulfilment now in Jesus as Son of God and Messiah. These are all important connections to make in Romans 1:2. However, there is one thing that Paul says about Jesus in connection with the theme of sonship which makes him so different and unique, as Tom Wright states

[m]any were descended from David's seed according to the flesh; James the brother of the lord could have made that claim, as could various blood relatives of Jesus who are known in the early church . . . *only one Davidic descendant had been raised from the dead. This, Paul declares, marks him out as the 'son' of Israel's God: that is, the Messiah.*[46]

[43] Cf. Isa. 40:9; 52:7; 60:6; 61:1; Nahum 2:2.
[44] Cf. Matt. 1:1; 20:30–31; 21:9; Luke 1:27, 32; 2:4; 3:23–31; Acts 2:30; 13:22–23; 2 Tim. 2:8; Rev. 5:5.
[45] Thomas R. Schreiner, *Romans*, BECNT (Grand Rapids: Baker, 1998), p. 40.
[46] Wright, *Resurrection*, p. 242. Wright also argues an excellent case for accounting for the importance of the resurrection in order to properly understand Paul's letter to the house churches at Rome. For an in-depth discussion of this theme see Dirk, *Unlocking Romans*.

While there are cases such as the widow of Nain's son and Lazarus who were raised from the dead I guarantee that if you were go to the Middle East today you will not find either of them hanging out with their friends and family – both died again. There is only one person who died and has been physically raised never to die again, Jesus the Messiah, the Son of God. Jesus is truly 'the firstborn from among the dead'.[47]

c. Jesus: resurrected as Son of God in power (1:3–4)

As we consider more closely Jesus' sonship, there are several key aspects that affect our understanding of his filial relationship to God. The first of these is the twin phrases *who as to his earthly life* (3) and *who through the Spirit of holiness* (4) which some scholars take as a reference to the two natures of Jesus, i.e. Jesus' *humanity* over against his *divinity*.[48] In other words, Jesus was the Son of David in regard to his *birth* but he is the eternal Son of God with respect to his *divine* nature. Those holding this view also understand the participle (*horisthentes*, 4) to mean 'declare' or 'show', and so the resurrection did not make Jesus the Son of God but openly 'declared' him in a powerful way to be what he always was, God's eternal Son. The two phrases *as to his earthly life* and *through the Spirit of holiness*, however, could equally be understood to refer not to the two natures of Jesus but to two phases of his historical career, the pre- and post-resurrection phases, in the sense that prior to the resurrection Jesus was the Son-of-God-in-weakness and humility but afterwards he was the Son-of-God-in-power. Understood in this way would also require us to take the participle (*horisthentes*, 4) to mean what it usually means in the New Testament, 'to appoint' (cf. Acts 10:42; 17:31) rather than 'to declare' so that Jesus' resurrection from the dead was his appointment to a new phase, a higher rank, where he is installed or enthroned as the messianic king. This also demands that we view the prepositional phrase *in power* adjectivally (rather than adverbially) as a description of Jesus' sonship – *appointed the Son of God 'with' power* which rules out any idea of adoptionist Christology, namely, that Jesus *became* the Son of God at the resurrection. In other words, even though Jesus has always been the eternal Son of God, at his resurrection he entered into a new phase of sonship in that he was enthroned as the Son of God in power.

---

[47] Col. 1:18.
[48] E.g., Robert Mounce, *Romans*, NAC 27 (Nashville: Broadman & Holman, 1995), p. 61.

The last and related point which these verses raise concerns the way that some recent interpreters have understood the participial *horisthentes tou huios* 'declared' as Son (4) as a formula or a roundabout way of describing Jesus' 'adoption as Son'.[49] It should be said some scholars who argue this do not doubt for a moment the fact that Jesus was the eternal Son of God but nevertheless they couch Jesus' sonship in adoptive terms.[50] I am not convinced by this view because the term 'adoption as son' (Gk *huiothesia*) is not found in this text and, moreover, is a term Paul always and only uses to describe Christians (cf. Rom. 8:15, 23; Gal. 4:5; Eph. 1:5) and never to describe the sonship of Christ. Rather, Paul in Romans 1:2–4 uses the term *son* twice (Gk *huios*, 3, 4) and by so doing underscores Jesus' sonship to be of an entirely different order to that of believers. In fact, it is precisely because Jesus is the eternal and unique Son of God (and not an adopted son) that he can be the conduit through whom the former slaves of sin and death are brought into God's family. Jesus' sonship is unmatched and sets him apart from the believer's adoptive sonship. Put differently, Jesus is the Son of God from eternity; we are the adopted sons and daughters by grace, an important distinction made by Tom Smail who comments:

> It is he who in the uniqueness of his resurrection is designated the Son of God in power (Romans 1:4) while we are sons through an act of *huiothesia* (adoption, son-making) . . . Thus the distinction between Jesus and us needs to be carefully observed. *The language of incarnation belongs to him, and the language of adoption to us . . . and if we try to reverse them confusion will result.*[51]

Summary

Jesus sits at the centre of the biblical narrative of sonship where his filial relationship to his Father is identified, tested and confirmed at strategic points in his earthly ministry: his birth, baptism, temptation, transfiguration, death and resurrection. In the former, the Holy Spirit is involved in conceiving Jesus the Son (Luke 2) where the focus of attention is not on the king of the day (who assumed such a title for himself) but on Jesus' humble birth in a guest room.

---

[49] Scott, *Adoption as Sons*, p. 242.

[50] Ibid.; R. B. Gaffin, *The Centrality of the Resurrection: A Study in Paul's Soteriology* (Grand Rapids: Baker, 1978), pp. 117–119.

[51] Thomas A. Smail, *The Forgotten Father: Rediscovering the Heart of the Christian Gospel* (London: Hodder and Stoughton, 1980), p. 144 (emphasis added).

The Son's subsequent flight and return from Egypt in Matthew 2 is a new exodus and demonstrates Jesus is the true son of Israel's God. Whereas Jesus' baptism is the moment when God identifies him as his Son who must suffer for sinners (Matt. 3), it is in his temptations that we see his filial relationship to the Father tested and confirmed by his complete obedience to the Father's will (Matt. 4). On a mountaintop Jesus is transfigured (Luke 9) as the Father declares his love for his Son, with his death – understood by Luke as his exodus – looming ahead. Finally, it is in his resurrection that Jesus stands firmly in line with David as he is gloriously resurrected as the Son of God with power (Romans 1). All of these key points in Jesus' historical career show his Sonship not only evolved out of the earlier Old Testament narratives but also brings them to their completion and fulfilment, proving through a life-time of obedience that he is the Son which both David and Israel failed to be.

John 1:14, 18; 5:16–30; 1:12–13; 3:1–10; 8:31–58; 11:51–52; 20:21–23
6. The Son of God and the children of God

Sinclair Ferguson, the Scottish theologian and pastor, tells how on one occasion he was being interviewed for a position when he was suddenly asked the question: 'How would you describe your relationship with God?' He was initially unsettled by the question as he was unsure whether the interviewer was inquiring as to how much time he had spent in prayer and Bible study earlier in the day or if there was some secret sin lurking in his life which was a hindrance to his fellowship with God. He thought for a moment and then gave the following response which proved to be illuminating: 'as a servant. And yes as a son!' In the end Ferguson tells how he did not get the job for which he was being interviewed, nevertheless it was an enlightening moment, as he concluded: 'it dawned on me with an altogether new sense of wonder, because I was nothing less than a child of the living God!' It was a defining moment because he went away and wrote his pastorally sensitive book *Children of the Living God*.[1]

The filial term which Ferguson uses for believers in the title of his book will become clear in this chapter but it is important having looked at the first three Gospels in our previous chapter to now look at the fourth Gospel. Indeed, no study of our theme would be complete without due consideration of John. There are at least two main reasons for this: first, at the heart of John's Gospel, as D. A. Carson notes, lies the *identity* of Jesus – '*who Jesus is*',[2] namely, the

---

[1] (Edinburgh: Banner of Truth, 1989); story from p. 1.
[2] D. A. Carson, *The Gospel According to John*, PNTC (Grand Rapids/ Cambridge: Eerdmans, 1991), p. 95, italics original.

Son or Son of God – the term 'son' (*huios*) occurs forty-five times in the gospel, forty-one of which refer specifically to Jesus (e.g., 1:34, 49; 3:18; 5:25; 9:35; 10:36; 11:4; 19:7; 20:31).[3] Jesus' filial relationship to the Father is therefore fundamental to any proper understanding of this Gospel: this is how the book opens, where Jesus is distinctly described as God (1:18) and 'the Son of God' (1:34), but it is also how it comes to a climax towards the end, as John 20:31 makes clear: 'these are written that you may believe that Jesus is the Christ, the Son of God, and that by believing you may have life in his name.'[4] The second reason for our focusing on John's Gospel is that Jesus is the conduit for others to become members of God's family:[5] It is only through believing in the Son that we can ever become 'children of God' (Gk *tekna theou*, e.g., 1:11–12).

It is important to note the filial distinction which John makes in his Gospel (and letters) between Jesus and believers which sets his writings apart from the other New Testament authors: Jesus is always and only identified as 'Son' (Gk *huios*) and believers are always named 'children' (Gk *tekna*). Thus, as regards the former, 'Jesus is the definition of all that sonship means'[6] and is presented in this Gospel as having a filial consciousness throughout. This distinction in the language used to describe Jesus as 'son' and believers as 'children' means there is no blurring of these lines, which might at first glance seem insignificant. It suggests that for this author that Jesus' filial status is unique and immediately sets his relationship to God apart from that of Christians as God's spiritual offspring. In other words, Jesus' sonship is of an entirely different order to that of his disciples: he is *the Son* and we are God's *children*. Indeed, this difference is made clear in another way towards the end of the Gospel where immediately after Jesus appeared to Mary Magdalene he sent her to tell the disciples that he was 'returning to my Father and your Father, to my God and your God' (John 20:17). Thus, just as Jesus' identity as 'Son' sets his filial disposition apart from that of

[3] Andreas J. Köstenberger, *A Theology of John's Gospel and John's Letters* (Grand Rapids: Zondervan, 2009), p. 380, n. 142.

[4] Commentators disagree over the purpose of the Gospel and whether it was written for Christians or to bring others to faith. In regard to the former and 20:31, the verb 'to believe' could be taken to mean 'to continue to believe' or 'to come to believe' for the first time. I side with commentators who take the latter view that it is a tract for bringing unconverted Jews, proselytes and God-fearers to faith in Jesus as Messiah.

[5] James M. M. Francis, *Adults as Children: Images of Childhood in the Ancient World and the New Testament* (Bern: Peter Lang, 2006), p. 162.

[6] Thomas A. Smail, *The Forgotten Father: Rediscovering the Heart of the Christian Gospel* (London: Hodder and Stoughton, 1980), p. 144.

Christians – 'believers do not (as in Paul) share sonship with Jesus'[7] – so his relationship to the Father is not in every way the same as that of believers.

There are many places we could turn to in this Gospel for our theme and we must be selective. We begin with a couple of texts which show clearly the uniqueness of Jesus' sonship, the basis for our consideration of the believer's filial relationship to God.

1. Jesus the only Son, who is God (John 1:14, 18)

a. Jesus, the only Son . . . (1:14)

John's Gospel begins like none other – there are no genealogies, no references to Jesus' birth, no baptism; rather, in the opening verses we are immediately aware of being in different terrain to that of the synoptic Gospels. At the outset of his Gospel John draws back the curtain of history and gives us a glimpse of eternity where the Word is in perfect union with the Father. This Word enjoys intimacy with the Father ('the Word was *with* God', i.e., face to face), is a distinct person ('The Word was *with* God'), and is himself divine, 'The Word *was* God' (1:1). But *who* exactly is this Word whom the evangelist tells us stepped out of eternity into history and put on flesh (14)? There are two crucial verses to help us here, one of which is like an eyewitness account: *We have seen his glory, the glory of the One and Only, who came from the Father, full of grace and truth.* The main issue to consider here is the identity and meaning of the words *the One and Only* (Gk *monogenēs*).

The word *monogenēs* has been much debated and has, for example, been translated by the KJV as 'only begotten'. But this is misleading because it suggests a pagan or a metaphysical relationship between the Father and the Son, an idea that is foreign to Scripture. Other translations like the NIV understand this word to mean 'one and only' and it is used this way, for instance, to describe Isaac as Abraham's only or one-of-a-kind son (Heb. 11:17; Luke 7:12). Thus in verse 14, *monogenēs* is best understood to mean 'only' as 'of sole descent'.[8]

But the word *monogenēs* in 1:14 stands alone and if it means *the One and Only*, we are prompted to ask, 'the one and only *what?*' Evidently, the context of verse 14 refers back earlier to the Word

[7] Francis, *Adults as Children*, p. 160.
[8] Murray J. Harris, *Jesus as God: The New Testament Use of* Theos *in Reference to Jesus* (Grand Rapids: Baker, 1992), p. 85.

made flesh and so it is not describing the Father; rather, it is identifying a separate but related 'person'. Exactly who that 'person' is can be determined from the way that *monogenēs* is used elsewhere in the New Testament. In four (out of a total of eight) times the term *monogenēs* is found alongside another word which it is describing, namely 'son'. John 3:16, for example reads, 'For God so loved the world that he gave his one and only Son.' Even on occasions where the word *monogenēs* occurs on its own it is clear that it means 'only son' (e.g., Luke 9:38; Heb. 11:17). Thus, if we were to fill in the blank or supply the needed word in 1:14: *the glory of the one and only [monogenēs] ____*, the appropriate word would be 'Son'. [9] This 'one and only *Son*' is a clear reference to Jesus, the significance of which, as Leon Morris comments, is that 'no one else stands in the same relationship to God the Father as Jesus Christ'. [10]

b. . . . who is God (1:18)

In addition to Jesus being 'the one and only Son', there is a second important credential which makes his filial relationship to the Father so unique and important for us as we prepare to consider the idea of believers as God's spiritual offspring. This is found a few verses later in 1:18 which reads: *No one has ever seen God, but God the One and Only [monogenēs], who is at the Father's side, has made him known.*

In 1:18, John puts the word *monogenēs* ('one and only Son') alongside the word *theos* ('God')[11] which is a highly unusual and striking combination because 'no other passage puts these words together like this'.[12] These two words agree grammatically; the *theos* attributes or adds something more about this 'one and only Son' by identifying Jesus even more closely as God; in short, it is an ascription to Jesus of deity; thus, taken together the two words mean: 'the only Son who is God'. [13] This 'only Son, who is God', John tells us,

---

[9] Harris, *Jesus as God*, p. 91.

[10] Leon Morris, *Jesus is the Christ: Studies in the Theology of John* (Grand Rapids: Eerdmans, 1989), p. 92.

[11] There is an important textual problem here. Some manuscripts have the word 'Son' rather than 'God'. However, most scholars conclude that the latter is the more likely reading because one of the rules (of textual criticism) for deciding such matters is that the more difficult reading is more likely to be the original reading. In other words, it is highly probable that a scribe wrote 'God', which would explain why this would be changed to 'Son' (rather than the other way round) and which also agrees with how Jesus is mostly described in the rest of the Gospel. For a full and exhaustive explanation of these matters of textual criticism see Harris, *Jesus as God*, pp. 73–103.

[12] Carson, *John*, p. 139.

[13] This is Harris' translation of the entire phrase; see *Jesus as God*, p. 92.

is the One who *came from the Father* (14) and *who is at the Father's side* (18). Hence, *he* is the only who *has made him* [i.e., the Father] *known* (18). This last phrase is one verb in the original language and is the word from which the English word 'exegesis' is derived. In other words, 'Jesus the only Son, who is God', is *God's exegesis*, the One uniquely qualified to reveal the Father, an appropriate way for the prologue to end since the rest of the Gospel of John is a further delineation of this; as Jesus himself declares later: 'Anyone who has seen me has seen the Father' (John 14:9).

Now that we have established the uniqueness of Jesus' relationship as Son to the Father, we shall explore how Jesus' life as a true Son provides a model for our understanding of our role as the children of God.

2. Like father, like son (John 5:16–30)

a. The Son carries on the work of the Father (5:17)

One reason for considering this passage is the heavy concentration of filial language: Jesus is repeatedly described as *Son* – it occurs no less than eight times,[14] not counting the expressions *Son of God* (26) and *Son of Man* (27). The language of sonship in this passage therefore provides us with the very essence of what it meant for Jesus to be in relationship with his Father. As we read this passage we have what one scholar calls '*a parable of apprenticeship* – a son learning a trade from his father'.[15] This provides the wider framework for understanding this passage. So, as we consider these verses we clearly see Jesus modelling a perfect lifestyle as Son which is not surprising since 'sonship . . . is . . . a functional category'[16] where the cultural assumption applied, namely that sons usually followed their father into the same occupation by doing the same kind of work. This principle of like father like son is conveyed well in Matthew 5:9, where we read: 'Blessed are the peacemakers, for they will be called sons of God.' God is viewed as the supreme peacemaker and those who replicate his behaviour are considered his 'sons'. It is this aspect that lies at the root of the filial relationship between Jesus and his Father.

Immediately prior to this verse, Jesus had healed a man who had

---

[14] Vv. 19 (twice), 20, 21, 22, 23 (twice), 26.

[15] John Ashton, *Understanding the Fourth Gospel*, 2nd ed. (Oxford: Oxford University Press, 2007), p. 227 (emphasis original).

[16] D. A. Carson, 'God is Love', *Bib Sac.* 156 (1999), p. 135.

been an invalid for thirty-eight long years (5:5), a cure which took place on the Sabbath (5:9). Jesus' actions provoked the Jews to question their validity, questions which centre on the precise identity of the one who made the man well. The Jews immediately ask the healed man: '*Who* is this fellow who told you to pick [your mat] up and walk?' (5:12). The narrator's remarks also hone in on the *identity* of the healer, as 5:13 makes clear: 'The man who was healed had no idea *who* it was.' The man's ignorance concerning the identity of the one who performed the miracle is followed by the repeated and unequivocal disclosure of his (i.e., Jesus') identity: he is the Son of God (5:19–26), that's *who* he is!

But Jesus, rather than getting bogged down in the nitty-gritty of the arguments about the Mosaic Law, provides his own self-authorization for his actions: *My Father is always at work to this very day, and I, too, am working* (17). The intimacy of the Father-Son relationship is immediately apparent in the way that Jesus describes God as *My Father*, which sets relationship on an entirely different plane. Equally, Jesus' point is that he is only doing what his Father has been doing and continues to do through him: *My Father is . . . at work . . . and I . . . am working.* Jesus is functioning and carrying on the work of his Father. 'Thus', in regard to John 5:17, Carson concludes, 'when Jesus makes the claim that His Father is "always at work to this very day", He is implicitly claiming to be God's Son, with the right to follow the pattern of work that God Himself sets in this regard'.[17]

Jesus' 'work' has been learned from his Father which in this context is the ushering in of the kingdom of God, evidenced through the healing of a chronically crippled man, instructing him to carry his mat, as well as the rest of his saving activity. What the Pharisees categorically failed to see is that Jesus was the fulfilment of the Sabbath ('the Scriptures', v. 39) and that he is free from the minutiae of their traditions. Thus, if the Father's work continues without pause, then the Son's does too, and his work is of the same kind as his.[18]

b. This Son always obeys his Father (5:18–19)

The response to Jesus' statement in verse 17 (*My Father is always at his work . . . and I, too, am working*) is met with murderous intent by his Jewish adversaries. We read their response: *for this reason the Jews tried all the harder to kill him.* They wanted him dead because

---

[17] Carson, 'God is love', p. 135.
[18] For some of this I am drawing on Carson, *John*, p. 248.

in their eyes Jesus was guilty on two counts: *not only was he break-ing the Sabbath, but he was also calling God his own Father, making himself equal with God* (18). The latter claim was tantamount to blasphemy since in their strict monotheistic understanding there is only one who is God. His opponents were correct, Jesus *is* indeed God, though he does not explicitly say so here; rather he responds by providing the basic ingredients for an understanding of his equal-ity with the Father, which is spelt out in functional terms, as verse 19 makes clear: *the Son can do nothing by himself* but can *only do what he sees the Father doing, because whatever the Father does the Son also does* (19). John knows nothing of a theology that is theoretical or ethereal; rather he grounds it in the practical realities of life and in Jesus' behaviour. Moreover, Jesus' filial relationship is exemplified in a life lived out in total obedience to his Father upon whom he is utterly dependent and subordinate. This is clear in that *the Son can do nothing by himself* (19). He relies on his Father to take the lead and obeys accordingly.

But, then, in an astonishing turn of phrase what Jesus says next is arresting: *whatever the Father does the Son also does* (19) which is nothing less than 'a claim to deity'[19] and goes beyond a mere filial claim of being *like* his father; rather Jesus *actually does what his Father does*, thereby making 'his Sonship unique'.[20]

c. The Son (like the Father) also gives eternal life (5:26)

We consider one last point as regards Jesus as the Son of God before we turn to believers as the children of God. If, as noted, Jesus the Son is being taught by his Father and does what the Father does, it is not so surprising that this continues in another way, this time in the sense of 'the Father educating the Son *to give life*'.[21] Jesus is also able to offer what the Father offers, namely eternal life, which as van der Watt points out is all part and parcel of the '*family rela-tions* between the Son and the Father'.[22] Thus, a few verses later we read: *For as the Father has life in himself, so he has granted the Son to have life in himself* (26). The 'life' in context here is 'eternal life' as an earlier verse makes clear: 'I tell you the truth, whoever hears my word and believes him who sent me has eternal life' (5:24). In other words, Jesus in another way has been given the right to execute the

---

[19] Carson, 'God is Love', p. 136.
[20] Ibid.
[21] Jan G. van der Watt, *Family of the King: Dynamics of Metaphor in the Gospel according to John* (Leiden: Brill, 2000), p. 207 (emphasis added).
[22] Ibid. (emphasis added).

same function as the Father, to give eternal life to those who come to the Father through him. We indeed find this to be the case, for a few chapters later Jesus authoritatively declares 'I give them eternal life, and they shall never perish'.[23] This same right is also assumed in the so-called High-Priestly Prayer on behalf of those who will yet come to believe: 'For you granted him authority over all people that he might give eternal life to all those you have given him.'[24] Once again functionality lies at the heart of the relationship between Jesus the Son and his Father – Jesus is entrusted with the giving of eternal life to others and everyone who believes in him will be saved and have everything they need for this life and the one that is to come.

That having Jesus is everything is well illustrated by a story of wealthy man and his son who owned a rare collection of works of art. They had everything, including works of Picasso, Raphael, Van Gogh, to name just a few artists. The father and his son would often sit together and admire their great works of art. But then a war broke out. The son went off to fight and died shortly after in action on the battleground. The father grieved deeply for his only son. Not long after his death, there was a knock on the father's door. A young man stood at the door with a large package in his hands. He said: 'Sir, you don't know me, but I am a soldier for whom your son gave his life. He saved many lives that day, and he was carrying me to safety when he was struck down and died. He often talked of you and your love for art.' The young man then held out a package. 'I know this isn't much. I'm not really an artist, but I think your son would have wanted you to have this.' The father opened the package. It was a portrait of his son, painted by the young man, and as the father looked at it he saw how well the artist had captured the personality of his son. He thanked the young man and offered to pay him for the picture. 'Oh no, sir,' he replied, 'I could never repay what your son did for me.'

After he left, the father hung the painting over his mantelpiece and visitors to his house often commented on it. Not long after the father died and there was a great auction of his paintings. Many wealthy people gathered for the sale. On the platform sat the painting of his son. The auctioneer began the sale: 'We will start with the picture of the son. Who will bid for it?' There was a strange silence and then someone from the back shouted, 'We want to see the Picassos and Raphaels.' The auctioneer was persistent and asked 'Who will start the bidding? 100 pounds?' Others at the auction also

---

[23] John 10:28.
[24] John 17:2.

became impatient and shouted: 'We didn't come to see this painting. We want to see the Van Goghs, the Rembrandts.' But the auction-eer persisted, 'Who will purchase the son, the son?' Finally, a voice from the back of the room was heard. It was the family gardener who had worked for the father and his son. 'I'll give 10 pounds for the painting.' Being poor, it was all he could afford. 'We have 10 pounds, any advance to 20 pounds?' The crowd became more impa-tient and after one last chance to advance on the price of 10 pounds, the auctioneer declared: 'SOLD'. Those present demanded that he quickly move on to the sale of the rest of the paintings, however, the auctioneer suddenly and dramatically declared: 'The auction is now over.' 'What about the rest of the paintings?' demanded those present. 'I'm sorry,' the auctioneer said, 'but I was instructed that the only painting to be sold today was that of the son. Whoever bought that would inherit the entire collection, including the mas-terpieces you also see on show here today. In other words, whoever took the son gets everything!' In the spiritual realm, the good news of the Christian faith is still the same, that whoever receives the Son has everything![25]

Having looked at the filial identity and credentials of Jesus and of how he is uniquely 'qualified', these become the foundation for how believers as the children of God are to live.

3. The children of God (John 1:12–13; 3:1–10)

We turn from looking at Jesus the Son to believers as 'children of God', and the first occurrence of this expression in the Gospel. As noted earlier, the filial identity of Jesus and that of believers are related because it is only those who *received him* [i.e., Jesus the Son] *to those who believed in his name, he gave the right to become children of God* (12).

Jesus is sent into the world as God's emissary, and in 1:12–13 the focus is on the need to exercise faith in the Son in order to become God's spiritual offspring. John strikes the note of human responsibility by doubly emphasizing the need in verses 11–12 to *receive* Jesus by people putting their *faith* in him. Such faith is not to be understood as wishy-washy or 'easy believism' but rather is a whole-hearted trust in who Jesus is (the Son), his character and claims, followed by open confession of that faith to others. Thus, if

---

[25] This illustration is taken from Harold A. Buetow, *Embrace Your Renewal: A Thought a Day for Lent* (New York: St. Pauls, 2004), pp. 82–84.

John was asked 'Who are the people of God?' he would invariably couch his response bifocally – those whose *faith* is *filially* focused in Jesus. As Marianne Meye Thompson rightly points out, the 'children of God are those who *believe in* the name of *the Son of God (huios theou)*'.[26]

A second and more fundamentally important emphasis in these verses (as well 3:3–8, below) is divine sovereignty, in that the new birth begins with God.[27] In other words, something must *happen to us* for us to be able to become members of God's family. Within the same context of the need to exercise faith in the Son, John in verse 13 particularly stresses the divine nature of this new birth by placing the verb 'born' at the end of the sentence (in the original) for maximum effect. In other words, a person only becomes a child of God by being born of God. For John, the new birth is both dynamic and divine and it puts into the shade any kind of humanly engineered birth which here sits in immediate juxtaposition: *children born not of natural descent, nor human decision or a husband's will, but born of God* (13). Such a birth is not self-generated or self-defined but finds its spring and origin in God the Father where new life, eternal life, begins. Put another way, spiritual birth has got nothing to do with human initiative and everything to do with supernatural activity.

The supernatural activity of the new birth is further developed in John 3:3, 7 and the classic encounter between Nicodemus and Jesus. It is important to note in passing that the doctrine of regeneration (as it is called theologically) is an important, though not an exclusive one to John (cf., 1 Pet. 1:3). It is a reminder of the two ways by which we become members of God's family and that such a state is not our natural condition. For John this is explained by means of a 'new birth' where the language used is drawn from the biological or physical realm. Paul, however, as we shall see in the next chapter, is unique among the biblical writers in that he uses legal language to talk of being 'adopted' (e.g., Gal. 4:5) into God's household.[28] It is important not to confuse these two ideas as they are they are different and distinct and add to the richness of Scripture's presentation of salvation.

---

[26] Marianne Meye Thompson, 'Children in the Gospel of John', in Marcia J. Bunge (ed.), *The Child in the Bible* (Grand Rapids/Cambridge: Eerdmans, 2008), pp. 206.

[27] Theologians have tried to determine whether faith precedes the new birth but as Carson points out John is not concerned with spelling out the relationship between these; see Carson, *John*, p. 126.

[28] See Trevor J. Burke, *Adopted into God's Family: Exploring a Pauline Metaphor*, NSBT 22 (Nottingham: IVP, 2006), pp. 21–29.

Nicodemus is often viewed as a typical example of the person who experienced a new birth.[29] The scene is a vivid one as Nicodemus furtively makes his way through the dark streets of Jerusalem to seek out Jesus. He is a Pharisee, and Pharisees, unlike the Sadducees, believed in the resurrection (Acts 23:8) because, as someone rather wittily has put it, they could 'Far-I-See!'[30] He was also a member of the Jewish ruling council, the Sanhedrin, the highest body in charge of Jewish affairs. Though a learned person and an expert in the Jewish Scriptures, Nicodemus misunderstands (as does the Samaritan woman, John 4)[31] the kind of birth Jesus is talking about – he thinks Jesus is talking of a second physical birth. Jesus' surprise at his ignorance is captured nicely by John (3:10) where the original language is very emphatic: 'You are *the* teacher of Israel and you do not understand these things?'

Nicodemus was supposed to be the instructor *par excellence*, the modern-day equivalent of a 'Reverend Doctor Professor',[32] so he should have known what Jesus was talking about for a couple of reasons, at least. First, the language of birth used here is very reminiscent of Old Testament passages where in respect of the nation of Israel we read 'God . . . gave you birth' (Deut. 32:18). There are also the Old Testament prophecies of Jeremiah and Ezekiel which provide the promise of God giving a new heart and a new Spirit (Ezek. 36:25–27; Jer. 31:31–34). Nicodemus' ignorance of these things prompts Jesus' response: *You should not be surprised* (3:7). Finally, the double emphasis that *no one can* see (3:3) and *no one can* enter (3:5) underscores the point made earlier that something must happen to Nicodemus before he can ever become a member of God's household. This is further emphasized in 3:7 when Jesus says: *You must be born again/from above* (anōthen)[33] where the verb stresses the absolute or divine necessity that Nicodemus '*must* be born again/born anew'. As in 1:12–13, this comes about through the supernatural intervention of God or being *born of the Spirit* (3:8).

---

[29] Most commentators are of the view that Nicodemus became a follower of Jesus. For an alternative view see Andreas J. Köstenberger, *John*, BECNT (Grand Rapids: Baker, 2004), p. 119.

[30] On the other hand, the Sadducees did not believe in the resurrection (Acts 23:8) because as the same person has put it, they were 'Sad-u-see'!

[31] The initial 'misunderstanding' which needs to be corrected is a recurring motif in John's Gospel.

[32] Carson, *John*, p. 198.

[33] This Greek word is deliciously ambiguous and is all of a part of John's extended double meaning; it includes 'from above' in a figurative sense (e.g. John 3:7, 31; 19:11) or literally 'from head to toe' (e.g., John 19:23) or 'from the beginning' (e.g., Luke 1:3).

The seriousness of what Jesus has been saying is captured well in Leon Morris'[34] comment:

> Jesus is not saying that rebirth is on the whole a good idea. He is not just recommending it for people in some special situation, perhaps with difficult problems of their own. He is making it of universal application. This is true of everybody. There is no exception.

In other words, *you* (the personal pronoun is plural and means everyone in Nicodemus' position) *must* be born again/from above!

But birth is only the beginning of this new relationship and 'implies a continuing existence within God's family as a child'[35] where the need to live in compliance with the wishes of the Father is paramount. This was a given in the ancient Mediterranean family, the background against which the author is writing, where these new offspring were entrusted with the responsibility of honouring their heavenly Father and the household of which they were now a part. Children were supposed to remain entirely focused on acting in accordance with their new identity. Thus, for any child of God to live a life which dishonours their family was not only frowned upon but also brought the name of their 'Father' into disrepute. More than this, it was a betrayal of identity and origin. These are all important matters as we turn now to look at a different kind of filial association in John 8:31–58.

4. The children of the Devil (8:31–58)

These verses pick up from where we left off in John 3 and the discussion of the new birth, only this time John is concerned with the functionality of a different kind of filial relationship. It asks the question: what is the crucial litmus test of how we can tell God's true progeny from those who are illegitimate offspring and do not belong in the household? The answer – *behaviour*. That there are two opposing 'households' in view will be clear in what follows which, according to one scholar, suggests the drawing of

> the battle lines in the history-long struggle between the realm of God and the realm of the devil … According to the New

---

[34] Leon Morris, *Expository Reflections on the Gospel of John* (Grand Rapids: Baker, 1988), p. 92.
[35] van der Watt, *Family of the King*, p. 179.

Testament the devil has sons, a family, a household, and a kingdom. The conflict between these two communities forms the very structure of the eschatological vision of history. Between the two solidarities there can be no compromise.[36]

The encounter and the discourse that ensues is a very logical one and centres on a clash between Jesus and the Pharisees. It begins with the latter claiming to be *Abraham's descendants* (33). *Abraham is our father* (39), they bragged, and we are his offspring. In their eyes, physical descent from the patriarch made them his 'children' rather than being *slaves of anyone* (33); indeed, sonship and slavery are opposites and two very different statuses and as far as the Pharisees were concerned they were free from the latter because they could trace their ancestry back to the patriarch. They were not slaves, but Abraham's children.

But for Jesus, the test of true belonging and, more importantly, of divine sonship is more ethically than physically rooted; it is not a matter of merely *claiming* descent but of *conduct* and lifestyle. In other words, as Jan van der Watt rightly points out in regard to these verses: 'The way in which a person *acts* is linked to his origin. A person acts according to who he is, and who he is, is determined by his birth (father).'[37] Thus, Jesus counters, *everyone who sins is a slave to sin. Now a slave has no permanent place in the family, but a son belongs to it for ever* (34–35). Jesus is about to challenge the Pharisees' claim to be Abraham's true progeny by first prefacing it with a reminder of his own filial status and identity: *if the Son sets you free, you will be free indeed* (36). Freedom and right behaviour come from a proper understanding of who Jesus really is, the Son of the living God.

In Jesus' mind, however, the Pharisees could not be free since it would be obvious in the way they live and act, especially in their conduct *towards him*. As things stand, Jesus makes clear that the reality of the situation is very different because the Pharisees are *ready to kill me* (37). *If you were Abraham's children*, Jesus volleys back, *then you would* do *the things Abraham* did (39). One Church Father of the fourth century, Theodore of Mopsuestia, got it exactly right as regards the huge mistake which the Pharisees were making, when he wrote: 'How can they be sons of Abraham when their *actions* demonstrate they are anything but sons?'[38] The encounter is

---

[36] Paul S. Minear, *Images of the Church in the New Testament* (Fortress: Westminster, 1960), p. 170.

[37] van der Watt, *Family of the King*, p. 189 (emphasis added).

[38] Marcio Conti, *Commentary on the Gospel of John. Translation with an Introduction and Notes* (Downers Grove: IVP, 2010), p. 81 (emphasis added).

concluded by Jesus telling the Pharisees: *As it is, you are determined to kill me* (40) and Abraham never behaved like that – the Pharisees' actions make a complete mockery of their filial claim; *ipso facto*, they are not Abraham's progeny!

Rather, Jesus goes on to tell his opponents that their filial descent is not divine but diabolical: *you belong to your father, the devil* (Gk *diabolos*, 44). The two words 'father' and 'devil' stand side by side, with the latter word being a further explanation of the former. Put more mathematically or in the form of an equation Jesus is saying 'your real father = the devil'. Those desires and behaviours replicate their father's who was a *murderer from the beginning* (44), which is probably a reference to the fall in the garden when Adam and Eve were robbed of spiritual life and death entered the entire human race. Second, there is the abandonment of truth and speaking lies which is the devil's *native language* (44). Crucial in this fierce conflict between Jesus and his Jewish adversaries is that fact that the authenticity of a filial relationship to God will be evident not in what a person says but rather in what s/he *does*. As one scholar has concluded, 'Jesus insisted that true sonship is a *relationship* revealing spiritual lineage and characterized by *action* that expresses moral and spiritual likeness to the one who is claimed as father.'[39]

In the first epistle of John this point is also made abundantly clear: 'This is how we know who the children of God are and who the children of the devil are: Anyone who does not *do* what is right is not a child of God'.[40] Seeking to kill someone, in this case Jesus, doesn't square with 'doing right' in any book, and so the Pharisees by their behaviour demonstrated they were not divine progeny but the devil's.

5. Children of God: a metaphor for the church reconfigured around Jesus the Son (John 11:51–52)

We noted earlier how John's language of the children of God makes it clear that as believers we are born again and become members of God's new household. A radical change takes place where we exchange one community or 'family' for another. In other words, our filial relationship to God is not our native condition[41] and so

---

[39] Matthew Vellanickal, *The Divine Sonship of Christians in the Johannine Writings*, AnBib. 72 (Rome: Biblical Institute Press, 1977), p. 256 (emphasis added).

[40] 1 John 3:10.

[41] Smail, *The Forgotten Father*, p. 145.

when we become the children of God we not only have a new identity but also a new sense of belonging. When that happens we are introduced into the most intimate social structures, where irrespective of race, age, or gender we become members of the church, the family of God.

The epithet *children of God* is one of a number of rich metaphors in the Gospel of John which he uses to describe the church.[42] Although the word 'church' is not used in this Gospel, and is often underplayed, the subject of 'ecclesiology does figure prominently in John's overall theology'.[43] Van der Watt writes specifically of the fourth Gospel, 'if ecclesiology is defined in terms of the social gathering of the people of God, the family imagery is of course the way in which the ecclesiological relations are described . . . The church is God's family with everything this implies.'[44]

As we move further through the Gospel, the life of these children of God brought about by the work of the Holy Spirit (John 3:5) continues to be sustained and empowered by his indwelling and permanent presence (14:16–17). Thus, the 'Spirit rests and remains upon the Son, *and* upon those who, by receiving and abiding in the Son, have become "children of God"'.[45] Finally, with the instruction 'As the Father has sent me, I am sending *you*' (John 20:21), the children of God are tasked with continuing the mission of the Son so that the world may know that the Father has sent him. In light of this, John's ecclesiology is rich and profound and while it is not appreciated as much as Paul's thinking about community, his use of filial language is one important way in which he constructs for his readers a theology of the church.

With this in mind, one of the more enigmatic and neglected references to the expression *children of God* is found in 11:51–52 where in the context of the plot to kill Jesus, Caiaphas the high priest *prophesied that Jesus would die for the Jewish[46] nation, and not only for that nation but also for the scattered children of God to bring them together and make them one.* Though Caiaphas

---

[42] R. Alan Culpepper, *The Gospel and Letters of John* (Nashville: Abingdon, 1998), p. 100. Andreas J. Köstenberger, *The Missions of Jesus and the Disciples According to the Fourth Gospel* (Grand Rapids: Eerdmans, 1998), p. 166. For a fuller discussion of community imagery see Minear, *Images of the Church*.

[43] Johan Ferreira, *Johannine Ecclesiology*, JNSTS 160 (Sheffield: Sheffield Academic Press, 1998), p. 201.

[44] Van der Watt, *Family of the King*, p. 438.

[45] Andreas J. Köstenberger and Scott R. Swain, *Father, Son, and Holy Spirit: The Trinity and John's Gospel*, NSBT 24 (Nottingham: Apollos, 2008), p. 146 (emphasis original).

[46] Even though the word 'Jewish' is not in the Greek text it is clearly understood from the context.

does not know what he is saying, God does, and he speaks through Caiaphas in a prophetic manner. We are immediately struck again by the communal note being made here: John stresses the individual response of faith in Jesus as Son of God and in this way individuals enter into a new community – they are *children* (not singular 'child') who belong to one another in the family of God.

This communal aspect runs through the Gospel as a whole; for example, Jesus is portrayed as a shepherd who gathers his flock together: 'I have other sheep that are not of this sheep pen. I must bring them also. They will listen to my voice, and there shall be *one flock* and one shepherd' (10:16). Jesus' death serves the purpose of gathering *the scattered children of God, to bring them together and make them one* (52). Though the vertical dimension of being 'God's children' is important, the horizontal aspect of identity is as well, because it is by virtue of belonging to God that we belong to one another.[47] Significantly, it is the death of Jesus which is the means of reconfiguring the church, the children of God, around himself as the Son of God. In other words, Jesus' death is central and the means by which life is imparted (i.e., we are *made* the children of God) and are subsequently united into one church. The death of Jesus was mentioned immediately prior to our verses, where it is described in substitutionary terms: 'it is better that one man die *for the people* than the whole nation perish' (11:50).

Caiaphas, however, is merely thinking at the political level of how Jesus' death would remove him from the context and shore up his own standing. Thus, as far as he as high priest is concerned there is only one solution: either Jesus dies or the nation dies; Caiaphas' leanings are clearly toward the former. But John is working with a different agenda and his thinking is more ecclesial (than political) for if Jesus dies on behalf of the nation then the nation lives. However, John goes on to state that Jesus' death is not only *for that nation but also for the scattered children of God*. This latter expression has been understood differently by commentators but it is interesting to first note how 'gathering' functions as *inclusio*: the 'gathering' of the Sanhedrin in 11:47 which decides the death of Jesus is the trigger for the 'gathering' of the scattered children of God.[48] John's discussion is heavily couched in Jewish terms and his reference to the *scattered children of God* would be understood as referring to Jews of the diaspora, who one day would be gathered from the four corners of the earth (Isa. 11:12; 43:5–7). As we have noted already, this kind of

47 Thompson, 'Children', p. 207.
48 Köstenberger, *John*, p. 353

language was seized on by New Testament writers who drew the connections that the true children of God are those who believe in Jesus the Son of God (John 1:12–13; cf. 1 Pet. 1:1) brought together into *one* community (cf. John 10; 14 – 17).

Similarly, the Old Testament prophets describe a streaming of the Gentiles into the mountain of the Lord (e.g., Isa. 2:2–3; 56: 6–8; Zech. 14:16). In context, the reference to the 'holy nation' describes the church and this phrase *the scattered children of God* refers to the Gentiles, in anticipation of the Gentile mission (cf. John 12:20–21).[49] Although these *scattered children* have not yet been brought in they are described as though they have, which presupposes the idea of predestination and election. This fits well with the author's earlier comments in 10:16: 'I *have* other sheep that are not of this sheep pen. I must bring them also. They too *will listen* to my voice and there shall be one flock and one shepherd.' In other words, this is a church which will be (and already is) composed of scattered children reconfigured around Jesus the Son.

6. The children of God now participate in the mission of the Son (20:21–23)

The mission of Jesus is the central focus in the Gospel of John, where the Father sends his Son into the world. All other missions (e.g., the Spirit, John 15:26; the disciples, 15:27, see below) are a part of but are nevertheless subsumed under and subservient to the mission of the Son (e.g., John 3:16).[50] In Jewish life, and in order to safeguard a message, the father of the house would never send a hired servant but only a son, preferably a firstborn, in order to convey an important message to another person. Mission in the Gospel of John, we might say, is a family affair; the Father educates his Son in that he prepares him with the requisite knowledge (1:18), authorizes him in the execution of it (John 3:35; 13:3; 17:2), and ensures its successful fulfilment (John 19:30) by the gathering of others, the children of God, into the family.[51]

On the basis of this, and still with the familial context of the mission in mind, God's mission is furthered and continues through his children being sent out by Jesus, the Son, with the authority of

---

[49] Ibid.
[50] Andreas J. Köstenberger and Peter T. O'Brien, *Salvation to the Ends of the Earth: A Biblical Theology of Mission* NSBT 11 (Leicester: Apollos, 2001), p. 209.
[51] van der Watt, *Family of the King*, p. 296.

the Father: 'So Jesus said to them again, *Peace be with you! As the Father has sent me, I am sending you* (20–21). Indeed, it 'is precisely the children of God who recognize and confess the Son of God, and therefore they stand together with the Son over against a hostile world'.[52] Like Jesus, the disciples are also called (1:35–51), trained and educated for the task (20:23) and sent out (21). The 'success' of their endeavours, however, is entirely dependent on the groundwork already laid by Jesus the Son: the disciples will harvest a crop for which 'others have done the hard work' (John 4:38), and they will bear fruit which they did not produce (John 15:8, 16). In this way the mission of God through his Son leads to growth as the sons and daughters of God are commissioned to continue what the Father had given the Son. The note of continuity in the Gospel is important, as Eckhard Schnabel[53] points out:

> By virtue of being sent by Jesus, the disciples are co-workers of God the Father: they do the work of the Son (Jn. 13:12–14) . . . Jesus was sent by God in order to do the 'work' that the Father had entrusted to him, and Jesus faithfully carried out this work . . . And it is this work that the disciples are commissioned to continue.

Finally, and not without significance for the increasingly troubled world in which we live, the mission of these children of God is to be carried out within the context of peace (21) for it is, as we read elsewhere in the New Testament, only 'peacemakers' who are 'blessed' and identified elsewhere as 'the sons of God' (Matt. 5:9). Of all people, there is an obligation for God's children to endeavour to live in peace with everyone.

Summary

For John, Jesus is uniquely the Son of God and believers are described as God's children. As sonship is a functional category, Jesus does what his Father does and carries on the work of his Father by his implicit obedience to his will. Christians are described as the children of God, part of John's language for the church

---

[52] Marinus De Jonge, 'The Son of God and the Children of God in the Fourth Gospel', in James I. Cook (ed.), *Saved by Hope: Essays in Honor of Richard C. Oderersluys* (Grand Rapids: Eerdmans, 1978), p. 53.
[53] Eckhard J. Schnabel, *Early Christian Mission: Jesus and the Twelve*, vol. 2 (Downers Grove: IVP and Leicester: Apollos, 2004), p. 379.

into which they have now entered through the new birth and by believing in the Son.

Another more sinister familial allegiance is evidenced in the fourth Gospel, namely those who are children of the devil, that is, certain Pharisees who were seeking to kill Jesus. The Pharisees' claim to be Abraham's progeny is exposed by Jesus in his encounter with them because the patriarch never behaved like that. Their parentage is of a different order, and is more diabolical because they belong to the devil who was a murderer from the beginning.

Finally, the metaphor of 'children of God' is also an important one for John's understanding of the church. These children play a role in its future ingathering as they, like Jesus the Son, are sent into the world.

Romans 8:3, 12–25; Ephesians 1:5; Galatians 4:4; Romans 8:16–25
7. Adopted sons and daughters empowered by the Spirit

William Cowper, the renowned hymn writer of the eighteenth century and very good friend of John Newton, grew up in a well-established family in England with excellent connections. Cowper was a grandson of the Lord Chief Justice and was destined for a stellar career in law. He studied law at the Inner Temple and was called to the bar, at which point a cousin obtained for him an appointment in the Office of the Journals in the House of Lords. Prior to taking up this prestigious appointment, Cowper had to appear before the bar of the House to answer questions, a prospect which proved to be so daunting that he suffered what in eighteenth-century terms was called a huge melancholy – or depression – and was eventually pronounced insane. Cowper's plight was so desperate that he even attempted suicide on three separate occasions, with the result that his family had him committed to a lunatic asylum. Happily, after two years in the asylum in the care of a Dr Cotton, Cowper eventually recovered. An indispensable catalyst in Cowper's remarkable healing was the opportunity to live with the local minister and his wife, Rev. Morley and Mrs Mary Udwin of Huntingdon. In fact, he liked the couple so much Cowper stayed with them for more than two years, during which time he was not only able to enter fully into the life of the household by bonding with the couple's children but was also given biblical teaching and instruction. So remarkable was his recuperation and the care he received from the Rev. Morely and Mrs Udwin and their offspring that Cowper in a later correspondence to his aunt, Judith Madan, could find no better way to describe his relationship to them as an 'adopted son in this family'.[1]

[1] For these and further details see Jonathan Aitken's excellent biography

The term 'adopted as son' (Gk *huiothesia*), as noted earlier, is a uniquely Pauline expression among the writers of the New Testament. The word occurs five times in Paul's writings (Gal. 4:5; Rom. 8:15, 23; 9:4; Eph. 1:5), being used most often in his *magnum opus*, the letter to the Romans. We consider Paul's 'adoption' term because it falls under the umbrella of sonship, the latter being the larger, overarching theme in Scripture. In other words, the hierarchy runs sonship → adopted sons and daughters, and not vice versa. Paul uses the expression 'adoption' twice in Romans 8, a chapter which has been rightly described as the 'inner sanctuary within the cathedral of Christian faith; the tree of life in the midst of the garden of Eden, the highest peak in a range of mountains'.[2] This chapter, where Paul provides one of his most extensive discussions of sonship as well as of the Spirit, is strategically situated at the midpoint of the letter. To put our finger on the pulse of this chapter therefore is to feel the heartbeat of the entire letter.

1. Adoption in theological perspective

Theologically speaking, adoption is less well known than other terms in Paul's writings (e.g. justification, redemption), so it is appropriate we introduce it a little more fully. In fact, adoption has sometimes been misunderstood as the positive side of justification. But while justification and adoption are both legal terms, the former is Paul's primary salvific term and denotes how God puts a person right with himself. Adoption is a related but nevertheless theologically distinct idea in the mind of the apostle and we would do well not to confuse them. The relationship and distinction between these two terms is clear in the sense that God does not justify us and leave us destitute with nowhere to go; rather, he goes one step further and adopts us into the warmth and security of his family! Put differently, Paul's theology does not end in the courtroom, but is the basis for God's adopted sons and daughters being placed into the more intimate environment of the family, the church. In fact adoption, it could be argued, is the pinnacle of Pauline soteriology and as J. I. Packer has reminded us, 'adoption is . . . the highest privilege that the gospel offers; higher than justification'[3] owing to the 'richer

John Newton: From Disgrace to Amazing Grace (London: Continuum, 2007), p. 207.
  [2] Douglas Moo, *The Epistle to the Romans*, NICNT (Grand Rapids: Eerdmans, 1996), p. 467.
  [3] J. I. Packer, *Knowing God* (London: Hodder and Stoughton, 1988), p. 230.

relationship with God it involves'.[4] In short 'adoption is . . . the apex of redemptive grace and privilege'.[5]

Adoption adds a more nuanced view of Paul's understanding of salvation. There are many terms which Paul uses to describe what God in Christ has done for sinful humanity and each term is different and distinct. For example, justification draws from the realm of the law courts, propitiation (Rom. 3:25) from the language of *cultus* or sacrificial system, redemption (Rom. 3:24) from the slave market and reconciliation (Rom. 5:11) borrows from the realm of friendship. Adoption is different, however and complements these other expressions because it draws on a completely different conceptual field, that of the ancient family. Moreover, in the ancient Roman world of Paul's day, adoption had primarily to do with a person being *transferred* from one household to another, with all the attending privileges and responsibilities this brought. The importance of all these different terms to express what God in Christ has done for sinful humanity is not therefore for Paul a dull, monolithic notion. Rather, salvation according to the apostle is rich and kaleidoscopic. Or to change the metaphor, salvation could be likened to a ray of white light which when passed through a prism breaks up into the beautiful colours of the rainbow. Salvation, according to the Apostle Paul, is not in black and white or monochrome but in glorious technicolour. Thus, when we encounter Paul's unique expression of adoption it is to understand salvation through a different lens, a lens which we do not often take time to look through. When we do, we begin to appreciate how multifaceted Paul's view of the saving grace of God really is. If this is true, adoption is not just on the circumference of Paul's thinking, and should occupy a more central place in our theology than it currently does.[6]

2. Adoption and the Trinity (Rom. 8:3, 14–16; Gal. 4:4; Eph. 1:5)

Adoption is first and foremost a Trinitarian action where God the Father, Son and Holy Spirit work together in order to bring us into the household. Let us look at each of these in turn.

[4] John Buchanan, *The Doctrine of Justification: An Outline of Its History in the Church and of its Exposition from Scripture* (London: Banner of Truth, 1962), p. 277.
[5] John Murray, *Collected Works*, vol. 2 (Edinburgh: Banner of Truth, 1976), p. 233.
[6] I have argued this case in greater depth in Trevor J. Burke, *Adopted into God's Family: Exploring a Pauline Metaphor*, NSBT 22 (Nottingham: Apollos, 2006), pp. 32–45.

a. God the Father (Rom. 8:3; Gal. 4:4)

Though Paul does not mention adoption until Romans 8:15, he makes it abundantly clear that it begins with the Father, a point evident in Romans 8:3: *What the law was powerless to do . . . God [the Father] did by sending his own Son in the likeness of sinful man.* In a similar passage in Galatians Paul states that the Father takes the initiative in sending his own Son into the world at the climactic moment in salvation-history: *But when the time had fully come, God sent his Son . . . so that we might receive the full rights [adoption] of sons* (Gal. 4:4). Our adoption as God's sons and daughters begins with the action of God the Father's sending his Son to be born as a human being (yet without sin). Charles Spurgeon describes what the Father has done in the following terms:

> Observe, concerning the first advent, that *the Lord was moving in it towards man.* 'When the fullness of time was come, God sent forth his Son.' We moved not towards the Lord, but *the Lord towards us.* I do not find that the world in repentance sought after its Maker. No, but the offended God himself in infinite compassion broke the silence, and came forth to bless his enemies. See how spontaneous is the grace of God. All good things begin with him.[7]

In this respect, the Roman social context of the apostle Paul's day is quite enlightening because if an adoption was ever to take place it would only do so at the behest and initiative of the head of the household, the *paterfamilias.* The adoption procedure involved, in the first instance, the severing of the old *potestas* followed by the establishing of the paternal authority of the new father. This was carried out by the *paterfamilias* selling off his offspring into civil bondage (*in mancipio*), thereby making him a slave. On the release of his son the latter was still the property of the father and could by right be sold into bondage by him again and again. In order to avoid the son becoming a kind of familial football a law was laid down in the Twelve Tables (established by the second Decemvirate *c.* 450 BC) which stated that when a son was sold three times by his father the latter ceased to have any authority over him. It was from this law that the *adoptio* was derived. We can immediately see the relevance this background has for Paul – himself a Roman citizen who only uses his adoption term in letters written to churches under Roman

---

[7] Charles Spurgeon, sermon no. 1815: 'The Great Birthday and our Coming of Age'.

rule – who is of the view that it is God the Father who begins the procedure of bringing us into his household. In other words, adoption for Paul is primarily and profoundly a paternal initiative. Our adoption as God's sons and daughters finds its spring and origin in the saving purposes of God the Father who takes centre stage in his 'family'. One theologian says that if Christians were to truly reflect for a moment on the ramifications of the child of God being able to call the creator of the heavens and the earth 'Abba', 'it defies comprehension and calculation'[8] but for every spiritual son and daughter it is true!

Indeed if adoption is about anything is it is first and foremost about belonging to God the Father and his family. We not only belong to God but also to each other and if truth be told we cannot make progress in God's family without each other. Our African brothers and sisters in Christ are very conscious of this and have a deep understanding of community, connectedness and belonging, as one of their proverbs makes clear: 'If you want to travel *fast* go on your own; if you want to travel *far* go with a partner.' We need each other and we cannot make it on our own in the Christian life; in other words, there are no 'Lone Rangers' in the household of God nor should anyone feel lonely or excluded in the local church. One can understand how it is easy for many in our fractured society to feel isolated and severed from others, but this should not be the experience of those who now belong in God's family.

The experience of isolation has been very poignantly highlighted by Marla Paul, a columnist for the *Chicago Tribune* daily newspaper, who wrote a revealing piece about loneliness. In her article she confessed her sadness and frustration over her own inability to build and sustain friendships. She lamented that 'sometimes it seems easier to just give up and accept disconnectedness as a dark and unshakable companion; but, that's not the companion I want'. However, Paul concluded she was 'going to keep longing, searching, trying, and hoping that someday she will be able to discover and develop community'. After she had written her column, Paul thought nothing more of it but a few days later she was inundated with letters from others experiencing the same kind of isolation. One person responded: 'I've often felt that I'm standing outside looking through the window of a party to which I was not invited.'[9] In these days when people crave connectedness, the church should

---

[8] Sinclair B. Ferguson, *The Christian Life: A Doctrinal Introduction* (London: Hodder and Stoughton, 1981), p. 86.

[9] I was first alerted to this story by my pastor friend, Lewie Clark. Marla Paul later wrote a book *The Friendship Crisis* (Chicago: Rodale Books, 2005).

be a warm and welcoming environment for Christians and non-Christians alike where the former can show the love of Christ to those who do not profess the name of Jesus. Certainly no Christian should ever feel excluded from the 'party', the time especially when the church on a Sunday celebrates the risen, glorious Lord Jesus Christ, who welcomes all. Indeed, it is especially important as members of the God's household that 'we accept one another just as Christ has accepted you' (Rom. 15:7). Given that God the Father has adopted us, we now belong to him (and to one another), a point well captured by Alister McGrath when he writes:

> Adoption is about being wanted. It is about belonging. These are deeply emotive themes, which resonate with the cares and concerns of many in our increasingly fractured society. To be adopted is to be invited into a loving caring environment. It is about being welcomed, wanted and invited. Adoption celebrates the privilege of invitation, in which the outsider is welcomed into the fold of faith and love.[10]

b. God the Son (Rom. 8:3; Gal. 4:4; Eph. 1:5)

God the Father, however, does not act alone but does so in concert and unison with his Son, Jesus Christ (and the Holy Spirit[11]). It should not surprise us that Jesus the Son has a fundamentally important role to play in our adoption as God's sons and daughters since as we observed in an earlier chapter he is the perfect Son who is superior to all other sons before him (i.e. Adam, Israel and David). Thus, Paul writes *God sent his own Son in the likeness of sinful man to be a sin offering* (Rom. 8:3), for no one else would do, and that God *purposely* sent Jesus because as the Son of God he is the only means whereby we become God's children: *God sent his Son . . . so that* we might receive the adoption to sonship (Gal. 4.4). This is a crucially important point to grasp in light of the fact that Jesus as the Son of God is the only Son 'qualified' to do the work of God. Moreover, every time Paul mentions the believer's adoption as sons and daughters he ties it inextricably to the *person* (who Christ is) and the *work* (what he has done) of Jesus Christ God's only Son on the cross of Calvary.

Paul makes the same point in his letter to the church at Ephesus where he tells us that the blessing of adoption comes about *through*

---

[10] Alister McGrath, *Knowing Christ* (London: Hodder and Stoughton, 2001), pp. 144–145.
[11] See next section.

Jesus Christ (1:5), the equivalent of the 'in Christ' formula that is so much part of Paul's vocabulary in this letter. Most importantly then, the shedding of the blood of Jesus Christ his only Son on the cross 'is . . . the means . . . for the sinner to be adopted into the family of God'.[12] Our adoption as God's children was free but it did not come cheaply; rather, it was of infinite cost, the death of Jesus, God's own Son.

The role of the Son complements that of the Father in that Jesus is the means whereby we become God's children. In one sense, the significance of this for believers is that for the Apostle Paul 'what defines Israel is no longer ethnicity or Torah but *spiritual sonship and being in the Messiah*'.[13] Thus, if we take adoption out of its Christological context we will be sure to misinterpret it. Tom Smail concludes on the uniqueness of Jesus' role as far as the believers' sonship is concerned: '[it is] only as a result of an event of son-making and adoption (*huiothesia*) whose objective basis is in the work of the Son [that] . . . we are now able to address God as *Abba* and to enter into the inheritance that belongs to those who are his children.'[14]

c. God the Spirit (Rom. 8:14–16)

Understandably, much attention has been paid to the roles of the Father and the Son in our adoption as God's children since it is easier for us to identify with the personal or familial roles of these two members of the Trinity. But while the roles of the Father and the Son vis-à-vis the believer's adoption into God's household are clear, the same cannot be said of the Spirit. We do not have a proper understanding of the Spirit's function and as a consequence have underplayed the work of the Spirit in adoption. A closer look at

---

[12] Harold Hoehner, *Ephesians: An Exegetical Commentary* BECNT (Grand Rapids: Baker Academic, 2002), p. 197 (emphasis added); Gordon Fee, *God's Empowering Presence: The Holy Spirit in the Letters of Paul* (Peabody: Hendrickson, 1994), p. 667, makes a similar point: 'this "adoption" was effected for us historically through the death of Christ'.

[13] Michael F. Bird, *Introducing Paul: The Man, His Mission and His Message* (Downers Grove: IVP, 2008), p. 49 (emphasis added). See later in this chapter where Paul holds out hope for Israel.

[14] Thomas A. Smail, *The Forgotten Father: Rediscovering the Heart of the Christian Gospel* (London: Hodder and Stoughton, 1980), p. 146; Fee, *God's Empowering Presence*, p. 407, also states: 'Paul sets forth the work of Christ as an objective, historical, once-for-all reality. In that objective, historical work the Son procured "sonship" for all who believe in him, which Paul makes personal for him and for them by the final purpose clause "so that we might *receive* adoption as sons".'

the Spirit language and the Spirit's role in the believer's adoption in Romans 8 is significant for the fact that Paul here never uses inanimate terms (e.g., water, wind, fire) as do the evangelists in the Gospel writings (e.g., John 3:8) to describe the Holy Spirit. Rather, the Spirit is described in very intimate and personal ways. Paul, for instance, uses verbs that often denote personal agency, and this is immediately apparent in Romans 8, 'Paul's great Spirit chapter'.[15] Paul juxtaposes two ways believers can choose to conduct themselves: they can 'live according to the flesh' or 'according to the Spirit'.[16] To allow oneself to follow the dictates of the former is to have one's mind set on what that nature desires but to live in accordance with the Spirit is to 'have their minds set on what the Spirit desires'. In Romans 8:9 Paul is confident of the Roman believers' present standing in Christ, for he speaks in the past tense as he reminds them of what they once were: 'you, however, are controlled not by the sinful nature' (Gk 'flesh') 'but by the Spirit, if the Spirit of God lives (Gk *oikeō*) in you'. When it comes to understanding who and who is not a believer, we would do well to heed James Dunn's comments on this last verse: 'Rom. 8:9 rules out the possibility *both* of a non-Christian possessing the Spirit and of a Christian *not* possessing the Spirit.'[17] Who is a Christian, according to the apostle Paul? – a person in whom the Spirit of God dwells.

The human traits vis-à-vis the Spirit continue in Romans 8:14 where Paul describes the Spirit as the one responsible for giving direction and guidance since *all who are led (Gk agō) by the Spirit of God are the sons of God* . Two verses later the Spirit is the one who *bears witness* (Gk *summarturei*) *with/to our spirit that we are children of God* (16, ESV). And later in the chapter Paul tells his readers that Jesus Christ the Son is the one who is presently 'interceding for us' (8:34), a role he also ascribes to the Spirit earlier in verse 26: 'the Spirit intercedes for us with groanings that words cannot express.'

The manner in which Paul personifies the role and activity of the Spirit is profound and unequalled in the biblical canon and clearly demonstrates the fact that the apostle does not think of the Spirit as a force, energy or influence. Rather, the Spirit is a person, an integral member of the divine family who plays a vital role in the believer's adoption into God's household. Put differently, the Spirit

---

[15] James D. G. Dunn, *The Theology of Paul the Apostle* (London: T&T Clark, 1998), p. 438.

[16] Rom. 8:5, ESV.

[17] James D. G. Dunn, *Baptism in the Holy Spirit: A Re-examination of the New Testament Teaching on the Gift of the Spirit in Relation to Pentecostalism Today* (Philadelphia: Westminster Press, 1970), p. 95.

is not only God's empowering presence[18] as Gordon Fee has rightly reminded us, but the Spirit is also God's *personal* presence and an inseparable member of the divine family.

Part of the answer to the question of the role of the Spirit in adoption is given in Romans 8:15 where Paul uses the expression *Spirit of adoption*. Paul contrasts *a spirit of slavery* here with the *Spirit of adoption*; in the case of the former there is a clear allusion to the Old Testament in that the Spirit does not lead people back to Egypt, a place synonymous with fear and bondage. Scholars and commentators have understood the expression 'Spirit of adoption' differently. Some scholars argue that the Spirit of adoption is a reference to the Spirit as the agent of adoption: the Spirit *effects* adoption.[19] This reading, however, can be contested on two counts. First, it is hard to find a grammatical category for the phrase to be understood in this way[20] and second as we have already observed the *Father* – not the Spirit – is the chief instigator as far as our adoption into God's family is concerned, as John Murray rightly notes: 'It is the Father who, by way of eminence, is the agent of adoption. The evidence particularly in the Pauline epistles, indicates that it is to the Father believers sustain the relation of sons by adoption and it is therefore the Father who adopts.'[21]

Others understand this expression to mean 'the Spirit which anticipates adoption',[22] viewing adoption as an exclusively end-time event (8:23). The anticipatory dimension, as it relates to the consummation of adoption, is certainly part of Paul's understanding but this by itself does not sufficiently acknowledge the 'now' or 'present' aspects adduced earlier in verses 14 and 16. Still others take the phrase to mean 'the Spirit who expresses adoption'[23] in the sense that the Spirit does not actually make us God's adopted sons

---

[18] This is the main title of Gordon Fee's excellent magnum opus.

[19] Fee, *God's Empowering Presence*, p. 566 (author's own emphasis).

[20] James M. Scott, *Adoption as Sons of God: An Investigation into the Background of HUIOTHESIA* (Tübingen: Mohr, 1992), p. 261, n 143; Brendan Byrne, '*Sons of God'- 'Seed of Abraham': A Study of the Idea of the Sonship of God of All Christians in Paul Against the Jewish Background*, AnBib. 83 (Rome: Rome Biblical Institute, 1979), p. 100.

[21] John Murray, *The Epistle to the Romans*, 2 vols. (Grand Rapids: Eerdmans, 1960, 1965), p. 295. And as H. B. Swete comments: 'The Spirit of the Son is sent into the hearts of the adopted sons … it does not make them sons, for they are such by their union with the Incarnate Son, but it makes them conscious of their sonship'; see *The Holy Spirit in the New Testament* (London: Macmillan, 1931), p. 204.

[22] E.g., C. K. Barrett, *The Epistle to the Romans*, 2nd ed., BNTC (London: A.C. Black, 1991), p. 153.

[23] Murray, *Epistle to the Romans*, p. 295.

but assists us in testifying to this new filial disposition. This is true, the Spirit does bring the assurance of our newly adopted status, but this is more relevant to Paul's argument in verse 16 which follows (see below).[24]

A better way to understand the phrase 'Spirit of adoption' is to view the two as so connected with the sense that the 'Spirit . . . goes with . . . adoption'.[25] Taken this way, the Spirit and adoption are not only closely connected but are in fact inextricably linked together; in short, they are unitedly and reciprocally related.[26] This is further supported by what Paul has stated earlier in 8:9, where just as the Spirit is inseparable from Christian *beginnings* (cf. Gal. 3:3), so also by using the phrase 'Spirit of adoption' Paul is saying there can be no possibility of adopted sons and daughters of God without that same Spirit. This interpretation is assured by what Paul says in a similar passage in Galatians 4:6 where he uses another distinctive phrase, the 'Spirit of his Son', not found anywhere else in the Pauline corpus, to demonstrate how sonship and the Spirit are inseparable parts of the earthly life and ministry of Jesus. What Paul wishes to drive home to the Galatian (and Roman) Christians by the use of the phrase 'Spirit of his Son' is that just as it is impossible to think of the Spirit divorced from the sonship of Jesus, so it is equally inconceivable to think of that same Spirit apart from the Christian's adoption as son/daughter (cf. Rom. 8:14; Gal. 4:6; Rom. 8:15).[27] In other words, just as we can say 'no Spirit, no Christian'[28] we can also say 'no adopted son/daughter, no Spirit'.

3. Sonship and inheritance (Rom. 8:16–25)

One of the results of being a son or daughter of God is the inheritance into which the believer has already entered. Paul links the two together in Romans 8:17: *Now if we are children, then we are heirs – heirs of God and co-heirs with Christ.* And he states in Galatians 4:7: 'So you are no longer a slave, but a son and since you are a son, God has made you also an heir.' Sonship is a prerequisite for heir-

---

[24] Moo, *Romans*, p. 502, argues that the Spirit is *both* the agent and assurer of adoption.

[25] Byrne, '*Sons of God*'- '*Seed of Abraham*', p. 100; Scott, *Adoption as Sons*, p. 261, n 143.

[26] Herman N. Ridderbos, *Paul: An Outline of His Theology* (Grand Rapids: Eerdmans, 1995), p. 199, states: 'There is in the Pauline pronouncements a peculiar relationship of reciprocity between adoption as sons and the gift of the Spirit.'

[27] Richard Longenecker, *Galatians*, WBC 41 (Nashville: Nelson, 2010), p. 174.

[28] Dunn, *Theology of Paul*, p. 494.

ship, a point we noted in the Old Testament in respect of the nation of Israel when God declared 'Israel is my firstborn' (Exod. 4:22) after which they were delivered from Egypt and took possession of the 'land' (their inheritance) which God had promised to give them.

One of the much debated issues today is whether the inheritance of which Paul here speaks is tied physically to the land. In these verses Paul does not connect the two nor does the land as a physical idea appear to feature much, if at all, in the New Testament or indeed the apostle Paul's letters. In Romans 4:13 Paul talks more in terms of a universal principle where Abraham would be 'heir of the world'. And whenever Paul in Romans 8:17 says that the children of God are *heirs of God and co-heirs with Christ* the blessings he has in mind are more relational and spiritual rather than spatial or territorial precisely because they come about through union with God and with his Son, Jesus Christ.[29] Thus, the privileges which come to us as a result of our adoption into the family of God are that we can look forward to an 'eternal inheritance' (Heb. 9:15); 'not . . . a strip of land on the eastern Mediterranean shore but of eternity itself'.[30] Again the writer to the Hebrews writes of the patriarch Abraham 'for he was looking forward to the city with foundations, whose architect and builder is God'. In the New Testament the believer's goal is no different: 'For here we do not have an enduring city, but we are looking for the city that is to come.'[31]

In saying this, it does not mean that God is finished with Israel. Quite the opposite, for as Romans 9 – 11 demonstrate, Paul uses the term 'Israel' no less than ten times to refer to ethnic Israel, and in 11:26 where Paul says 'all Israel will be saved' it does seem to include an ethnic component.[32] God has plans for Israel in the future but in his strange providences God will use the Gentiles to make the Jews jealous after which they will turn and exercise faith in Jesus as Messiah and embrace the sonship (cf. Rom. 9:4) that is rightly theirs.[33]

---

[29] Thomas R. Schreiner, *Romans*, BECNT (Grand Rapids: Baker, 1998), p. 428.

[30] Gordon Fee, *Pauline Christology: An Exegetical-Theological Study* (Peabody: Hendrickson, 2007), p. 545.

[31] Heb. 11:10; 13:14.

[32] See the link <http://www.henrycenter.org/tag/doug-moo/>.

[33] N.T. Wright, 'Romans', in NIB 10 (Nashville: Abingdon Press, 2002), p. 496, sounds the caveat: 'In Paul's thought, ethnic, national Israel will not rule the world. *God will rule the world* and will do so through Jesus the Jewish Messiah, in such a way as to bring all nations equally into God's family' (emphasis added). In fact, Romans, especially chapters 9 – 11, as Moo (*Romans*, p. 291) points out, is 'ultimately . . . not about Israel – it is about God'. Romans is the most *theo*logical or *God*-centered Pauline letter: the noun *theos* occurs 153 times.

4. Sonship, the Spirit and the moral imperative (Rom. 8:12–17)

a. Sons and daughters led and empowered by the Spirit (8:13, 15)

Paul begins Romans 8:12–17 with an emphatic statement that relates to what he stated in the first eleven verses of the chapter, but which also charts the course for what he has to say on sonship.[34] The first time Paul uses the language of sonship in regard to believers is verse 14 where he states that 'as many as' *are led by the Spirit of God are sons of God* where the phrase 'as many as' may be taken inclusively ('all who are led are sons') or exclusively ('only those who are led are sons'), which may be deliberately ambiguous on Paul's part.

The language which Paul uses is that of the Old Testament because Israel as God's son was led (Deut. 32:12; Isa. 63:13). But as Paul writes to the Roman Christians, now both Jew and Gentile, there is to be no returning for them to the previous old ways of bondage because as the apostle goes on to remind them, they *did not received a spirit that makes [them] a slave again to fear* but have instead *received the Spirit of adoption as sons* (15). And so, just as Israel had been led out of Egypt, a place synonymous with bondage, so also for these New Testament believers there can be no going back to the past sinful ways. The chains of sin have been severed (cf. Rom. 6:2) and they are now free as liberated children of God.

But *how* are the sons of God to do this and *what* exactly is the leading to which Paul refers in this verse? It is possible Paul may be thinking in practical terms regarding a future direction or leading a person is to take, such as following a particular career or knowing God's will regarding the choice of a life's partner or seeking guidance over an important purchase one it to make (e.g., a house or car). Of course these are ways God leads us today, but rather than thinking about the future direction one is to take on these important matters, the leading to which Paul refers in 8:14 is more existentially focused and has much more to do with the present than with a course a person is to take in the days ahead. The 'leading' to which Paul refers must be understood within the context of the passage,

---

[34] Moo, *Romans*, p. 493, prefers to attach vv. 12–13 to vv. 1–11 but there is good reason for considering vv. 12–17 as hanging together. First, Paul in light of having reminded the Roman believers of how they used to live (vv. 5–8) now proceeds to exhort them 'Therefore...' with what they are to do. Second, the sibling language with which the passage opens 'brothers and sisters' fits the familial language that is so pervasive throughout: 'sons', 'children', 'adopted sons', etc. Third, the Nestle Aland 27th edition and the United Bible Society texts regard vv. 12–17 as a unit in their layout of the text.

where the phrase *led by the Spirit* (14) is immediately preceded by *if by the Spirit you put to death the misdeeds of the body you will live* (13). In other words, 'the ethical responsibility for God's sons and daughters to live circumspectly pervades Paul's thesis of adoption'.[35] There are two aspects to this which we will now consider: first, the believer's responsibility to act accordingly and second, the divine energy which is provided for them to do so.

b. The individual response: you must put to death the misdeeds of the body (8:13)

First, Paul emphasizes the individual responsibility for each Christian: he states *you must put to death the misdeeds of the body* (13). This means that each child of God has the moral obligation to mortify the sinful nature or the flesh by not giving it leg room or the opportunity to breathe or survive.[36] The verb *put to death* denotes an ongoing activity or a continual killing of the flesh, the sinful nature, rather than a once-and-for-all act. Every day you and I get up we have moral choices to make and the practical implications of this are profound: for example, am I going to give in to the dictates of the sinful nature or am I going to make good moral choices in order to live as a child of God? Am I going to look at an image on the internet which I know is dishonouring to God and the 'new family' of which I am now a part? Am I going to begin a relationship with someone I know could potentially lead me away from other believers and the church, my brothers and sisters in Christ? Am I going to engage in a particular behaviour which I know could quickly become a habitual activity and potentially ensnare me for life? All of these are tantamount to going back to 'Egypt' and slavery all over again and are not in keeping with the conduct of God's children. We need to choose wisely and, as we shall now see, help is given for us to do just that.

c. The divine energy – the Spirit enables God's children to mortify the sinful nature (8:13)

Thankfully we are not left unaided as God's offspring. God's sons and daughters are not left to their own devices, for Paul makes it

[35] Trevor J. Burke, 'The Characteristics of Paul's Adoptive Sonship Motif', *IBS* 17 (1995), p. 64.
[36] See also Sinclair B. Ferguson who understands v. 13b as the proper context for v. 14; *The Christian Life: A Doctrinal Introduction* (London: Hodder and Stoughton, 1981), p. 88.

clear that none of this is to be done on our own energy, strength or power; rather, it is *by the Spirit* you are to put to death the misdeeds of the body.[37] This phrase 'by the Spirit' sits at the end of the sentence for emphasis and 'indicates that the Spirit is the primary agent in Christian obedience'.[38] The verb 'led' is in the passive voice which means that the Spirit is the gift and empowering presence of God who now brings a moral duty for God's children to live accordingly. There is an end-time feel to what Paul says in this chapter, and the 'leading' to which Paul here refers is pregnant with moral content. By this I mean that the Spirit is the one who is powerfully and supernaturally available to all the sons and daughters of God to live appropriately *now*, the time between the first and second coming of Christ, the Son of God. What Paul is describing is nothing less than the ethics of the *eschaton*, the moral duty for all of the children of God to live circumspectly. In other words, holiness and godly living are not an optional extra for those who belong to God's new household. Rather, the moral responsibility of what Paul is describing is as C .E. B. Cranfield states: 'the daily, hourly, putting to death of the schemings and enterprises of the sinful flesh by means of the Spirit is a matter of being led, impelled, controlled, by the Spirit'.[39] There ought to be a consistency between acknowledging one is a son and conducting oneself as a child of God, something the church would do well to heed, especially when there is sometimes little difference in lifestyle between those who claim to belong to God's family and those who do not, a point about which L. H. Marshall is keenly aware: 'The ethical implications of Adoption are obvious. A "son of God" must behave in a manner worthy of his august descent, and only those who behave so are truly "sons" . . . only as men behave like God can they really prove themselves to be sons of God'.[40]

In context, then, Paul is describing how the new child of God should live, behave and conduct him/herself and the expression *by the Sprit you* [are] *to put to death the misdeeds of the body* is pregnant with moral content where the new privilege of filial belonging brings with it accompanying moral duties and responsibilities of a life of holiness. Sinclair B. Ferguson sounds the right note when he concludes:

---

[37] The dative expression 'by the Spirit' is best understood as a dative of agency: 'through the Spirit' we put to death the misdeeds of the body.

[38] Schreiner, *Romans*, p. 422.

[39] C. E. B. Cranfield, *Romans 1–8*, ICC 1 (London: Continuum T&T Clark, 2004), p. 395.

[40] L. H. Marshall, *The Ethics of the New Testament* (London: Hodder and Stoughton, 1960), p. 259.

the leading of which Paul speaks has very clear and definite content here. It is connected intimately with the help the Spirit is said to give in verse 13, 'to put to death the misdeeds of the body'. *The guidance the Spirit provides is that of clear-cut opposition to sin.* To claim to experience the ministry of the Spirit of adoption and yet to dally with sin is to be utterly deceived. The Spirit of adoption is the same Person as the Spirit of holiness of whom Paul had spoken earlier (Rom. 1:4). *His presence brings a new attitude to sin.*[41]

It is a salutary point to ponder how Paul's reference to the adoptive sonship of believers in Romans 8:15 is deliberately sandwiched in between references to Jesus as the Son of God (8:3, 29). The former reference reminds us that our sonship by adoption cannot be entered into apart from the sonship of Jesus while the latter makes it abundantly clear that God's goal for his spiritual progeny is to be 'conformed to the image/likeness (*eikōn*) of his Son'. In other words, there ought to be in the life of God's children a continual and growing likeness to Jesus whose image we ought to be mirroring to those who are non-family. When those outside the Christian family see the name of the Father and the church family being dishonoured by profligate and prodigal sons and daughters, it is no wonder some are turned off and there is little impact made on a world which is lost.

5. The witness of the Spirit: the assurance of the believer's filial relationship to God (Rom. 8:16)

As noted earlier, Romans 8:12–17 is part of a very closely reasoned argument, evident by the many conjunctions Paul uses. No such connecting word, however, is found in verse 16 where the relationship to the previous verses is more thematic and where the filial metaphor discussed earlier in verse 15 is picked up and carried forward.

There is little to doubt the fact that Paul 'still has the metaphor of adoption in mind'[42] in verse 16, a verse which is located in a passage containing a most unusual number of compound verbs (nine are used in the space of fourteen verses); one is used in verse 16, namely, the verb 'to bear witness to/with'. The major interpretative issue here centres on this compound verb which could be taken in one of

---

[41] Ferguson, *The Christian Life*, p. 88 (emphasis added).
[42] Williams, *Paul's Metaphors*, p. 65; see also Fee, *God's Empowering Presence*, p. 567.

two ways: did Paul mean that 'the Spirit bears witness to our spirit'[43] or that 'the Spirit bears witness with our spirit'?[44] Proponents of the former argue that the verb does not connote the idea of association but of intensifying the verb 'testify' and that such an understanding of the verb does not sit comfortably in this context, as Cranfield notes: 'What standing has our spirit in *this* matter? Of itself it surely has no right at all to testify to our being sons of God?'[45] But there are several good reasons for taking this to mean *'with* our spirit': first, the context suggests that after having already been adopted into God's family (Rom. 8:15) God sends his Spirit to bring an awareness and assures us of the reality of our new filial disposition; second, the verb in question has the meaning 'to' in only two New Testament passages (Rom. 2:15; 9:1); third, this word was still used to mean 'bear witness with' in papyri dating back to the second century; fourth, a plurality of witnesses is necessary to establish the truth of a matter (e.g. Deut. 19:15; 2 Cor. 13:1) and this has particular significance if a Roman adoption procedure is in view where several witnesses were required in order to verify that a *bona fides* adoption had taken place.[46] For these reasons it is better to understand the Spirit's role in as *bearing witness with our spirit* (ESV) that we are God's sons and daughters.

We should not misunderstand this as some kind of mystical experience as though God's Spirit whispers to us 'You are God's son' which 'would be tantamount to a new revelation from God over and above the revelation given to us in Scripture'.[47] Rather the role of the Spirit in sonship is to bring an appreciation and understanding of our new filial disposition. Put another way, the Spirit of God strikes a chord with the human spirit of the newly adopted child, indicating to him or her that they have indeed come home.

This concurs with the role of the Holy Spirit elsewhere in the New Testament in that his work is always reiterative and not innovative,

---

[43] Greek grammarians refer to this as a dative of indirect object. For this view see Daniel B. Wallace, *Greek Grammar Beyond the Basics: An Exegetical Syntax of the New Testament* (Grand Rapids: Zondervan, 1996), pp. 160–161, who argues for this interpretation.

[44] In grammatical terms, this is called a dative of association.

[45] Cranfield, *Romans*, p. 403 (emphasis original).

[46] A. N. Sherwin-White, *Roman Society and Roman Law in the New Testament* (Grand Rapids: Baker, 1978), p. 149, states that any matter in Roman law had to certified by several witnesses (five or seven) and we can assume this would have been no different in the Roman socio-legal practice of adoption; see also James D. Hester, *Paul's Concept of Inheritance: A Contribution to Paul's Understanding of Heilsgeschichte*, SJTOP 4 (Edinburgh: Oliver Boyd, 1968), p. 60–62.

[47] Sinclair B. Ferguson, *Children of the Living God* (Edinburgh: Banner of Truth, 1989), p. 73.

because the Spirit always acts on the basis of what God in Christ has already done (John 14:26; 16:14). And earlier in this chapter Paul has struck a soteriological and Christological note that God had sent his Son in the likeness of sinful flesh to be a sin offering for us (8:3). Thus, when doubts creep in, as they invariably do and will throughout our Christian life, it is at such critical moments that the Spirit bears witness with our spirit, bringing a new consciousness and appreciation that we belong to God and his family. James Dunn rightly points out in regard to this verse that 'adoption is given its existential reality by the presence and witness of the Spirit'.[48] The Spirit's role is vital in reassuring the child of God of their new sense of belonging in God's household.

6. Sonship, the Spirit, and the climax of salvation[49] (Rom. 8:17–25)

This passage is brimming with language of the end times and there is a distinct familial flavour to the terms Paul uses (i.e., *children of God*, 19, 21, and *adoption as sons*, 23). In these verses Paul is describing the final adoption of the children of God, which will not be entered into lightly because they along with the whole cosmos are caught up in this limbo period as everything moves inexorably towards a glorious future.

a. Adopted sons and daughters, now (8:14, 16)

Paul had earlier stated that the Roman Christians have no longer received a spirit of slavery but have received the Spirit of adoption. The reality of the situation for the believers to whom Paul is writing is that they are *already* God's sons and daughter. Earlier Paul had repeatedly used the present tense, as in verse 14: *those who are* led by the Spirit are *the sons of God*. He sounds the same note in verse 16: *The Spirit himself testifies with our Spirit that we* are God's children. There can be no doubting Paul's point, namely that right *now* we are members of the family of God, and this is of immense reassurance and comfort to the believer.

[48] Dunn, *Theology of Paul*, p. 424.
[49] See further on this in Trevor J. Burke, 'Adopted as Sons: The Missing Piece in Pauline Soteriology', in Stanley E. Porter (ed.), *Paul as Jew, Greek and Roman*, PAST 5 (Leiden: Brill, 2008), pp. 259–287.

b. Adopted sons and daughters, not yet (8:23)

But that is not the entire picture, for while we are God's sons and daughters in the present ('now') there is the tension between this and what is yet to be (the 'not yet'), and Paul sounds the latter note here: *Not only so, but we ourselves, who have the firstfruits of the Spirit, groan inwardly as we wait eagerly for our adoption as sons, the redemption of our bodies* (23). Our filial disposition therefore spans the present and the future, it is a reality now but its full consummation lies ahead. In other words, the adoption papers have already been signed and filed and the new relationship has already begun, but the child has not yet gone to live in their new home, which is still under construction.[50]

So, what happens in the intervening period between the 'now' and the 'not yet', between the present and the future for the children of God? It is this subject which Paul takes up in 8:17–25 where again the Spirit plays an important role in regard to sonship, for the Spirit is the overlap between the ages as Paul makes clear in verse 23. This is our next topic.

c. Suffering and sonship: you can't have one without the other (8:17–25)

Significantly, Paul describes this waiting-room period as one of adversity, and weaves together the three themes of sonship, suffering and the Spirit, wrapping it all up in a cosmic framework. The suffering which Paul describes in 8:18–25 must be understood within the context of what he has said earlier in verse 17: *Now if we are children then we are heirs – heirs of God and co-heirs with Christ, if indeed we share in his sufferings in order that we may share in his glory.* Paul prefaces the suffering of the inanimate and human orders in 8:18–25 by first describing the suffering of God's Son, Jesus Christ. A cursory reading of the 'if' clause in verse 17 might suggest that believers *may* suffer, but this is a real condition that must be met if God's children are to enter into their inheritance. In other words, there is a proviso here that just as Christ himself suffered, God's spiritual offspring cannot expect any different since they must tread a similar path that he trod. In the physical realm some children might shirk their responsibilities (and difficulties) towards an elderly parent and still think they will inherit, but not so in the spiritual realm:

[50] Brenda Colijn, *Images of Salvation in the New Testament* (Downers Grove: IVP, 2010), p. 187.

Perhaps we have known grown sons who were quite content to leave the care of their aging parents to others, but when the old folks passed on, they came promptly forward to claim their inheritance. It cannot be this way with our divine sonship, Paul says. If we are going to be associated with Christ in receiving the inheritance, we must also be associated with him in the difficulties that sonship entails.[51]

Certainly the suffering of the adopted sons and daughters of God is not the same as Jesus, God's Son, as he suffered vicariously and in our place. Nevertheless suffering and sonship are two sides of one and the same coin and the former is to be expected if one is to enter into the glorious inheritance. Tom Smail succinctly puts it in the following terms: 'shared sonship means shared suffering'.[52] In a different context where the filial language is lacking, Peter also reminds his readers of the certainty of suffering when he states: 'Dear friends, *do not be surprised* at the fiery ordeal that has come upon you to test you, as though something strange were happening to you'.[53]

What is most striking about Romans 8:18–25 is that alongside the legal imagery of adoption is the most unusual and arresting maternal imagery which Paul employs to describe the inanimate order. In fact, the created order's destiny is contingent and dependent on what God has planned for his spiritual offspring, as Paul writes that creation *waits in eager expectation for the children of God to be revealed* (19, TNIV). In Romans 8 there is not only an incontrovertible link between the renewal of the inanimate creation and God's adopted sons and daughters but also that the inanimate order is the passive partner in the unfolding cosmic drama and transformation of all things. In these verses Paul is retelling the Genesis story as God's purpose for the cosmos unfolds. In verses 20–22 Paul describes the inanimate order (rocks, mountains, seas, rivers, birds), the *ktisis* ('creation') which he says was subjected to frustration not by its own choice *but by the will of the one who subjected it*. Then in verse 23 there is a shift to the animate order, humanity, which Paul describes as God's children. There is a clear link between the two orders as verse 19 makes clear: *creation* waits *in eager expectation for the children of God to be revealed*. The inanimate order is the passive partner in the outworking of this cosmic drama as its transformation is contingent on what will happen to the human order,

---

[51] Merrill Proudfoot, *Suffering: A Christian Understanding* (Philadelphia: The Westminster Press, 1964), p. 30.
[52] Smail, *The Forgotten Father*, p. 151.
[53] 1 Pet. 4:12, TNIV.

here described as God's children. In other words, the main player in this passage is not the inanimate creation, important as this is, but on what God is going to do through his adopted sons and daughters.

The language which Paul uses to describe both orders is also significant: the inanimate order is identified using the language of *biological birth* whereas the human creation draws from a different conceptual field, legal *adoption*, which is exclusively reserved for believers. Importantly, Paul never blurs the distinction between the two orders. That the latter is the more dominant idea in the passage is clear in two main ways: first, by the way in which the inanimate creation is looking forward to its emancipation via the children of God; and second, the language of natural birth which is used to describe the inanimate creation is dropped – the 'baby' is never born, as Beverly Roberts Gaventa makes clear: 'in this passage, the birthing metaphor captures creation's cry for liberation, but the birth metaphor has its limits: creation does not in fact give birth'.[54] This is because the birthing imagery (20–22) gives way to the imagery of adoption (23) for it is the sons and daughters of God who are the conduit or the channel through whom the glorious transformation in the cosmos will come about.

d. Our adoption as God's children and the Spirit as the firstfruits (8:23–24)

How can we be sure that the final consummation of our adoption as sons and daughters will come to pass? There is a certainty about Paul's language as verse 22 makes clear: *We know . . .*' Part of the reason why Paul has this assurance is found in the prevalence of the language of *hope*, where he employs both the verbal (24–25) and noun forms (20, 24). A second reason why Paul is confident is found in verse 23 where he says that we who have *the firstfruits of the Spirit . . . wait eagerly for our adoption . . . the redemption of our bodies.* Paul is using Old Testament imagery once again because the firstfruits were just that, *first*fruits, a harbinger as well as a guarantee that more was to come. The Spirit then is one proof of the authenticity of our sonship but also of the certainty that it will be completed in the end. While the participle *having* (23) has been understood by some to mean that believers groan *despite* the fact they have the Spirit, the more likely interpretation – given Paul's confidence above – is that the presence of the firstfruits of the Spirit causes the believer to long for the consummation of sonship. In other words, we groan

---

[54] Beverly Roberts Gaventa, *Our Mother Saint Paul* (Louisville: Westminster John Knox, 2007), p. 57.

inwardly *because* we have the firstfruits of the Spirit and so the Holy Spirit not only anticipates what is to come but causes the believer to look forward to what lies ahead, the day when their sonship will be openly and publicly proclaimed. Thus, although God's children share in the currently ongoing suffering with the inanimate order, the former has the advantage because they have the Spirit within. 2 Corinthains 5:2–5 is a good commentary on this passage:

> Meanwhile we groan, longing to be clothed with our heavenly dwelling, because when we are clothed, we will not be found naked. For while we are in this tent, we groan and are burdened, because we do not wish to be unclothed but to be clothed with our heavenly dwelling, so that what is mortal may be swallowed up by life. Now it is *God* who has made us for this very purpose and *has given us the Spirit as a deposit, guaranteeing what is to come.*

e. Adoption as sons, the redemption of the body (8:23)

At the end of verse 23 Paul makes a statement that is related to our adoption as God's children, namely *the redemption of our bodies.* The relationship between these two phrases has often been a matter of discussion. Some see the latter as being subsumed under the former. Charles Hodge, for instance is of the view that the latter is included in the former 'as one of its prominent parts'.[55] However, the way these two phrases are arranged is better understood as the 'redemption of the bodies' giving a further explanation of the adoption. In other words, Paul is fusing them together and describing them as one reality, as Cranfield states, 'The full manifestation of our adoption is identical with the final resurrection of our bodies at the Parousia, our complete and final liberation . . . to which we have been subjected'.[56]

Believers await the consummation of their adoptive sonship, the very climax of redemption, when through the Holy Spirit they are transformed and resurrected as sons. What Paul is describing here therefore rules out any suggestion of annihilation of the body or of having a mere spiritual existence. In other words, the redemption of the body will be one that is a real, physical entity. On that day our salvation, i.e., adoption as God's children, will be complete.

---

[55] Charles Hodge, *A Commentary on Romans* (Edinburgh: Banner of Truth, 1972), p. 276.
[56] Cranfield, *Romans*, p. 419.

Summary

Paul's unique filial expression 'adopted as sons' (Gk *huiothesia*) in Romans 8:15 falls under the wider biblical theme of sonship, and should be considered as another important but overlooked term for the apostle's understanding of salvation. Adoption is a Trinitarian action, involving the Father, who initiates the adoption through the Son, and the Spirit who brings assurance of salvation. Those whom God has adopted into his new family have also been given the Spirit who empowers them to live morally upright lives, as children who are led by the Spirit in order to honour their heavenly Father. And it is the Spirit, no less than the 'Spirit of adoption' (Rom. 8:15), who witnesses to God's children of the reality of their new filial disposition. Sonship also brings the accompanying blessing of inheritance, which for Paul is relational and not territorial because it is no longer focused in a place but in the person of God the Father and his Son Jesus Christ. Lastly, adoption spans the present and the future, the now and the not yet, as the sons and daughters of God experience suffering by virtue of being a part of the created order, waiting for the future consummation of their salvation.

Ephesians 1:4–6; 2:1–10; 4:11–16
8. Children of wrath who become strong and stable sons and daughters of God

Cecil Frances Alexander, the nineteenth century Irish children's hymnwriter, composed many hymns – four hundred in total – which are known, loved and sung throughout the worldwide Christian church. What perhaps is not known about Alexander is her reason for writing some of these hymns, which was to enable Sunday school children to grasp doctrine in simple language that was easily understood. Moreover, as the Apostle's creed was recited at every Anglican service, her hymns were especially written in order to explain some of its major tenets. For example, the Christmas carol 'Once in royal David's city'[1] was an explanation of the birth and incarnation of the Saviour, Jesus Christ. Another well-known hymn 'There is a green hill far away' describes the crucifixion and death of Christ, which was specifically written for her god-children in order to help them understand the creedal statement 'Suffered under Pontius Pilate, was crucified, dead and buried'. Frances Alexander was ahead of her time in that she saw children not only as an integral and important part of the worship service but also as part of the visible church, and her hymns went some way towards enabling them to understand better and grow in their Christian faith.

In the fourth chapter of his letter to the church at Ephesus, the apostle Paul transitions from instruction (1 – 3) to exhortation (4 – 6) where he, like Cecil Frances Alexander, uses filial language to encourage the believers to

---

[1] It should also be said that Alexander's hymn 'Once in Royal David's City,' also reflects Victorian values and the way children were perceived.

no longer be infants, tossed back and forth by the waves, and blown here and there by every wind of teaching and by the cunning and craftiness of men in their deceitful scheming. Instead, speaking the truth in love, we will in all things grow up into him who is the Head, that is, Christ (4:14–16).

Paul's use of the family term *infants* (*nēpioi*) here is a striking metaphor and contributes to, but is also different from, the terms *children* (*tekna*) and *sons* (*huioi*) which we have so far considered. Indeed the apostle's use of this expression is a warning to the Ephesian believers that they are not to remain in such an infantile state. It is, according to James Francis who comments on this text, 'incompatible with a firm grasp of Christian principles on the part of the ... Christian'.[2] The Ephesian believers, like the children under hymnwriter Alexander's tutelage, need to grow and become stable sons and daughters in the Lord, a text to which we will turn in a moment. But we need to retrace our steps, for this is not the first time Paul has used such filial language in Ephesians, a letter which has rightly been described as being 'relentlessly relational'.[3]

In this chapter we shall look at three main issues: what God has done, what we once were, and what God wants us to become as his children.

1. What God has done: adopted you as his sons and daughters (1:4–6)

a. The paternal initiative in adoption

Paul begins this short, powerful epistle – a long-time favourite of John Calvin's and of many Christians throughout the history of the Church – with a deep, dense, doctrinal opening. Theological terms tumble from Paul's pen in one long sentence (in the original language) comprising 202 words, including election (v. 4), predestination (v. 5), redemption (v. 7) and sanctification (v. 4). Paul blesses God for all the wonderful things he has done for us and uses no less than seven verbs: blessed (v. 3), chose (v. 4), destined (v. 5), bestowed/given (v. 6), lavished (v. 8), made known (v. 9) and gather up/bring together (v. 10). It is as if Paul ransacks his first-century mind and extensive theological vocabulary in order to try to articu-

---

[2] James M. M. Francis, *Adults as Children: Images of Childhood in the Ancient World and the New Testament* (Bern: Peter Lang, 2006), p. 213.
[3] Klyne Snodgrass, *Ephesians*, NIVAC (Grand Rapids: Zondervan, 1996), p. 19.

late the amazing and inexhaustive riches of God's grace. Eugene Peterson, in his typically fresh and brilliant manner, describes these seven words as 'rocket verbs', 'each one detonated by God'[4] because God is the subject of each and God is the one doing all the action. The sovereignty of God in salvation blessing is to the fore in the opening of this letter, where our being brought into his family finds its spring and origin in the action of the Father. That's where salvation starts, evident by the eight references to 'Father' in the letter[5] which, according to Marianne Meye Thompson, 'is more than any other letter'.[6]

The jewel in the crown in this majestic opening to the letter, however, is found in verse 5, where Paul describes believers as God's adopted sons and daughters. The metaphor which Paul uses here for sonship by adoption (*huiothesia*) is the same one he used in his letter to the Romans (8:15, 23) which we considered in the last chapter. Immediately prior to this Paul uses two verbs, 'chose' and 'predestinate', in connection with his adoption term, both of which are a reminder that God had us in view in the past. The phrase *he chose us in him* is one to dwell deeply on for it involves a trinity of relations spanning eternity and history – *He* (God the Father) chose *us* (you and me) in *Christ* (God the Son) – as John Stott comments: 'Mark well the statement: *He chose us in Christ.* The juxtaposition of the three pronouns is emphatic. God put us and Christ together in his mind. He determined to make us (who did not exist) his own children through the redeeming work of Christ (which had not yet taken place).'[7]

However, the above two verbs (election and predestination) have sometimes been misunderstood as though salvation could be reduced to mere mathematical formulae and that God in a cold, calculated manner decided to arbitrarily pick out some and cast the others aside. Quite the opposite is the case because Paul tells us that God *in love*[8] *predestined us to be adopted as his sons* and daughters. The Father's love here emphasizes that God is intimately and

---

[4] Eugene H. Peterson, *Practice Resurrection: A Conversation on Growing up in Christ* (Cambridge/Grand Rapids: Eerdmans, 2010), p. 57.

[5] 1:2, 3, 17; 2:18; 3:14–15; 4: 6; 5:20; 6:23.

[6] Marianne Meye Thompson, *The Promise of the Father: Jesus and God in the New Testament* (Louisville: Westminster John Knox, 2000), pp. 121–122.

[7] John R. W. Stott, *The Message of Ephesians: God's New Society*, BST (Leicester: IVP, 1979), p. 36 (emphasis original).

[8] The position of the prepositional phrase 'in love' has been a matter of debate and could either go with v. 4 or v. 5. One commentator makes the point that predestination has always to do with God the Father and 'is never connected with the thought that we are . . . predestined in Christ'; see R. Schnackenburg, *Ephesians: A Commentary* (Edinburgh: T&T Clark, 1991), p. 43.

affectionately connected to his spiritual offspring and underscores the amazing grace – God's 'adopting grace'[9] – which he has lavished upon us. What God has done for us has been well stated by James I. Packer:

> God adopts us out of his free love, not because our character and record shows us worthy to bear his name, but despite the fact that they show the opposite. We are not fit for a place in God's family; the idea of His loving and exalting sinners as He loves and has exalted the Lord Jesus sound ludicrous and wild – yet that, and nothing less than that, is what our adoption means.[10]

In addition to the unmistakable Old Testament background of sonship which lies behind Paul's adoption term, there is also good reason to believe that Paul is borrowing from the ancient Roman socio-legal practice of adoption in the first century (and not the twenty-first century). This is because the father, the head of the household (or *paterfamilias*), rather than both parents, took the initiative in adopting a son (an adult male and not an infant as is the case today). So, in the spiritual realm, God the Father is the prime mover in bringing us into his family as his sons and daughters, language which marks the boundary and sets the church in Ephesus apart from the surrounding society. In other words, adoption finds its spring and origin in the purposes of God the Father. However, unlike a Roman father in antiquity who only adopted in order to perpetuate the family name and line, God has no such 'selfish' interests in view because he already has a Son and heir and he 'adopts because he *loves* to adopt'[11] which was also the basis of God's relationship with the nation of Israel as God's son in the Old Testament (e.g., Exod. 4:22–23; Deut. 7:7).[12]

b. The paternal pleasure in adoption (1:5)

Paul proceeds to inform his readers that God not only has an eternal purpose in adopting us but also takes great delight in bringing us into his household: *he adopted us as his sons . . . in accordance with his pleasure and will* (5). The apostle's use of the preposition (*kata*) 'according to' emphasizes that such an action was the 'norm' or

[9] Mark Stibbe, *From Orphans to Heirs: Celebrating our Spiritual Adoption* (Oxford: Bible Reading Fellowship, 1999), p. 44.

[10] J. I. Packer, *Knowing God* (London: Hodder and Stoughton, 1988), p. 241.

[11] Ernest Best, *Ephesians*, ICC (Edinburgh: T&T Clark, 1998), p. 125.

[12] Ibid.

'standard' while the term 'pleasure' (*eudokia*) used elsewhere by Paul in relation to his passionate concern for his own people, Israel (Rom. 10:1), connotes the warmth and joy with which the Father executed this plan in making us his adopted children. Mark Stibbe captures the essence of God's action when he says: 'It pleased him to enfold us in the eternal family of faith. It brought him joy and thrilled his heart. Even though this adoption would not be cost-free, God did not undertake this task by gritting his teeth and clenching his fists. No, it was his pleasure as well as his will.'[13]

Adoption is also in accordance with God's will, an important theme in the letter which recurs more frequently here than any other Pauline letter (e.g., 1:5, 9, 11; 5:17).[14] The emphasis here is that what God had purposed in eternity (i.e., our adoption as sons and daughters) cannot be thwarted, changed or overturned. God planned and purposed the believer's adoption in the past and his will was sovereignly brought to pass in his time. Included also in the word 'will' is the fact that we do not find God but that God has found us and 'willed' or wanted us to be included as members of his family. Children willed and wanted, that's the language of acceptance and belonging as adopted children in God's household.

c. Paternal and filial cooperation: Father and Son in unison (1:5)

God the Father, however, never acts alone in the believer's adoption – he always does so in conjunction with his Son, Jesus Christ, as Paul states: *he predestined us to be adopted as his sons through Jesus Christ*. Paul had struck a similar Christocentric note a little earlier when he states that believers are 'chosen *in him*' (1:4). Paul uses a proliferation of prepositional phrases in these opening verses which are an important and characteristic feature of his letters and theology, especially his letter to the Ephesians, as the following shows:

- 'in Christ' (1:3, 9, 12)
- 'in him' (1:4, 11, 13)
- 'through Christ' (1:5)
- 'in the One he loves' (1:6)

The prepositional phrase *through Jesus Christ* is virtually equivalent to the more frequent expression 'in Christ' where the Son is the *agent* through whom the believers' adoption is secured. God adopts us through the death of Christ on the cross at Calvary; Jesus is the

---

[13] Stibbe, *From Orphans to Heirs*, p. 53.
[14] Snodgrass, *Ephesians*, p. 37.

broker and the only one through whom Christians are enfranchised as adopted children, which immediately underscores a qualitative distinction between Jesus' sonship and ours as believers. He is the eternal Son (*huios*) of God and we are adopted children (*huiothesia*) through God's grace. Paul also signals the importance of the death of Christ and our union with him in bringing about our adoption in his letter to the Galatians: 'God sent his Son ... *to redeem* those who were under the law, so that we might receive adoption as sons' (Gal. 4:4–5, ESV). Our adoption as God's children may be free but it did not come cheap, but rather it was all of grace and at incalculable cost, the death of Jesus, God's own Son.

The point Paul is making is unmistakably Christological because when believers are adopted into God's family it is uniquely and exclusively through the death of his Son and the shedding of his blood on the cross. John Murray concludes his comments on the significance of the opening of Ephesians 1 and of the close connection between 'adoption' and our being 'united with Christ': 'We cannot think of adoption apart from union with Christ ... union with Christ and adoption are complementary aspects of this amazing grace. Union with Christ reaches its zenith in adoption and adoption has its orbit in union with Christ.'[15]

In short, our adoption as God's sons and daughters does not, better, cannot, take place without or apart from Christ, the Son of God. For Paul, the two are inextricably linked together. That's what God has done for us.

2. What you once were: 'sons of disobedience' and 'children of wrath' (2:1–10)

a. Sons of disobedience (2:1–3)

It is a useful and instructive practice for us as Christians, in order to appreciate what God has done in our lives, to sometimes look over our shoulder into the past to see where we once were. This also helps to orientate us in the present and move forward into the future. In this regard, Klyne Snodgrass points out that in Ephesians 2:1–7 'the past, present, and future of God's salvation in Christ are all in view'. In verses 1–3, which we are mostly interested in, Paul deals with the past, which accentuates the blessings of salvation in verses 4–10. The past tenses are unmistakable in verse 1 where Paul

---

[15] John Murray, *The Epistle to the Romans*, 2 vols. (Grand Rapids: Eerdmans, 1960), p. 170.

describes how *you were dead in your transgressions and sins* and *you used to walk/live* (2). As regards the former, the Ephesians' previous condition was not simply a disease but was much more serious – they were *dead* in sin, unaware of their eternal plight and in grave danger. As Paul puts it later in the letter, they were 'separated from the life of God' (4:18) and little different to a corpse in the sense of being spiritually unresponsive to God's voice through his word. The phrase *used to walk* is a further explanation of their sinful past, where the verb 'walk' has moral connotations and is often used in the Old Testament to describe God's people and the notion of walking in the way of the Lord (e.g., Deut. 5:33; Ps. 1:1). Here, however, before the Ephesians ever became God's children they were walking in the opposite direction, far away from him, as they wallowed in their sins.

Paul then provides three reasons for this bondage to the sinful practices which once held his readers captive. They were enslaved to *the ways of the world* (2) and subject to *the ruler of the kingdom of the air* (2), but more importantly for our purposes all this was due to *the spirit of the ruler who is now at work in those who are the sons of disobedience* (2, author's translation). Regarding this last description, it is possible to understand the word *spirit* in an impersonal (i.e., 'kingdom' or 'domain') or personal (i.e., 'ruler', the evil one, the devil) sense. What sways us more towards the latter, however (though the former cannot be entirely discounted) is the personal language which Paul goes on to use to describe the former bondage of the Ephesian Christians. Twice in as many verses – which some translations overlook (e.g. NIV) – the past, unregenerate condition of Paul's readers is described as *sons of disobedience* (*huioi tēs apeitheias*, 2) and *children of wrath* (*tekna physei orgēs*, 3). Thus, this 'ruler of the spirit of the air' is none other than a title for the person of Satan, a primary title used in John's Gospel ('the ruler of this world', 12:31), who has his own personal offspring to do his dirty work, doubly described here as *sons of disobedience* and *children of wrath*.

The former filial description, the *sons of disobedience*, is a reminder how Satan was (and is) at work among the Ephesians prior to their coming into God's family. When Paul uses the participle *energountos* ('working') it is a 'power-denoting term'[16] and means more than a simple 'working in'. Rather, it is better to translate it with the use of the adverb 'powerfully' giving the sense that Satan was 'powerfully working' in his offspring, the *sons of disobedience*. What Paul is describing here, then, are progeny who were

---

[16] Clinton E. Arnold, *Ephesians*, ZEC (Grand Rapids: Zondervan, 2010), p. 132.

not merely characterized by a lack of trust or a failure to believe in Christ, but those who were in absolute, open defiance and rebellion against God and his ways.

b. We were children of wrath (2:3)

Paul continues to discuss the Ephesians' past way of life in verse 3 where he describes the consequences of their sins which resulted in their alienation from God, evidenced by the fact that they are under the wrath of God. More than that, Paul uses a second filial expression parallel to the earlier expression *sons of disobedience*, when he states *we were by nature children of wrath* (*ēmetha physei tekna orgēs*, see ESV). The word *physei* (*by nature*) has been understood differently, with three main views being advanced: the word can denote origin (e.g., Gal. 2:15), a natural condition or quality (e.g., Rom. 11:26), or it may describe the created world or nature (e.g., Rom. 1:26). The best fit in the present context is the first (though the second may be included as a consequence of 'birth') where Paul is more than likely describing 'origin' or 'descent'. In other words, it is because of ancestral descent, traced back to Adam (Rom. 5:12–21), that we were *children of wrath*. This together with the earlier adjective *all* and the repeated plural filial descriptions in verses 2 and 3 means that everyone without exception is affected, and Paul includes himself (*we* and *us*). Moreover, we all lived among them at one time where both body (*cravings of our sinful nature*, lit. 'flesh') and mind (*following its desires and thoughts*) were given over in slavish and devoted service to this tyrant.

As a consequence of this, everyone is on a collision course with God and is exposed to his *wrath*. The contrast of the wrath of God here with the earlier manifestation of God's love (1:4–6) in adoption could not be more striking, but it is not a contradiction, for wrath and love are two sides of the character of God. Moreover, such anger is not to be associated with pagan deities whose anger was irascible, unpredictable and irrational. Rather, God's holy, righteous anger is a more settled notion or as C. K. Barrett put it so well: 'wrath is God's *personal* . . . reaction to all sin'.[17] Because God is holy, he naturally and immediately recoils from all and any sin. The subject of wrath and God's righteous anger is a hotly debated topic among theologians and has even been described as an outdated and unbiblical metaphor that does not resonate with Christians today. Further, it is asked, why would a God of love punish his Son, who was innocent and had done nothing wrong? Such an action is considered

---

[17] C. K. Barrett, *The Epistle to the Romans*, BNTC (London, 1957), p. 133.

by some to be nothing less than a 'form of cosmic child abuse'.[18] In response, it should be said that Jesus' going to the cross was not a case of a Son having his arm twisted behind his back in order to do what he did not want to do. On the contrary, as the Gospel of John makes clear, Jesus says he came willingly to lay down his life for his sheep (John 10:15), that is, on behalf of and as our substitute. Further, John goes on to record Jesus as stating: 'No one takes [my life] from me, but I lay it down of my own accord. I have authority to lay it down and authority to take it up again.'[19] Rather than his death being a form of child abuse, Jesus in actual fact is *a consenting adult* who freely offers his life as a ransom by dying on the cross for our sins, a point Paul goes on to make in verses 4–5.

c. But now we are saved (2:4–10)

That was the past but in verses 4–10 Paul deals with the 'now' or the present and goes on to describe how God's righteous anger has been removed – through the substitutionary death of his Son – in a passage that has been described as 'the most effective summary we have of the Pauline doctrine of salvation by grace through faith'.[20] The difference between the two eras is made clear by Paul's use of a strong contrasting conjunction in verse 4: *But because of his great love for us* we who once *were dead* are now *alive with Christ* (5). *God raised us up with Christ* (6) and *expressed his kindness to us in Christ Jesus* (7) and *we have been saved* (8). When we consider the bondage which we were once in and the change that has taken place now we have been saved through faith, is it any wonder that the world cannot understand why a young Christian woman should serve the Lord in a rundown inner city area rather than take a high-salaried job in the city in banking or commerce, or why a young Christian man should give his entire life to serve in a slum in a city in the Majority World rather than pursue a career in science in a well-endowed medical school or university? It's grace, sheer grace, and it's all God's doing!

But the change which God has brought about for Paul's readers and for us is that they and we are not to merely tread water; rather we are to go forward and progress in the Christian life and so the filial language of 2:2–3 is picked up again in 4:11–16, to which we must fast forward.

---

[18] Steve Chalke and Alan Mann, *The Lost Message of Jesus* (Grand Rapids: Zondervan, 2003), p. 182.
[19] John 10:18.
[20] C. L. Mitton, *Ephesians*, NCBC (London: Oliphants, 1976), p. 155.

3. What you must be(come) (4:11–16)

a. No longer infants but grown-up children (4:11–16)

The church, universal and local, which is so much a part of any proper understanding of this powerful and much loved epistle, is comprised of people of many different backgrounds and at various stages of Christian growth. None of us can ever claim to have 'arrived' to full maturity but each of us is on a learning curve, a journey where growth is not automatic and development takes time. Although we live in a world of instant coffee and instant information, there is no 'quick fix' or 'yellow-brick road'[21] in the Christian life because progress here is not an act but a process, not a straight line from A to Z, more like the course of a river which during its youthful stage finds the most direct route, but whose maturity is evident by the way it meanders and curves its way down to the sea. For the child of God there will also be periods of what seem to us like meandering, apparently going off course into bypath meadows, or periods of waiting, but it is often during such times that real growth and maturity in character can take place.

I remember immediately after formal training for pastoral ministry at seminary I was not entirely sure whether God was leading me to pastor a church or to go overseas to teach in a theological college in the Majority World. The latter was where God seemed to be leading, but my wife and I were not fully sure. I took some 'time out' in a secular job for eighteen months and sought, with the help of our pastor, elders, church family, and family and friends, to determine God's mind and will. It was not an easy time but in the end God led my wife and I abroad to Nigeria to a seminary to teach, which is what I have been doing ever since. (The pastoral ministry came later when I was teaching in a seminary in Wales.) During this period it was a time for us to determine God's will and I especially learnt that *waiting* time – for God to open a door – is never *wasted* time because during such times God is growing patience in us and preparing the way for what he has in the future.

Maturity in the Lord is very much on the mind of the apostle Paul in these verses, which is not only evident by the repeated expressions to do with growth but also by the fact that such growth is described within the context of community, the church. As regards the former, Paul writes that the Ephesian Christians must *become mature, attaining to the whole measure of the fullness of Jesus Christ* (13), *grow up into him who is the Head, that is Christ* (15), even as

---

[21] Peterson, *Practice Resurrection*, p. 184.

*the whole body, joined and held together by every supporting liga-
ment, grows and builds itself up in love, as each part does its work*
(16). The heavy concentration of this growth language has been
noted by Eugene Peterson in his recent book *Practice Resurrection*,
in which Ephesians is the main text and which he describes as 'a
conversation in growing up in Christ'.

As regards the latter, the aspect of community, Paul in the earlier
verses (11–13) has identified that growth can only take place in
community and in relationship to other believers and leaders in the
church. Paul's ecclesiology or doctrine of the church would not
have it otherwise. It is within the context of this new community we
call the church that growth needs to take place. Part of the problem
today, however, is that growth is not always as high on the ecclesial
agenda as it ought to be; the church, at times, is big on birth but low
on growth. Peterson's remark on this is insightful because, as he
points out, the church often

> runs on the euphoria and adrenaline of new birth – getting people
> into the church, into the kingdom, into causes, into crusades, into
> programs. We turn matters of growing up over to Sunday school
> teachers, specialists in Christian education, committees to revise
> curricula, retreat centers, and deeper life conferences, farming
> it out to parachurch groups for remedial assistance. I don't find
> pastors and professors, for the most part, very interested in
> matters of formation in holiness. They have higher profile things
> to tend to.

The church can appear like a teenager who mistakenly assumes that
growing up means lots of doctrine, lots of Bible study, lots of ethical
concern, lots and lots of projects, all of which are important and
necessary (see below), but they sometimes miss the point, for these
'have little to do with becoming a mature person, with growing up.
We know a thing, a truth, a person only *in relationship*'.[22]

The divine purpose for the Ephesian church is further fleshed out
in verses 11–13 where Paul speaks of God gifting leaders, pastors,
evangelists, teachers in order to *prepare God's people for works of
service so that the body of Christ may be built up* (12). In other
words, God provides the church with godly leaders whose aim it
is to prepare the whole community (*God's people*) who in turn will
play a role in serving, edifying and strengthening the family of God.
The goal of the sound instruction of these leaders is the fostering
and developing of *unity in the faith and in the knowledge of the*

[22] Ibid., p. 65.

171

Son of God (13). In other words, not only is church the communal context in which believers are to grow, but unity amongst the
members in God's family is also one sure sign of maturity.

b. Be(come) stable and strong sons and daughters (4:14)

A second purpose[23] of God for this community – this time expressed
more negatively – is found in verse 14 where Paul uses a (*hina*)
purpose clause which goes all the way back to verse 11 where the
apostle states that *he [God] gave* or gifted pastors and leaders, in
order that *we will no longer be infants, tossed back and forth by the
waves, and blown here and there by every wind of teaching and by
the cunning and craftiness of men in their deceitful scheming* (14).
The filial term which Paul uses on this occasion is *infants* (*nēpioi*)
and is different to other metaphorical expressions we have so far
considered, such as *children* (*tekna*) and *sons* (*huioi*). This word
speaks of immaturity and stands in sharp contrast to the mature
person mentioned in verse 13. So, rather than using the term *infants*
to describe the 'innocence' of these believers, Paul's use of the word
conveys the idea of Christians who are young or vulnerable and are
therefore more easily taken advantage of. We get a good idea of the
meaning of this word when we compare how it is used elsewhere
by Paul and other writers in the New Testament. Two examples
will suffice: Paul, after he left Corinth, expected his converts to
have grown up spiritually but instead of being ready for a diet of
meat they were still drinking *milk* (1 Cor. 3:1–2). Rather than being
attired in clothing suitable for adults, the Corinthians, spiritually
speaking, were still running around in nappies (or diapers)! The
same word is used in Hebrews 5:13 to describe the infantile status
which the author no longer wishes his readers to be in. The one who
lives on milk is still acting like an infant and not ready for 'solid
food' which is the diet 'for the mature, who by constant use have
trained themselves to distinguish good from evil'.[24] Important here
is the contrast not only between diet (feeding on God's word) but
also between the more mature believer (over against an immature
Christian) who is more morally equipped to discern between what
is right and wrong.

When he employs the term *infants*, Paul knows full well that
his readers have not yet reached the final goal of maturity. The
Ephesians' inexperience and lack of insight which the word describes
underscores their gullibility and lack of understanding and percep-

---

[23] Arnold, *Ephesians*, p. 267.
[24] Heb. 5:14.

tion. This present state of spiritual infancy and immaturity coupled with the vivid nautical language of being *tossed back and forth by the waves* and *blown here and there by every wind of teaching* emphasizes the instability as well as the manner in which they can be easily influenced and misled. The first phrase is used to describe the raging waters of Lake Galilee (Luke 8:24) as well as the person whom James tells us doubts God when he or she prays. When we pray James tells us we must believe and not doubt, for the one who doubts is like a wave of the sea 'blown and tossed by the wind'.[25] In the latter, it is the waves themselves which are driven by the wind, but here in Ephesians it is probably a picture of a boat tossed in the storm and carried about.

The second phrase *blown here and there by every wind of teaching* carries with it the idea of a violent swinging about that makes a person dizzy. Here in Ephesians Paul talks of winds of doctrine against which Christians were having difficulty keeping an even keel. The unsteady and rudderless could easily be turned from their course. The image then is one of drifting and being at the whim and mercy of the elements, the wind and waves, the perilous consequence of which have been well summarized by Clinton Arnold: 'Without the firmness and stability that comes from growth stimulated by the ministry of the various members of the Christian community believers are as vulnerable as a boat adrift on a stormy and tempestuous sea. They are totally at the mercy of the waves and the wind which can carry them off course.'[26]

All this is to say that Paul's point is that Christians who remain in an infantile state are helpless and easy prey and this is counteracted by being 'fitted out properly with the Word of faith'.[27] Being part of a community and being grounded in Scripture is crucially important for Paul's readers, especially in light of what he had earlier prophesied to the Ephesian elders in an emotional and concluding speech on the beach at Miletus as he prepared to leave them. On that occasion Paul told them, 'after I leave, savage wolves will come in among you and will not spare the flock. Even from *your own number men will arise and distort the truth* in order to draw away disciples after them. So be on your guard!'[28]

The importance of growing in our knowledge of God's word is important. Paul as a pioneer missionary would have encountered

---

[25] Jas 1:6.
[26] Arnold, *Ephesians,* p. 267.
[27] R. C. H. Lenski, *St Paul's Letters to the Galatians, Ephesians and Philippians* (Minneapolis: Ausgburg, 1961), p. 538.
[28] Acts 20:29–31.

during his travels many false teachers (or sophists, so-called 'wise men') who would show up in a town, give a very plausible and persuasive speech to their assembled audience, seek monetary reward, and then quickly scarper out of town. There was not much content in what they said and in such a prevailing context it would have been imperative for Christians to be able to sift the wheat from the chaff and not to be blown off course on their faith. The word *teaching* (14) is in the singular and while it can refer elsewhere to Christian teaching (e.g., Rom. 12:7), the phrase *every wind* describes a variety of false teaching both from within and without the church. Spiritually immature children are often unstable, and can be turned every way by the winds of erroneous doctrines, easy prey to the tricksters who have no interest in their spiritual welfare. In fact, Paul describes these charlatans as engaging in *craftiness* (14) which is the word *kybeia* from which the term 'cube' or 'dice' is derived and is a vivid metaphor and depiction of those who play dice with the gullible in order to cheat and lead them astray. Mature Christians, on the other hand, are alert and wary to such con artists and are solid and unshakable in their faith. This is what Paul desires for the Ephesians family of God where 'Christian maturity is marked by stability of life which is a recognizably *adult* characteristic'.[29]

Growth, of course, can take many different forms, including unnecessary or unhealthy 'growth' such as obesity. Then there is apparent growth which is not maturity at all, but a mere pretence of 'growth' such as the tree that I saw recently on a visit to a local Japanese garden. Because the Japanese hold old age in such high esteem, this tree was 'aged' by pruning it in such a way as to give the appearance of maturity when the tree is really younger than it was made to look. Such 'growth' is phony and not real at all. Paul, however, wants there to be wholesome growth and what he writes here is most instructive, especially for younger Christians who sometimes mistakenly think that if they get up to speed on what the cults such as Mormons or Jehovah's Witnesses are teaching they will be able to defend their own views. There is some truth in this, but our priority is not to learn what others believe but rather to first know and understand what we as Christians believe. We do that by being well grounded in Scripture and Christian doctrine, which are the best and most important antidotes and remedies for counteracting false teachers and their teaching. 'The conviction that Christian

---

[29] W. A. Strange, *Children in the Early Church: Children in the Ancient World, the New Testament and the Early Church* (Carlisle: Paternoster Press, 1996), p. 68 (emphasis added).

doctrine matters' as Sinclair Ferguson rightly points out, 'is one of the most important *growth points* of the Christian life'.[30]

c. Grow up into Christ, the Head of the church (4:15–16)

The church is not an organization but a vibrant, living organism, a family of believers whom Jesus has bought with his own blood (Eph. 1:7). The Christological note is important and continues from 4:13 where Paul stated how God's children need to grow into maturity. In 4:15 this same note is sounded where Christ is the goal, since the verb *grow* can be understood not only as an exhortation but as a command to continue to *grow up into him* (15). In other words, Christ is the source[31] for these infant Ephesian Christians whereby they develop and mature because it is *from him* [Christ] *the whole body, joined and held together . . . grows* (16).

However, the church is not a passive recipient of God's work through Christ for there is also an onus or a responsibility placed on believers to facilitate growth and ensure their own maturity, which in turn impacts the whole body of Christ. The note of personal accountability is especially struck at the end of verse 16 where Paul, using the analogy of the body, says *every supporting ligament, grows and builds itself up . . . as each part does its work*. Paul is describing a church where there is not only unity in diversity, but also a community in which individuality or personal responsibility is not overlooked or lost. Each individual member in the family of God has a vital and indispensible part to play in the overall growth of the community. Thus, for example, if we are not regularly meeting with other members of the body of Christ at church on a Sunday or if we are not actively using our gifts for the overall nourishment and benefit of the church, the community will not grow as Christ intends it.

Summary

Paul's letter to the Ephesian Christians is spiritual dynamite; the apostle reminds them of three main things: what God has done for them, what they once were, and what they must become. Thus as regards the past, Paul takes them on a journey back into eternity past when God through his Son had chosen and predestined them to

---

[30] Sinclair B. Ferguson, *The Christian Life: A Doctrinal Introduction* (Hodder and Stoughton, 1981), p. 1.
[31] Andrew T. Lincoln, *Ephesians*, WBC 42 (Waco: Word, 1990), p. 261.

be adopted as his sons and daughters, a saving action which was for his own pleasure and glory. This was necessary because of what they once were, namely children of wrath and sons of disobedience who followed their sinful desires because they were under the control and domination of the ruler of this world, the evil one. But now they are saved and have become God's offspring it is incumbent upon them to no longer be like infants tossed about like a cork on the ocean, but to grow into strong and stable sons and daughters of God. They are to do this primarily through growing in community as members of God's household and as they grow up into Jesus Christ, God's Son.

1 Thessalonians 1:9–10; 4:16; 5:1–11
9. Sonship and the second coming of God's Son

Paul's first letter to the Thessalonians has long been considered a treatise on the second coming of Jesus Christ, which is not surprising given that each of the five chapters of this short letter ends with a reference to the *parousia* (Gk 'coming') or return of the Lord. For example, at the end of chapter 1 Paul states how the inhabitants of Macedonia and Achaia *tell how you turned to God from idols to serve the living and true God, and to wait for his Son from heaven whom he raised from the dead – Jesus Christ who rescues us from the coming wrath* (1:9–10; cf. 2:19; 3:13; 4:13–18; 5:23).

Any proper understanding of this letter must therefore take into consideration the importance which it gives to the end times and Jesus' returning in glory. A closer reading of the contents of this letter – arguably the earliest penned by the apostle Paul – also shows that it is not only the second coming of Christ which is important. Indeed, this eschatological emphasis has often overshadowed, even at times obscured, the equally important theme of ecclesiology, or the church. This focus on community in the letter, however, has not cut much ice with some scholars, a point rightly noted by Abraham J. Malherbe:

> First Thessalonians has not impressed commentators for what it contributes to our understanding of the church. Such Pauline images of the church as temple, field, and body are not used in this letter. . . . If it is the elaboration of such images that . . . makes for a significant ecclesiology, then Paul indeed has not given much thought to the nature of the church in this letter.[1]

[1] Abraham J. Malherbe, 'God's New Family in Thessalonica', in Michael L. White and O. Larry Yarbrough (eds.), *The Social World of the First Christians:*

Certainly, unlike the Pastoral Epistles, for example, where Paul explicitly refers to the church as 'the household/family of God' (1 Tim. 3:15), the apostle nowhere describes the church in this way in 1 Thessalonians. Nevertheless, the profusion of family terms in this letter shows that Paul delineates a theology or a view of the church that cannot be overlooked. For example, he uses the familial terms 'father' (2:11),[2] 'nursing mother' (2:7), and 'orphan' (2:17)[3] to describe his relationship to the Thessalonians. It is also possible that Paul describes himself and his missionary colleagues as 'infants' (2:7), although commentators continue to vigorously debate this matter.[4] Paul also describes his Thessalonian converts twice as his 'children' in 2:7, 11. Alongside these expressions is Paul's favourite and most frequently occurring familial expression to describe the Thessalonians' relationship to one another, namely 'brothers and sisters'.[5] 'From beginning to end first Thessalonians breathes brotherly/sisterly language.'[6]

In addition to these terms, which Paul uses to describe *his* role and relationship to his Thessalonian converts, is the more important way in which he uses the same language to describe *God's* paternal relationship to them. On three separate occasions, two at the outset of the letter, God is referred to as 'father' (1:1, 3; 3:13). The Thessalonians, moreover, are twice described as God's spiritual offspring or as his 'sons' (*huioi*) in 5:5. Indeed, at the beginning of the letter Paul uses the phrase 'in God the Father' which as Gordon

Essays in Honor of Wayne A. Meeks (Philadelphia: Fortress Press, 1995) p. 116. Leon Morris, 'The Christian Family', in *1 and 2 Thessalonians*: *Word Biblical Themes* (Waco: Word Publishing, 1989), pp. 77–84, describes the Christians as 'the family of God'; Karl P. Donfried, *Paul, Thessalonica, and Early Christianity* (Grand Rapids: Eerdmans, 2002), pp. 154–155, is of the same view: 'Family structures, although transformed in Christ, are basic to the internal structure of the community . . . family structures lie at the heart of this new family in Christ'; see Trevor J. Burke, *Family Matters: A Socio-Historical Study of Kinship Metaphors in 1 Thessalonians*, JSNTS 247 (London: T&T Clark, 2003).

[2] See Trevor J. Burke, 'Pauline Paternity in 1 Thessalonians', *TynB* 51 (2000), pp. 52–89.

[3] This is clearer in the original language where the verb Paul uses is *aporphanizō* 'to be orphaned'.

[4] The issue centres on a disputed reading which has to do with the addition or subtraction of one Greek letter thereby changing the meaning. Thus, Paul may have been describing himself as 'gentle' (ESV) or he and his associates as 'infants' (TNIV). For discussion of this, see Gordon D. Fee, *The First and Second Letters to the Thessalonians* (Grand Rapids/Cambridge: Eerdmans, 2009), pp. 65–72.

[5] E.g., 1:4; 2:1, 14; 3:2, 7; 4:1, 10; 5:4, 25–27. Older English translations use the word 'brothers'.

[6] Burke, *Family Matters*, p. 165. This is the most concentrated usage of sibling language in any of Paul's letters; one in every four verses has a reference to this term.

Fee points out is 'the real surprise in our letter'[7] and has been understood by some commentators to describe 'the assembly . . . brought into being by God the Father'.[8] If this is so, and because the emperor of the day viewed himself as the 'Father' of his subjects who were his 'children', Paul is being subversive and undercuts any imperialist notion to show that *God* and not any human potentate is the sovereign, prime mover in bringing this new community into existence.

Coupled with this heavy concentration of familial language are the many affective expressions used by Paul. For instance, he reminds the church that they are 'loved by God' (1:4) and by Paul (2:8). The love of God, moreover, is to be demonstrated *within* ('may . . . your love increase and overflow for each other', 3:12) and *without* ('and for everyone else', 3:12) the community. Thus, in spite of Malherbe's initial demurring about whether this letter has anything to teach us about Paul's understanding of the church he nevertheless rightly concludes: 'I think the matter otherwise and wish to follow the . . . view of the church that underlies Paul's exhortations in this letter'. This is so, as Malherbe concludes, because the church is 'God's new family in Thessalonica'.[9]

It is not hard to find a reason why Paul should regard the believers as a church family in this, arguably his most emotive letter (cf. 3:1–6) – because just as in Philippi, Paul and his missionary[10] colleagues in Thessalonica had experienced much personal suffering and opposition to the gospel. After having planted the church in Thessalonica, they were hounded out of town, having only been there for two or three months.[11] This sudden severance from such a fledgling community has prompted some to conclude that this is the reason for the heavy use of familial terms in the letter. Paul badly misses the community and desires intensely to return in order to complete the task which he has begun (cf. 2:17 – 3:10). There is much to be said

---

[7] Fee, *Thessalonians*, p. 15.

[8] Abraham J. Malherbe, *The Letters to the Thessalonians*, AB 32B (New York: Doubleday, 2002), p. 99.

[9] Malherbe, 'God's New Family', p. 116. Linda McKinnish Bridges, *1 & 2 Thessalonians* (Macon: Smyth and Helwys, 2008), p. 119, also makes an excellent observation: 'Paul's words are . . . not a millennial event chart for eager sky watchers. Paul's word are written to create a sense of presence, *apostolic parousia* (Paul's coming), as he describes the *parousia* (the coming) of Jesus Christ.'

[10] Often the Acts of the Apostles is used to understand Paul the missionary. For an approach which uses the Pauline letters as the main text, see Trevor J. Burke and Brian S. Rosner, *Paul as Missionary: Identity, Activity, Theology, and Practice*, LNTS (London: T&T Clark, 2011).

[11] Though Acts 17:1–9 states that Paul was only in Thessalonica for three Sabbaths, most commentators are of the view that he must have been there for two or three months in order to have been able to establish a church in the city.

for this view but as we have been seeing throughout this book it is also possible that Paul is drawing on the normal social expectations of family members which he then uses in order to regulate the affairs of this young community.

We begin with Jesus' relationship of son to God, which sets the scene for a consideration of the Thessalonians as God's children.

1. The second coming of God's Son (1:9–10)

There is a general consensus among commentators that 1 Thessalonians is Paul's earliest letter. One text which supports this view is these verses, which are in essence a very early form of his missionary message (*kerygma*): *They tell how you turned to God from idols to serve the living and true God, and to wait for his Son from heaven, whom he raised from the dead – Jesus, who rescues us from the coming wrath*. Given that this is the apostle's earliest epistle, the mention of Jesus as 'Son' here is the first actual filial reference to Jesus in the whole of the New Testament. What we have here are the necessary components or ingredients of the good news in short summary form which we can collect under three main points or a 'triad . . . *turned, serve, wait*'.[12] This triple description of conversion and the Christian life echoes the trinity of graces, faith, love and hope mentioned at the beginning of the letter (1:3).

a. You turned from idols (1:9)

First, these believers whom Paul later describes as sons and daughters of God (5:5) have turned from idols, which is good evidence that the church comprised mostly Gentile believers who were essentially polytheistic as opposed to Jews who were strictly monotheistic. The plural *idols* is a reminder of the Thessalonians' pagan past and that the city itself was a potpourri and awash with gods. Imperial worship, the worship of Caesar, was prominent in the city as well as the religious cults of Dionysius, Serapis, Zeus, Aphrodite, and especially the local cult of Cabirus. The debased activities of those who engaged in the idolatrous worship of these false gods included a highly suggestive sexual content with an open display of phallic symbols. Sometimes a symbol of the phallus was placed in a basket and put on the head of a devotee at festivals as a sign of fertility which was obviously important to a people who depended

[12] G. K. Beale, *1 and 2 Thessalonians*, IVPNTC (Downers Grove: IVP and Nottingham: Apollos, 2003), p. 61, n 1.

on the land for their livelihood. On other occasions, phallic symbols were erected beside the tombs of the dead as a symbol of life-giving power and to represent a happy afterlife.[13]

It was from the debased worship of these false gods and dead images (as opposed to the living God) that the Thessalonians had *turned*. The verb 'turn' is in the past tense which is a once-for-all act. It is used by Paul of turning to God (2 Cor. 3:16) and commonly used in the Acts of the Apostles to describe conversion (Acts 3:19; 9:35; 11:21; 14:15; 15:19; 26:18, 20).[14] The verb implies not simply a change in attitude but also action, which is nothing less than true repentance. Conversion is first and foremost a turning *away from* (*apo*) what we once held dear never to go back to it again. Thus, idolatry in all its forms was for the Thessalonians to be a thing of the past.

Of course, when Christians today hear the gospel and repent of their sin the idolatry from which they turn may not be as dramatic or involve disengaging from the shameful activities in which the Thessalonians were involved in first-century Macedonia. Conversion too is not only to be understood as a change of attitude; if it is truly genuine it must be followed by a change of direction. For us today, this may mean turning away from making idols of *people* (a friend, spouse, colleague) or *things* (the latest car, computer, house, money or career) or like the Thessalonians the giving up of certain *lifestyles* and *activities* (drugs, alcohol, sexual infidelity) or anything which would deflect us from turning to God and the consequent need 'to seek first his kingdom and his righteousness'.[15] Whatever it was that once ensnared us, there must be some visible change in behaviour which authenticates an inner, spiritual transformation that has already taken place.

b. To serve the living and true God (1:9)

But conversion also involves a turning *towards* and the one verb 'turn' does double duty for the phrase *from idols* and the earlier phrase *to God*. If repentance more negatively means a turning away from sin, it also and more positively includes a turning towards (*pros*) God with a view *to serve the living and true God*. Whereas the worship of idols meant spiritual death and separation from God,

---

[13] Donfried, *Paul, Thessalonica, and Early Christianity*, pp. 23–24. See 1 Thess. 4:4 where one possible interpretation for the Greek word *skeuos* is the male sex member, i.e., penis.
[14] F. F. Bruce, *1 and 2 Thessalonians*, WBC (Waco: Word, 1982), p. 17.
[15] Matt. 6:33.

now as a result of their conversion the Thessalonians were to serve the living and true or real God. There was to be no mixing of their previous religious practices with Christian worship, emphasized by the fact that they were turning *to the one God* (implied by the use of the article before God – *ton theon*).[16] In other words, their allegiance and loyalty was to be given to God alone and not to be shared with other competing 'gods' on offer. The closest parallel to verse 9 is Jeremiah 10:10: 'But the LORD is the true God; he is the living God, the eternal King.' This God is not only the one who is alive but who gives life, the new life which only he can give. The significance of all this has been well stated by Howard Marshall: 'To be converted is to own this God as God, to accept his existence, to trust in him as the source of life and to give him love and obedience'.[17] It also means to serve God joyfully and wholeheartedly as his loyal subjects.

c. And to wait for his Son from heaven (1:10)

The early references to God as 'Father' in 1:1, 3 are now explicitly stated in the description of Jesus as God's *Son* (10). The Christian or child of God is not only one who has been converted and who serves but is also one who *waits* and looks expectantly for the sure and certain return of the Son of God. Paul elsewhere describes the return of Christ as 'the blessed hope – the glorious appearing of our great God and Saviour, Jesus Christ'[18] to which the believer can look forward. We noted in an earlier chapter how Paul connects the sonship of Jesus Christ with the incarnation and his coming into the world (e.g., Rom. 8:3; Gal. 4:4) and it is through his sonship that believers can become God's sons and daughters. But here in 1 Thessalonians he links Jesus' sonship with his return, which is significant because as one commentator has observed, 'uniquely in Paul's letters the Jesus Christ who is to come from heaven at the Parousia is called God's Son'.[19] Jesus entered humbly into this world as the eternal Son of God (Rom. 8:3) but it is only because *God raised him from the dead* (10) – a resurrection note Paul also sounds in connection with Jesus' sonship in Romans 1:4 – and is presently seated at the Father's right-hand side in heaven that he

---

[16] See Gene L. Green, *The Letters to the Thessalonians*, PNTC (Grand Rapids/Cambridge: Eerdmans, 2002), p. 107.

[17] I. Howard Marshall, *1 and 2 Thessalonians*, NCBC (London: Marshall, Morgan and Scott, 1983), p. 57.

[18] Titus 2:13.

[19] Ivor H. Jones, *The Epistles to the Thessalonians* (Peterborough: Epworth Press, 2005), p. 17.

will one day come in great glory and triumph as Son to wrap up history.

In light of the fact that Jesus the Son will return what are Christians to do? This is our next question.

2. Sons and dughters of God preparing for the return of Jesus the Son (4:16; 5:1–11)

a. Do not be like the rest who have no hope (4:16)

The filial language which Paul uses to describe Jesus as God's Son (1:10) within the context of his return is brought into service towards the end of the letter and in a passage heavily coloured with eschatological language. This time, however, Paul twice describes the Thessalonians as *sons of the light and sons of the day* (5:5; cf. Eph. 5:8). We earlier stated that Paul is not only concerned in this letter with the subject of the end times (i.e., eschatology) but he is also addressing the topic of the church, or ecclesiology. Alongside this dual emphasis is a third topic which Paul brings into focus in chapter 5, namely that of ethics, which together with the other two provides a trinity of foci – *eschatology, ecclesiology* and *ethics* – all of which are interwoven as Paul gives instructions on how these sons and daughters are to live in preparation for the Son of God.

But why exactly does Paul introduce the topic of the end times here and how does it relate to being church and to morality? The answer to the former question is closely tied with the previous topic in 4:13–18, where Paul had been addressing the fears of some within the church who were wondering what would happen to those believers who had died in Christ. Would they miss out on the events when Christ would return? Paul gives instructions that they would not miss out nor should Christians grieve like *the rest . . . who have no hope* (4:13). In fact, some believers had become so discouraged that they were reverting back to their pagan mindset and were grieving *like the rest of men who have no hope*. One writer, Theocriticus, typifies the ancients' mindset of life beyond the grave: 'Hopes are for the living, the dead are without hope.'

Certainly, Paul is not saying that Christians are not to grieve when a loved one or someone we are close to dies because Jesus himself demonstrated sorrow and grief as he wept at the graveside of his much loved friend, Lazarus (John 11:35). Paul, moreover, also displayed similar sadness when he learnt of the near-death experience of his collaborator in the gospel, Epaphroditus: 'He was ill, and almost died. But God had mercy on him, and not only him but also on me, to spare me sorrow upon sorrow'.[20] The point, as Gordon Fee rightly notes, is that 'believers who have hope in the resurrection do not *sorrow in the same way* as others, people who lack that hope'.[21] Christians who die in the Lord are not hope*less* but rather are hope*ful* where hope typically in the New Testament understanding does not convey the idea of uncertainty but of confident assurance of being physically raised at the last day when Jesus comes again in glory.

Nor are Christians to live in denial as if the person who has died is still with them. I find it intriguing how when a famous actor or Hollywood star dies the media use the euphemisms of 'his passing away' or 'she slipped from us' in order to avoid the reality that someone has actually *died*. The reality is that 'no life is complete until there's a death . . . [and] *denial of death is avoidance of life*'.[22] But for the believing Thessalonians and for all Christians there is hope and Paul writes to reassure his readers that when Christ returns *the dead in Christ will rise first* (16).

This background is vitally important because Paul uses it as the backdrop to go on to provide a necessary reminder of the need to live and be prepared for that coming day. The other two issues of morality and community will become apparent as we look more closely at the passage.

b. Don't look up, look out! (5:1–3)

Chapter 5 opens with the statement, *Now, brothers and sisters, about times and dates*[23] *we do not need to write to you* (1, TNIV), which has a familiar ring as a similar statement was made by the disciples in the Acts of the Apostles when immediately prior to the Day of Pentecost they asked Christ, 'Lord when are you going to restore the Kingdom to Israel?', to which the pre-ascended Jesus responded in similar language to that which the apostle Paul uses here: 'It is not for you to know the times or dates the Father has set by his own authority'.[24] Rather, the disciples are expressly told by Jesus to no longer look up but to *look out* and to get busy by taking the gospel to those who have yet to hear it. Thus immediately after the apostles' question Jesus tells them, 'You will receive power

---

[20] Phil. 2:27.

[21] Fee, *Thessalonians*, pp. 168–169 (author's own emphasis).

[22] Eugene H. Peterson, *Leap over a Wall: Earthy Spirituality for Every Day Christians* (San Francisco: Harper Row, 1997), p. 218 (emphasis added).

[23] This is an example of hendiadys where the two words 'times' and 'dates' refer to the same thing.

[24] Acts 1:6–7.

when the Holy Spirit comes on you, and you will be my witnesses in Jerusalem, and in all Judea and Samaria, and to the ends of the earth.'[25] Likewise, Paul follows his Lord's example as we shall see below, and rather than encouraging the Thessalonians to be overly preoccupied or fixated with the exact timing of Christ's return Paul reminds them that no one can know exactly when these events will occur; indeed, the evangelist Mark tells us that not even the Son knows the precise moment of his return (Mark 13:32). More importantly, the Thessalonians too are to live and serve God now by being a light, *sons of light* (5) in a dark, depraved world.

Before Paul provides instructions on how they are to do this, he first addresses those who do not belong to the community. *While some people are saying 'Peace and Safety'* (3), is a description of the 'outsiders' (4:12), 'the rest . . . who have no hope' (4:13) who were putting their confidence in the governing authorities, the emperor of the day, and the *Pax Romana* (Roman peace) which was promised to its citizens. The Thessalonians had benefitted greatly from such peace, even going to the extent of erecting a temple in honour of Julius Caesar and of Augustus as 'son of god'. Set against this context and the coming of Jesus *the* Son of God one can see how deliberately subversive Paul's gospel really is. Those who rely on such false hope and who think this way are misled because, says Paul, destruction will come upon them. Paul uses two very graphic metaphors of a *thief* (2) and the *labour pains on a pregnant woman* (3) in order to make his point clear. Both are telling images and vivid reminders of the suddenness and unexpectedness of Jesus' second advent – thieves do not announce their arrival and usually strike under cover of darkness (*at night*, 2) when no one is expecting them and the *labour pains* of a heavily pregnant woman can also suddenly occur without a moment's notice.

c. Live as sons and daughters of the light (5:4–7)

Then in 5:4 Paul turns to specifically address the entire Thessalonian community, evident by the plural pronoun and verbs, as well as the plural filial descriptions, and he does so in a most emphatic and specific manner: *But you, brothers and sisters are not in the darkness . . . you are all children of the light and children of the day* (4–5, TNIV). Paul uses the adjective *all* to stress the difference between the Thessalonians as God's children, which sets them apart from those who do not belong to the community. Wayne A. Meeks, in his ground-breaking work, *The First Urban Christians:*

[25] Acts 1:8.

185

The Social World of the Apostle Paul states that terms like 'sons', 'saints', 'beloved' and 'brothers and sisters' are all part of what he calls the 'language of belonging' which stands in contrast to others who outside the church are depicted as using the 'language of separation'.[26] Thus, the description of sons and daughters who belong to God's family the church sits alongside other language used earlier in this passage to describe those on the periphery of the community such as 'the pagans who do not know God' (4:5), the 'outsiders' (4:12), and 'the rest, who have no hope' (4:13, TNIV).

The twin expressions, *sons of the light* and *sons of the day*, are best understood adjectivally and mean 'sons *characterized* by light'[27] where the focus is on these Thessalonians as God's children to behave and conduct themselves in a way that is in keeping with members of the family of God. In other words, there is a moral[28] expectation for those who are members in this new household of God. In real families of Paul's day, sons and daughters were supposed to live and behave in a way that upheld the good name of the family, and for God's spiritual offspring we can expect nothing different. This ethical thrust, moreover, fits in with the importance of the theme of sanctification and godly living which is so pervasive in this short letter. Leon Morris rightly points out how the language of holiness or 'sanctification receives unusual attention in our two letters'.[29] For example, the word 'sanctification' itself occurs four times (3:13; 4:3, 7; 5:23) which is significant when set against the much longer letter of Romans where it only occurs twice (Rom. 6:19, 22). In addition to the language of sanctification is the use of the term 'holy' (2:10; 5:26) along with several references to the third person of the trinity, the '*Holy* Spirit' (1:5, 6; 4:8; 5:19).

The importance of this language thus sets the context for what Paul goes on to say in chapter 5 in regard to godly living and how God's sons and daughters are to conduct themselves: they should not *sleep* (6) but rather be awake or *alert* and *self-controlled* (6) as opposed to being *drunk* (7), the last of which is usually a night-time activity. Thus, in verse 4 Paul begins with the words *but you*, followed by a number of statements of fact (*you are sons of the light and sons of the day*, 5) which are closely followed by the imperatives or commands of what they are to do: *Let us not be like others, who are asleep, but let us be alert and self-controlled* (6). There is to be

---

[26] Wayne A. Meeks, *The First Urban Christians: The Social World of the Apostle Paul* (Yale: Yale University Press, 1983), p. 85.

[27] It is in fact an adjectival genitive; see Wallace, *Greek Beyond Basics*, p. 81.

[28] Green, *Thessalonians*, p. 237.

[29] Morris, 'The Christian Family', p. 87.

no spiritual somnambulating, sleepwalking, for those who belong in God's household! Those who do so end up in deep trouble. Rather, just as Jesus is the Light of the world so God's spiritual offspring are to live morally responsible lives and live as sons and daughters of light. Paul makes the important connection between the Thessalonians' new filial disposition – who they are – and what is now expected of them. Put another way, the *identity* of the Thessalonians as God's children cannot be separated from the *activity* in which they must now engage, links which have been rightly noted by Gene Green when he comments:

> This intimate relationship between their new existence and their new moral life touches a fundamental aspect of Christian ethics: What they *are* is what they should *do*. The moral exhortation finds its roots in the previous work of God in their lives. They have been made 'children of the light and children of the day' via salvation, and now they are to act according to that new state of being.[30]

This new language and orientation represents a seismic shift for these nascent Christians as they break from their past pagan way of life to a new way of living as God's children, as Wayne Meeks states: 'Whatever else is involved, the image of the initiate being [accepted as] . . . God's child and thus receiving a new family of human brothers and sisters is a vivid way of portraying what a modern sociologist might call the resocialisation of conversion.'[31] Meeks' point is that just as little children need to be taught how to conduct themselves socially as they grow up in the physical family, so the sons and daughters in this fledgling church needed to learn how to behave as Christians in God's household. Growing up in this new family to which they have now come to belong is significant for the fact that the same note of maturity noted earlier in respect of the nation of Israel as God's son in the Old Testament is now worked out in the New Testament for *sons of the light* as the new Israel of God, the church. This injunction to morality is not so surprising because the church at Thessalonica comprised mostly Gentile believers (as well as some Jews) who had *turned to God from idols to serve the living and true God* (1:9). Indeed, the morals and previous way of life of those who were Gentiles prior to their conversion would have been very different to their Jewish counterparts who had embraced the good news of the gospel. Clearly, the former needed to be

---

[30] Green, *Thessalonians*, p. 237 (emphasis added).
[31] Meeks, *First Urban Christians*, p. 88.

resocialized into the distinctively Christian way to live. This would not happen overnight – yet must begin to be visible to others in their behaviour – but would take time as they learned to walk in the ways of the Lord Jesus as they waited for his return.

Today there is much talk in some Christian circles about the second coming of Christ; indeed, in some quarters of the church there is an unhealthy fixation and preoccupation with these matters, to the extent that some people are confident they can predict the exact day when Jesus will return in glory. Certainly, there are signs which must precede his second advent (e.g., an escalation in catastrophic events, complete breakdown in families, Mark 13:8, 12), but Paul is no crystal-ball gazer; rather he is a realist. Moreover, it is instructive to note that Paul always links his *eschatology* with *ethics* and how believers ought to live in light of Christ's return. It is entirely biblical to talk and encourage one another about the return of Christ but Paul connects such talk with the believer's responsibility for *action* and the need to be ready and prepared for his unveiling. If Christ is coming, believers will be thinking and talking about the Son's second advent. But merely to engage in trying to determine *when* the Son will return, without proper preparation for *how* we ought to be living lives that are distinct to those outside the family of God will not only bring shame on such believers when Christ does return but is also a travesty of Paul's teaching on eschatology. A proper, biblical understanding of the return of the Son of God will mean that the conduct of God's new family of sons and daughters will become increasingly Christ-like and different to those who make no claim to belong to the household of God.

Summary

Paul's first letter to the Thessalonians has a distinctive end-time feel to it but is a letter that is as much about the church (ecclesiology) as it is about eschatology (end times). Early in the letter Paul reminds the Thessalonians of the coming of Jesus, the Son of God, as a prelude to underscoring what believers are to do as God's sons and daughters in the light of his return. He does this because some of the Thessalonians Christians were grieving like those who were not believers – 'like the rest, who have no hope' (4:13) – and were doing so because they feared that those Christians who had died would miss out when Christ returned in glory. Paul writes to reassure them that the dead in Christ will be the first to rise, but more important and in addition to the notes of ecclesiology and eschatology, Paul wraps it all in ethics and the necessity of living godly lives so that God's sons and daughters (5:5) will not be ashamed when the Son of God comes again.

Hebrews 1:1–13; 3:5–6; 2:10–18; 12:1–11
10. A sermon on sonship

When did you last hear a sermon on Hebrews or participate in a
Bible study of this book? Perhaps recently or maybe some time ago
or possibly never! – which in one sense may not be so surprising, if
the following comment is anything to go by:

> Hebrews has acquired a reputation for being formidable to
> understand and remote from the world in which we now live.
> Consequently, it has been neglected in the liturgy and preaching
> of the churches, in the curricula of seminaries, and in devotional
> reading of the laity . . . Hebrews tends to remain unappreciated in
> the classroom, the pulpit, and the pew.[1]

But Hebrews, if we take the time to read it through carefully, is not
only a profound theological discourse it is also a powerfully com-
municated message that addresses the reader in a direct up-close-
and-personal kind of way. The reader cannot miss what the writer is
saying because Hebrews is a speech-act and there is an oral quality
about the book that we do not find anywhere else in the New
Testament.[2] Hebrews, in fact, 'is crafted for the ear, not the eye'[3]
a point made clear by the numerous times the author[4] emphasizes

---

[1] William L. Lane, 'Standing Before the Moral Claim of God: Discipleship in
Hebrews', in Richard N. Longenecker (ed.), *Patterns of Discipleship in the New
Testament* (Grand Rapids: Eerdmans, 1996), p. 222.

[2] It was common practice, given that only two out of ten people could read
in the ancient world, for a letter to be read out loud to those gathered; see Ben
Witherington, *The Paul Quest: The Renewed Search for the Jew of Tarsus*
(Downers Grove: IVP and Leicester: Apollos, 1998), p. 89.

[3] Lane, 'Standing', p. 204.

[4] The authorship of Hebrews remains a disputed and open question with

what he is *saying* to his audience. For example, in Hebrews 2:5 we read: 'It is not to angels that he has subjected the world to come, about which *we are speaking*' (cf. 5:11; 6:9; 8:1; 9:5; 11:32). The emphasis on the oral nature of the discourse as a preached message is further heightened by the way that the book begins with an alliterative artillery (!) of words all beginning with the same Greek letter 'p' – *polymerōs ... polytropōs palai ... patrasin ... prophētais* (*In the past [God spoke] to our forefathers through the prophets at many times*), a common device used in speeches of the time which no doubt would have come across to the hearers with profound rhetorical effect.

But that's not all, for there are many other tools of the preacher's trade on display in this discourse, including rhyme (*emathen ... epathen*, 5:8) and repetition of words or phrases (e.g., *by faith ... by faith ... by faith*, in ch. 11), as well as a cornucopia of metaphors drawn from many different backgrounds, including the law court (6:16; 7:20), athletics (12:1–2), the classroom (5:11–14), and, of course, the household (2:10–11; 3:1–6). All this suggests that the author of Hebrews is a powerful preacher, for the message proclaimed not only begins in an arresting manner but is also judiciously illustrated and spiced with turns of phrase, all of which would have prompted those listening to sit up and concentrate![5]

Hebrews, then, as most commentators today agree, is a homily or a sermon[6] (or series of sermons) and, we might add, it is a sermon on sonship, primarily to do with the sonship of Christ, as evidenced by the repeated use of the noun 'Son' throughout.[7] Certainly there are other themes that are equally, if not more important, that the author addresses, including the covenant and the high priesthood of Christ. However, in both these instances the author points out that the Son is superior to the old covenant because he ushers in a new covenant based on better promises (Heb. 2:1–4; 8). And the Son is a superior high priest to Melchizedek, for while the author does not state this in so many words, he does say that Christ has become a priest on the basis of 'an indestructible life' (Heb. 7:16).

A good argument can therefore be made for 'the sonship of

various suggestions having been made, including the apostle Paul. Because of the sophistication of the Greek, Apollos and Luke have also been suggested, as have Barnabas and Timothy.

[5] For these and many other forms of speech used throughout the book see the excellent discussion in Andrew H. Trotter, *Interpreting the Epistle to the Hebrews* (Grand Rapids: Baker Academic, 1997), pp. 163–184.

[6] As Trotter, *Hebrews*, p. 79, makes clear, this is 'a sermon ... clearly reconstructed as an epistle'.

[7] E.g., 1:2, 3, 5 (twice), 8; 3:6; 4:14; 5:5, 8; 6:6; 7:3, 28; 10:29.

Christ [as] the dominant theme in the epistle',[8] a viewpoint shared by A. B. Davidson, the nineteenth-century Scottish Old Testament scholar, who writes that Christ's sonship 'is the fundamental idea of the epistle'.[9] And as noted above, if numbers are anything to go by, the designation 'Son' (Gk *huios*) is conspicuous throughout, for the author 'employs it generically or Christologically twenty-four times throughout the letter. The title "Son" or "Son of God" as it pertains to Jesus' person . . . dominates the Christolology of Hebrews'.[10] The person and work of Jesus Christ as the Son of God pervades the sermon; indeed, apart from the writings of John (both Gospel and letters), Hebrews more than any other New Testament writing particularly emphasizes the divine sonship of Jesus.

But while Hebrews is soaked in the language of sonship, it is not only Jesus' filial relationship to his Father which is an important theme; this Son is also seen to be in solidarity with believers as God's sons and daughters. For example, Jesus entered into the human condition and so was *made like his brothers in every way* (2:17) in order to bring them into the family of God; just as Jesus suffers as a Son so too must believers suffer because of their new identity and belonging to God's household (2:10); just as Jesus as Son learns obedience (5:8) so also do God's sons and daughters (12:5–11). Thus, J. Scott Lidgett rightly notes that the link between the filial relationship of Jesus and believers throughout the sermon is one that should not be overlooked:

> Sonship . . . explains and indeed constitutes the salvation he imparts . . . His earthly experience reveals the only way by which sonship can be imparted to and fulfilled in those whom 'He is not ashamed to call his brethren' (2.11) . . . the master-theme, the unifying conception, of the Epistle to the Hebrews is . . . Sonship and Salvation.[11]

This filial language, moreover, is important, for it relates to the context and reason for writing, which was the adversity and persecution which the recipients were undergoing. While there is much discussion why Hebrews was written, the text indicates the readers were Christians, mostly Jewish but also Gentile, who were

---

[8] J. Scott Lidgett, *Sonship and Salvation: A Study of the Epistle to the Hebrews* (London: Epworth Press, 1921), pp. 110–113, 254–255.

[9] A. B. Davidson, *The Epistle to the Hebrews* (Edinburgh: T&T Clark, 1882), p. 79.

[10] J. Daryl Charles, 'The Angels, Sonship and Birthright in Hebrews', *JETS* 33.2 (1990), p. 175.

[11] Lidgett, *Sonship and Salvation*, p. 13.

warned about the continuing need to be faithful (e.g., 5:11 – 6:12; 10:19–39), especially in the face of adversity and difficulty. Such sufferings were probably not sponsored by the state[12] but were more a result of new believers coming to faith in Jesus Christ, the Son of God. The author reminds his audience that although they are recent converts experiencing alienation as a minority in the world, their coming together means they are also of *the same family* (2:11) of Jesus. Thus, in the face of adversity and suffering from a world which is not only against them but also does not understand their new filial relationship, '*child imagery* contributes . . . significantly to the writer's purpose of *reaffirming identity and belonging*' for the members of this small house church.[13] This sermon on sonship, then, functions primarily as an exhortation and a reminder; belonging to this new family which is in solidarity with Jesus the Son is intended to give support and confidence to these recent converts so that they might live with the ultimate triumph of God in view even in the midst of difficulty and rejection by others.

We begin with the sonship of Jesus before turning to the sonship of believers.

1. The supremacy of Jesus the Son of God (1:1–13; 3:5–6)

a. The Son is superior to the angels (Heb. 1:1–13)

On a cursory reading of the beginning of Hebrews we are immediately struck by the fact there is no introduction or mention of the author's name or the addressees. Rather, the writer abruptly and immediately launches into a heavy discourse on angels where, in the first two chapters, the expression *the angels* (e.g., 1:4, 5; 2:2, 5) occurs no less than ten times. This extended discussion of angels provides one of the early keys to the sermon and its content since it is introduced in order to demonstrate the superiority of the sonship of Jesus. The writer does this because at that time and earlier, between the Old and New Testaments (known as the intertestamental era), angelology or the worship of angels was particularly prevalent. On the one hand, the worship of angelic spirits was unduly elevated while on the other the worship of Jesus was diminished. There is a contemporary ring about all this today as the veneration of angels and angelic beings is part of the wider New Age religious

---

[12] James W. Thompson, *Hebrews* (Grand Rapids: Baker, 2008), p. 8.
[13] James M. M. Francis, *Adults as Children: Images of Childhood in the Ancient World and the New Testament* (Bern: Peter Lang, 2006), p. 218 (emphasis added).

phenomenon which has swept through the United Kingdom and the United States. In today's world where people crave connectedness and a deeper experience and meaning to life, fascination with the unseen and the paranormal is a huge growth industry.

The author responds to this preoccupation with angels and deficiency in his hearers' Christology (the person of Jesus as the Son of God) by launching a polemic against the worship of these created beings.[14] He immediately deprecates this misplaced view of angels by reminding the believers that God has finally and climactically spoken *in these last days ... by his Son* (2). It is precisely because Jesus is the Son of God that he has been *made the heir of all things* (2). The Son, moreover, shares the *radiance of God's glory* and is *the exact representation of his being* (3). Since Jesus is God's Son he is the only one who could provide *purification for sins* (3); moreover, the proof that his perfect sacrifice on the cross was acceptable to the Father is that he *sat down at the right hand of the Majesty in heaven* (3), a clear indication that Jesus' work on the cross was finished and complete.

The superior status of the Son of God is developed further by the use of a number of rhetorical questions that follow – each requiring a negative response – questions which have a biting and sarcastic edge: *for to which of the angels did God ever say? ... or again ...?* (5); *In speaking of the angels he says ... But about the Son he says* (7–8); and *to which of the angels did God ever say?* (13). The crux of chapter 1, however, is verse 5, where the author counters this over-exaggerated view of angelology by combining two well-known passages on sonship from the Old Testament (2 Sam. 7:11–14 and Ps. 2:7) which, as we have already noted, are significant for the unfolding of our meta-narrative of sonship. He writes: *For to which of the angels did God ever say, 'You are my Son, today I have become your Father?' or again, 'I will be his Father, and he will be my Son'?* These Old Testament texts would have been rejected by Jews as having any messianic significance or association of the term 'Son'[15] to Jesus, a view that stands in contrast to Christian exegesis.[16] Moreover, these texts are also chosen to demonstrate that this 'Son-king' who now rules the nations does so by mirroring the filial relationship between Yahweh and King David's descendants, from whose seed the rights of dominion flow. Jesus the 'Son-king' supersedes David as 'son-king', for through his perfect obedience and

---

[14] For some of this argument I am relying on Charles, 'Angels', p. 171.

[15] S. Kistemaker, *The Psalm Citations in the Epistle to the Hebrews* (Amsterdam: W.G. van Soest, 1961), pp. 75–76.

[16] E.g., Acts 2:15–36; 3:11–26; 4:24–30.

compliance to the will of his Father he ushers in a greater kingdom, one that is eternal and will know no end.

There is also an important allusion to another Old Testament text in verse 6 which connects with the theme of sonship. The author writes: *And again, when God brings his firstborn into the world, he says, 'Let all God's angels worship him'*. With this phrase, the tables are quickly turned on the angels as they are not to be worshipped but are instead themselves expressly told – and none are excluded – to worship the Son: *Let*[17] *all God's angels worship him* (6). As the firstborn, Jesus stands in line with the nation of Israel as son (Exod. 4:22) whose relationship to Yahweh was special. Here in Hebrews, however, Jesus is unique, for *he* is to be worshipped, which clearly sets apart his filial relationship to the Father from any other 'sons' that we have so far encountered in the Old and New Testament. Revelation 22:8–9 provides further commentary on who Christians are to venerate, since immediately after John was given a number of visions of the future as well as a glimpse of eternity, he tells his readers, 'When I had heard and seen them, I fell down to worship at the feet of the angel.' John, however, had to be corrected and is clearly commanded: 'Do not do it! . . . Worship God!' The writer of the book of Hebrews would agree in regard to the one to whom his readers (and we as Christians) are to give allegiance and worship: angels 'No'; God's Son, 'Yes'.

b. Jesus the Son is superior to Moses the servant (3:5–6)

Having shown that Jesus is superior to angels the author moves on in chapter 3 to discuss Jesus in relation to Moses. There is none of the polemic in this chapter that we saw earlier in Hebrews 1 in the author's combating of a false view of angels. Rather, there are several similarities between Moses and Jesus, for both functioned as leaders and mediators: the former led the children of Israel out of Egypt into the Promised Land, their inheritance, while the latter had been sent into the world at the behest of the Father in order to lead lost humanity back to God. In addition, both Moses and Jesus are twice spoken as having proved faithful (3:2, 5–6) to God in all they did.

But even though Moses was a great figure and faithful leader, at the beginning of chapter Hebrews 3 these similarities soon give way to differences as the author continues where he left off in chapter 1 by prioritizing Jesus' person and his ministry. He does this firstly by issuing a command to his readers to 'fix your thoughts *on Jesus*

---

[17] The Greek verb is in the imperative mood, the mood of command. In other words, this is not an option for angels but an order for them to obey.

the apostle and high-priest whom we confess' (3:1). Having struck this Christocentric note, the writer goes on to draw a number of contrasts. He notes especially how Moses is described as a *servant in . . . God's house* (5) whereas Jesus' role is superior because he is *a son over God's house* (6). A servant can never expect to have the authority, the privileges or the inheritance rights of a natural-born son in the household. Again, Moses is a servant 'in' (Gk *en*) God's house, whereas Jesus is a son 'over' (Gk *epi*) God's house. The latter preposition 'is a marker of power . . . over someone or something',[18] again highlighting Jesus' superior *role* to Moses. Finally, by focusing on his filial *relationship* to the Father the author shows that 'Jesus occupies a more elevated position in the household of God'.[19] The upshot of all this is that not only are the author's readers to steer clear of worshipping angels but as Craig Blomberg helpfully comments: 'Professing Christians, therefore, should not imagine that revering Moses rather than Jesus can bring them the spiritual inheritance they would want'.[20] The Christian church would do well to take heed of such advice when we too can easily elevate preachers, pastors, and scholars by giving them iconic status.

2. Sonship and suffering: Jesus in solidarity with believers (2:10–18)

The uniqueness of Jesus' sonship already considered now becomes the basis for the author's discussion of the sonship of believers in Hebrews 2. The link between the two ideas is especially apparent because of the many conjunctions which connect 2:10–18 with the previous section and which also carry the argument forward. In verse 10, the first of many of these conjunctions 'for' (Gk *gar*) – omitted by the NIV – reads: *In bringing many sons to glory, it was fitting that God, for whom and through whom everything exists, should make the author of their salvation perfect through suffering.* This first conjunction then, 'introduces a statement implying the solidarity between the Son of God and the sons who are being led by God to their heritage'.[21] A number of parallels between the two filial identities can be drawn.

---

[18] BDAG, p. 365.

[19] David deSilva, *Perseverance in Gratitude: A Socio-Rhetorical Commentary on the Epistle 'to the Hebrews'* (Grand Rapids: Eerdmans, 2000), p. 137.

[20] Craig L. Blomberg, *From Pentecost to Patmos: An Introduction to Acts to Revelation* (Nottingham: Apollos and Nashville: Broadman & Holman, 2006), p. 418.

[21] William L. Lane, *Hebrews 1–8*, WBC 47A (Waco: Word, 1991), p. 53.

a. The Son shared our humanity (2:14, 17)

First, God the Son became a real, physical human being. The writer states: *Since the children have flesh and blood, he too shared in their humanity.* The description *children* who have *flesh and blood* is a reference to his hearers' human condition which is synonymously paralleled by a reference to Son's incarnation in that he too identified with them by assuming the same full humanity. The point is that if the solidarity of Jesus as Son is to be considered real, he must become a true human being.[22] Both expressions *children have flesh and blood* and *humanity* describe a full participation in a shared reality. Indeed, the adverb (*paraplēsios*) is one word and translated as 'in just the same way' and 'signifies a total likeness',[23] underscoring the extent to which the Son was prepared to go by being involved in the human experience. In other words, Jesus did not *seem* or *appear* to be human, as one early Church heresy (Docetism)[24] taught, he actually took on real flesh and blood. This demonstrates what Calvin calls the great condescension, the fact that God accommodated himself to our weakness by sending his Son into the world as a man. Jesus' solidarity with us is again emphasized a few verses later where the author states that in order to bring about salvation Jesus the Son *had to be made like his brothers in every way* (17a), which in the immediate context relates to many things (e.g., testing), including the fact that he assumed 'a shared and full human existence'.[25] The significance of the Son's actions, as Sinclair Ferguson has aptly noted, is that it is 'because he has entered our family that we enter into the family of God'.[26]

b. The Son shares in our temptations and sufferings (2:10, 18)

We noted earlier the temptations of Jesus in the Gospel accounts which centred on his filial relationship with his Father (e.g., Matt. 4:1–11). The idea of solidarity centres on the temptation of Jesus' sonship and those who are to become sons (2:10). The same alliterative style with which the letter opened with a play on the Greek

---

[22] F. F. Bruce, *The Book of Hebrews*, NICNT (Grand Rapids: Eerdmans, 1990), p. 84.

[23] Lane, *Hebrews*, p. 60.

[24] The Greek verb is *dokeō* which means 'to seem/appear'. In other words, Jesus only 'seemed or appeared to be human'.

[25] Lane, *Hebrews*, p. 64.

[26] Sinclair B. Ferguson, 'The Reformed Doctrine of Sonship', in Nigel M. de S. Cameron and Sinclair B. Ferguson (eds.), *Pulpit and People: Essays in Honour of William Still on his 75th Birthday* (Edinburgh: Rutherford House, 1986), p. 87.

letter 'p' returns in verse 18 – (*peponthen . . . peirastheis . . . peira-zomenois*) – *because he himself suffered when he was tempted, he is able to help those who are being tempted.* But literary style is no substitute for substance as is clear in what follows, as the word for 'tempted' can also mean 'tested' and here in the context the author is probably referring to Jesus' trials by what he *suffered*.[27] As Son, Jesus is therefore uniquely in a position to be able to come to the aid of others who are tempted like he was. If the temptations to which the author refers here are to Jesus' sufferings, Jesus is once again in solidarity with humanity by virtue of the fact that he suffered. However, the Son's sufferings were different to what we as God's children will ever have to face because he suffered so uniquely and vicariously for the sins of others, thereby bringing salvation. F. F. Bruce therefore rightly makes the important distinction that Jesus 'not only suffered *with them* but *for them*'. This is why the writer earlier describes Jesus as *the author of salvation* (10) because it was only through his unique sufferings and death that he as the Son of God[28] could ever bring *many sons to glory* (10).

We would do well to linger on the saving significance of the death of Jesus which enables those who trust in him to become sons and daughters of God. The author states, *In bringing many sons to glory, it was fitting that God . . . should make the author of their salvation perfect through suffering* (10). The context for verse 10 is of course verse 9 where we read that Jesus has tasted death for everyone. Verse 10 then is further commentary on this, where the connection between bringing many sons to glory is linked to the pioneer of their salvation, the latter being a description for Jesus. The word *archēgos* is translated by the NIV as 'author' but 'pioneer' or 'founder' is better and in the context describes Jesus as 'the pioneer who secures salvation'. How Jesus the Son accomplishes all this is fully described at the end of verse 10, *through suffering*. These sufferings of the Son, moreover, function as an *inclusio* (10, 18), the significance of which, as Lidgett points out, is that 'the saving work of the Son by its very nature involves and brings about . . . *solidarity between the Son and the "many sons"* that are brought "unto glory" *through him*'.[29] The writer to the Hebrews is similar to Paul in this respect, namely that the notion of believers as God's sons and daughters is tied and

[27] Ben Witherington, *Letter and Homilies for Jewish Christians: A Socio-Rhetorical Commentary on Hebrews, James and Jude* (Downers Grove: IVP and Nottingham: Apollos, 2007), p. 161.

[28] Commentators differ over whether it is 'God' or 'Christ' who brings the many sons to glory; for the former see Lane, *Hebrews*, p. 56; for the latter see T. Hewitt, *The Epistle to the Hebrews*, TNTC (London: Tyndale Press, 1960), p. 70.

[29] Lidgett, *Sonship and Salvation*, p. 173 (emphasis added).

inextricably bound up with the Sonship of Jesus. The Christological note should not be overlooked.

3. God's children must grow in the school of training and discipline (12:1–11)

As we turn to chapter 12, the shift from chapter 11 is clear and obvious: the statements of fact (the indicatives) in a chapter better known as the 'hall of fame of the faithful', to commands and exhortations to obey (the imperatives) in chapter 12. Notably, there is also a shift in person from the third person ('he') in chapter 11 to the first ('we', e.g., 12:1, 9) and second ('you', 12:3, 4, 5, 7, 8, 12, 13) persons. The tone of chapter 12 is therefore more personal and relational not only because of the change of pronouns but also because of the reintroduction of filial[30] and paternal language.[31] In fact, it may well be that behind this text, with its emphasis on sonship, suffering and the need for obedience to God, lies Deuteronomy 8:5 and the synoptic Gospels' texts of Jesus' encounter with the evil one.[32]

a. Suffering and sonship: Jesus and believers (12:1–5)

Chapter 12 begins with an unusual and doubly strong inferential word (found only here and in 1 Thess. 4:8) which means 'therefore' and connects back to chapter 11. The author's readers are to remember those saints who had preceded them in order to inspire them on their Christian journey. However, good as all these saints are, each one is flawed and so in chapter 12 the author calls upon his readers to make Jesus their primary role model. Though the word 'son' is not used here of Jesus, the note of solidarity between Jesus and the hearers of the sermon is again struck in verses 1–2 by exhorting them to *fix our eyes on Jesus* (2) and to *consider him* (3) before going on to exhort them as children of God more directly (12:3–12). In the face of persecution which the believers were experiencing, the writer holds up Jesus' suffering and response as a model for his readers to follow: *Consider him who endured such opposition from sinful men, so that you will not grow weary and lose heart* (3). Before we look at why these believers are to reflect on Jesus, it is highly significant how in an earlier chapter, and unlike prodigal son Israel

---

[30] Cf. vv. 5 (twice), 6, 7 (twice), 8.
[31] Vv. 7 (twice), 9.
[32] Christopher J. H. Wright, *Deuteronomy*, NIBC (Peabody: Hendrickson Publishers and Carlisle: Paternoster Press, 1996), p. 125.

for example, who refused to grow and learn, Jesus as a son 'learned obedience from what he suffered' (Heb. 5:8). Thus, his hearers have much to learn themselves and are to keep Jesus' sufferings ever before them so that *in your struggle* (4) they do not forget *that word . . . that addresses you as sons* (5) where once again '*sonship* unites Christ and believers in the experience of *suffering*'.[33] 'Suffering and sonship in fact go hand-in-hand'[34] here, though endurance is a continuing theme.

There are a number of things which the writer calls his readers to do or to remember when suffering occurs but before we turn to these, one key interpretative issue has to do with the actual reason *why* his readers are suffering. Have they done something wrong? Is there some specific sin about which he is correcting them? In other words, as one commentator asks in regard to the discipline described here: 'Is it punitive and corrective, or is it formative and educational?'[35] Certainly the author's citation of the original quotation of Proverbs 3:11–12 in verses 5–6 with the parallel expressions of *discipline* and *rebuke* (11) and *disciplines* and *punishes* (lit. 'flog', 12) shows that the discipline could involve punishment and correction. But there is nothing in this passage to suggest that the readers are being punished for being involved in some sin or other. Rather, as some commentators argue, 'the "sinners" and "sin" of verses 3–4 refer to those hostile forces that opposed Jesus and now beset the church'.[36] This does not mean his hearers were sinless, for clearly they were not, struggling as they were to maintain a Christian witness and at times failing, but it is significant that unlike Paul for example, the writer nowhere actually tells them to 'Put to death the sins within you'. Rather, he says, 'Endure in the face of hostility, verbal abuse, and public shame'.[37] Endurance, as we shall see then, is 'a sign of divine sonship'[38] and is a part and parcel of God's parental training.

There are a number of aspects which the writer calls his readers to

---

[33] Francis, *Adults as Children*, p. 219.

[34] Harold W. Attridge, *Hebrews* (Philadelphia: Fortress Press, 1989), p. 361.

[35] Fred B. Craddock, *The Letter to the Hebrews: Introduction, Commentary, and Reflections*, NIB 12 (Nashville: Abingdon Press, 1998), p. 151.

[36] Ibid., p. 151. David deSilva, *Perseverance*, p. 447, also cautions against seeing this passage as being one where 'suffering is somehow a punishment for sin; although this would be an appropriate assessment of the ideology of Proverbs, the author of Hebrews has muted those aspects of the text of Proverbs that speak of punitive discipline and moves instead in the direction of formative discipline'. His conclusion is worth pondering because the Greek word *paideia* and related forms (12:5, 6, 7, 8, 9, 10, 11) can be translated either as 'education' or 'discipline'.

[37] Craddock, *Hebrews*, p. 151.

[38] deSilva, *Perseverance*, p. 448.

remember during such times of adversity and hardship; exhortations and admonitions which are couched in the language of the family.

b. God's children need to remember God's word (12:5–6)

When hard times hit, sometimes the first thing we do is to go looking for advice and counsel from Christian mentors whom we know and respect and who are able to help us. Seeking advice from others we can trust is extremely helpful and encouraging, but when the storm breaks and the flood waters seem overwhelming, sometimes the last thing we do is to turn to the Lord and to his word. This appears to be what had happened to the hearers of this sermon, as the writer's statement or question[39] in 12:5 makes clear: *And you have forgotten that word of encouragement that addresses you as sons.* In a sermon loaded with Old Testament citations and allusions, this together with the present text he is citing (Prov. 3:11–12) functions as a rebuke to his readers and is a reminder to reflect on Scripture. Since in this passage the author is telling his readers to look to Jesus and his sufferings we should not forget the example which Jesus himself as Son left behind when he faced the onslaught of the evil one (Matt. 4:1–11) – he immediately cited Scripture, which no doubt sprung from a deep knowledge and meditation on it. As noted, this passage is a very personal and relational one and perhaps it is appropriate to ask: '*have* you *forgotten the word of encouragement that addresses you as sons?*' (5).[40] As God's children, we need to turn to God and his word in every circumstance of life, but especially in times of trial and adversity when we are buffeted by the raging waves that seem to overflow us.

c. God's children are treading a similar path to Jesus the Son (12:8)

As noted, in citing Proverbs 3:11–12 where sonship language is found, the author's purpose is to apply it directly to his hearers and is in effect calling them children (lit. 'sons') of God.[41] He does so in the hope that 'they will recall 5:8 (*Although he was a Son, he learned obedience through what he suffered*) and make the connection to themselves'.[42] The linkage of sonship and suffering is clear. Moreover, the latter is language which the hearers would

---

[39] Most commentators and translations take the phrase as a statement.
[40] Lane, *Hebrews*, p. 401, n. d, takes v. 5a as a question (cf. RSV, JB, TEV). He writes: 'The sylistically rhetorical character of the statement favors reading v. 5a as an interrogative.'
[41] Craddock, *Hebrews*, p. 151.
[42] Ibid.

have readily understood (e.g., Philo, the Jewish commentator, uses the same argument). He is in effect telling them they do not need to go looking for suffering but adversities of one kind or another will come searching for them. Such times are an inevitable, indeed expected, part of being a follower of Jesus the Son. Paul, as we observed in chapter 8, says a similar thing in Romans 8:17 where he links the sonship and suffering of Jesus immediately prior to going on to talk in depth about the suffering which the sons and daughters of God *will* face in 8:18–28.[43] In the former text he uses a conditional clause (NIV, 'if indeed') which is a real condition that must be met if God's children are to enter into their inheritance. It reads: 'Now if we are children, then we are heirs – heirs of God and co-heirs with Christ, if indeed we share in his sufferings in order that we may also share in his glory.' In other words, there is no sonship without suffering, for this is the path that every Christian (to one degree or another) will take.

Other biblical writers make the same point. In the letter of James, we read: 'Consider it pure joy, my brothers and sisters, whenever you face trials of many kinds.' And in the first letter of Peter the author states tells his readers they should not 'be surprised' at the painful trial they were undergoing as though this were something strange.[44] The question we need to ask ourselves is this: Are we ready as the children of God willing to *learn* like Jesus, God's Son in the school of suffering? (Heb. 5:8). I thought I was until this was put to the test when we went from Northern Ireland to a theological seminary in the Pacific Islands to work. We were told that the school to which our children were to go in Fiji was offering international GCSEs but a suddenly a new principal was installed and that syllabus dropped to be replaced by the International Baccalaureate diploma. After about a year it became apparent there were problems with the school meeting the standard required by the authorities and if our son remained in the school he would not have been properly qualified to gain entrance into a university in the UK. Providentially, the school he had attended in Northern Ireland had a boarding department and so on a hot and sticky dark September night I made the long journey from one end of the world (Fiji) to another (Northern Ireland) to leave him there. The year of separation was a particularly difficult for us all, not least as I initially said my goodbye in the car park of the school in Belfast knowing I had

---

[43] See discussion of these verses in Burke, *Adopted into God's Family*, pp. 187–190.
[44] Jas 1:2; 1 Pet. 4:12.

to make the 12,000 mile journey back to Fiji without him.[45] The next year proved to be a difficult and challenging one for our older son as well as for us as parents and his younger brother. But interestingly, it was also a time when he grew stronger as a Christian and developed in character and so did we! Following Jesus will mean adversity for every child of God, a point about which Horatius Bonar, the hymn writer, seems to agree:

> Go, labour on; spend and be spent,
> Thy joy to do the Father's will;
> It is the way the Master went;
> Should not the servant tread it still?[46]

d. God loves his children (12:6)

The author's hearers might have tempted to think that being allowed to go through adversity and suffering was a sign of God's disfavour and a withdrawal of his care and affection for them. Nothing could be further from the truth. Rather, the writer counters this view by underscoring the point that *the Lord disciplines those he loves* (6). The love of which the author speaks is one which undergirds the disciplinary training and examinations of life God takes each of us through. When suffering is understood from the divine perspective as something permitted by God, then it is seen not as proof of his rejection but rather as a sign of his affection and warm embrace. Further, God's discipline is not to be misconstrued as some divine despot getting his own back or as a lack of care or concern. No, God loves his children therefore he tests and toughens them, as William Lane helpfully comments: 'The imposition of divine discipline is an evidence of God's responsible love and commitment. Adversity and hardships are to be recognized as means designed by God to call his people to faithful sonship.'[47]

When suffering comes, God is not impassive like some cold, distant figure who stands aloof, detached from us or the situation in which we find ourselves. Rather, as we read elsewhere in Hebrews God, in his Son, is 'touched with the feelings of our infirmities' (4:15, KJV). God suffers when we suffer. For some this is a philosophical issue to try to resolve but for others, as in the case of

---

[45] To compound our situation, I was only back one week in Fiji when I received a telephone call from my older brother to say that my father had been taken seriously ill; he eventually died before I could make the same trip back home.

[46] Horatius Bonar, hymn 'Go Labour On', *Songs for the Wilderness*, 1843.

[47] Lane, *Hebrews*, p. 420.

Nicholas Wolterstorff, a philosopher and Christian whose son died at the tender age of twenty-five, it is the reality of life. He writes:

> For a long time I knew that God is not the impassive, unresponsive, unchanging being portrayed by the classical theologians. I knew of the pathos of God. I knew of God's response of delight and of his response of displeasure. But strangely, his suffering I never saw before. God is not only the God of the sufferers but the God who suffers. The pain and fallenness of humanity have entered into his heart. Through the prism of my tears I have seen a suffering God ... And great mystery: to redeem our brokenness and lovelessness the God who suffers with us did not strike some mighty blow of power but sent his beloved Son to suffer *like* us, through his suffering to redeem us from suffering and evil. Instead of explaining our suffering God shares it.[48]

God shares in our pain and our suffering because he has been there. Moreover, in times of difficulty and great affliction when we are often confused by what is happening in our lives we need to remember God is there, however dim his appearance might seem to us. It is especially then that we need to remind ourselves that God knows what he is doing; he is sovereign and in control. And 'when we cannot *trace* God's hand we know we can *trust* his heart' (attributed to Charles Spurgeon). God is *with* his beloved children in every situation in life, especially during times of immense anguish and deep distress, and so we are not abandoned, but can rather take comfort in the fact that even *in* and *through* the darker providences of life God is the one who will in the end make all things right.

e. God the Father's discipline and training authenticates the believers' filial relationship (12:7–11)

In 12:7–10 the writer moves on to drive home his point about genuine sonship by using an everyday example from the household. In the human realm, every son is trained and disciplined by his father; that's par for the course, what we normally expect. But then the writer puts the point negatively as follows: *If you are not disciplined (and everyone undergoes discipline), then you are illegitimate children and not true sons* (8). All children can expect to undergo training but to fail to experience this is to be shamed and to be dishonoured in the eyes of others. Indeed to shrink from and avoid

---

[48] Nicholas Wolterstorff, *Lament for a Son* (Grand Rapids: Eerdmans, 1987), p. 81. See also pp. 66–67 above.

such times puts a question mark over the legitimacy of one's filial relationship to one's father. It is put even more strongly because the 'son' who shirks these experiences has a *bastard* (*nothos*) status and is not a true son because he does not share what all God's children experience and therefore has no place in the family of God.

Moreover, the nature of such disciplinary sufferings – at the human level – is that they are short-lived, transient and fleeting (*for a little while*, 10) but *God disciplines us for our good* and, more importantly, with eternal consequences in view: *that we may share in his holiness* (10, cf. 12:14b). The point is that we cannot have a share in God's holiness apart from the correction given via discipline and suffering. In short, 'no pain no gain'. To have a share in God's holiness is a present reality and means to enjoy life in his presence (cf. 12:9).[49] Equally, suffering as the children of God plays a role in our sanctification and progression in holiness which will not be complete until we 'see the Lord' (14).[50]

Summary

Hebrews stands out as immediately different to other writings in the New Testament and, as is generally accepted today, is a sparkling and spirited sermon, a sermon on sonship. From the outset, the superiority of Jesus as Son over against angels (merely created beings) and Moses (only a servant) means he is the head of God's household and the only one worthy of our worship. As Son, Jesus is in solidarity with believers as sons and daughters of God where in a number of ways he experiences what we experience: he shares with our humanity by being born into the human condition, is tempted like us, and suffers as well, where, especially in regard to the latter, he as Son learnt obedience through adversity, something which filial-Israel failed to do earlier. As a consequence Jesus' life as Son is a perfect model for us as believers to follow when we are corrected and trained through God's good discipline, one piece of evidence of the Father's love for us as his children.

---

[49] David Peterson, *Possessed by God: A New Testament Theology of Sanctification and Holiness*, NSBT 1 (Leicester: Apollos, 1995), p. 72.
[50] Peter T. O'Brien, *The Letter to the Hebrews*, PNTC (Grand Rapids: Eerdmans and Nottingham: Apollos, 2010), p. 468.

1 John 2:29 – 3:3; 5:1–2
11. Children born and loved by God and called to love each other

The first epistle of John neither begins nor ends like other letters in the New Testament – the author tells us little or nothing about himself and the typical greetings we normally associate with the introduction (and conclusion) of a letter are conspicuous by their absence. However, two related aspects in the letter are clear: first, the church was facing some serious problems and second, the author has a clear pastoral strategy for dealing with them. We shall look at these in turn.

Most commentators are of the view that 1 John is a circular letter addressed to a number of churches. The author[1] is opposing the false teachings of those who once were in fellowship with them but have now seceded from the community, as 1 John 2:19 states: 'They went out from us, but they did not really belong to us. For if they had belonged to us, they would have remained with us; but their going showed that none of them belonged to us.' These former members held different views about the person of Christ (4:1–3). They were also in error concerning the Christian obligation to keep certain commands (2:4; 3:23) and they claimed to have a special anointing (2:20, 27). Even though some had left the community, they continued to exercise some influence over those who remained (2:26). Indeed, these secessionists appear to have gone as far as to embark on an itinerant teaching ministry among the churches in order to sow seeds of doubt among the believers (2:18–19, 26).

So, what should a pastor of a church do when faced with such grave and difficult problems? John has a clear, two-fold pastoral plan. First, he deals with the problems outside. He confronts the false teachers head-on by exposing their erroneous doctrines in as

---

[1] I am assuming a common authorship for the Gospel and letters.

public a way as he possibly can – by writing a circular letter to not one, but many churches. John does not wish the Christians he was pastoring to be in any doubt about the truth concerning the non-negotiables of the Christian faith. Thus, for example, he writes to inform the churches that Jesus was indeed a real, physical human being (4:2–3) and that he is the Christ (5:1). Moreover, those to whom he writes are not exempt from the practical outworkings of the Christian faith, namely, to go on loving one another (3:23) as Christ had taught them. Thus, as we read John's words, there is an 'unmistakable polemic edge'[2] to his message as he tackles head-on and condemns outright those who seek to twist and distort the truths of the Christian gospel and who fail to practise it.

In addition to the evident polemics and the negative side of John's pastoral strategy in addressing the schism, there is the more positive approach of inculcating and strengthening the ties of belonging within the community.[3] John does not explicitly describe the church as a 'family' but it is this idea which undergirds his understanding of community. Indeed, there are clear parallels between the Gospel of John and the first letter of John as far as this language is concerned in respect of Jesus and believers, but the latter has the edge for it is replete with filial language.

Regarding the latter, Jesus is repeatedly described as 'Son' (Gk *huios*, 2:24), 'the Son' (2:23; 4:14), 'his Son' (Gk *tou huiou autou*, 1:3, 7; 4:9; 5:9) or 'the Son of God' (Gk *ho huios tou theou*, 3:8; 5:5, 13). Repeatedly in the letter the author addresses his readers with the affectionate terms 'my dear children' (Gk *teknia*, 2:1, 12, 28; 3:7, 18; 4:4; 5:21), 'little children' (Gk *paidia*, 2:14, 18),[4] and 'beloved' (Gk *agapētoi*, 2:7; 4:1, 7, 11).[5] As in the Gospel, the author here also uses a different (though related) word 'children' (Gk *tekna*) to

---

[2] John Painter, *1, 2, 3 John*, SP 18 (Collegeville: Liturgical Press 2002), p. 17.

[3] This is the view of Terry Griffith, 'A Non-Polemical Reading of 1 John: Sin, Christology and the Limits of Johannine Christology', *TynBul* 49 (1998), pp. 253–276. I tend to agree with Painter who is of the view that it is not one or the other (polemical or pastoral) but 'both-and'.

[4] This is the diminutive form of the related Greek word for 'children' (i.e. *teknia*). *Teknia*, however, is a more affectionate expression similar to German word Frau*lein*, 'young woman', which is a more endearing term than the related word 'Frau', 'woman'. For more on John's use of this word in describing his relationship to his readers see Paul Trebilco, 'What Shall We Call Each Other? Part Two: The Issue of Self-Designation in the Johannine Letters and Revelation', *TynB* 54.1 (2003), pp. 51–73.

[5] John's first letter is almost poetic in parts and the language of love is almost lyrical and far surpasses any other letter in the New Testament; see Robert L. Yarbough, *1–3 John*, BECNT (Grand Rapids: Baker Academic, 2008), p. 174 for a table of statistics.

describe the *believers'* relationship to God as his spiritual offspring
– 'children of God' (Gk *tekna tou theou* 3:1, 2, 7, 10; 5:2). Thus, by
describing Jesus as 'Son' (Gk *huios*) and his readers as 'children' (Gk
tekna) the writer wants to make an important distinction – Jesus'
filial relationship is of a totally different order to that of Christians:
he is the Son of God by nature, Christians are the children of God
by grace. In addition, the terms 'brother' (Gk *adelphos*, 3:16; 4:20
[twice], 21; 5:16) and 'father/s' (*patēr*, 1:2; 2:1, 13, 14, 23; 3:1) fill out
his understanding of community. The upshot of all these familial
terms is that everywhere we turn in 1 John we are confronted with
the language of *relationship* and belonging which John uses to reassure his readers of their new identity as the family of God. John is
a very skilful pastor in that this language serves the purpose of not
only strengthening the bonds of belonging within the community
but also sets them apart from those outside the church, the ones
of whom he writes 'went out from us' because 'they did not really
belong to us' (2:19).

As John seeks to build up the community, he reminds the church
of a number of distinctives which show they really belong to God's
new family. We now turn to consider these.

1. Children born of God do what is right just as their Father is righteous (2:29)[6]

The birth of a child into a family brings many changes, much
excitement (as well as early starts!) and a lot of discussion about
who the newborn child resembles. In the quest to answer this, the
child's physical appearance is keenly scrutinized, including eye and
hair colour, their facial features such as shape of the nose, ears and
mouth, and of course, their build. As children grow older, in addition to these physical similarities to their parents is the unconscious
copying of certain mannerisms, ways of speaking, stance, attitudes,
and so on. It is an inescapable (and sometimes rather scary!) fact that
children exhibit something of the physical, moral and emotional
make-up of their parents.

Just as children share certain characteristics or features of their
biological parents so it is in the spiritual realm; the reason for this

---

[6] A number of commentators see the break at 3:1 as artificial and connect
2:28 with chapter 3; see John R. W. Stott, *The Epistles of John*, TNTC (London:
Tyndale, 1983), p. 115; Daniel L. Atkin, *1, 2, 3 John*, NAC 38 (Nashville:
Broadman and Holman Publishers, 2001), p. 127, and the Nestle Aland *Novum
Testamentum Graece* 27th edition.

John tells us is that believers have been *born of God* (Gk *gennaō*, 29). This is the first of ten occurrences of this verb in the letter[7] and it is significant that eight of the ten uses are in the perfect tense indicating that God has not only brought his 'children' into the family at a point in time but that this spiritual 'begetting' has ongoing consequences in the present as a result. Thus, although their spiritual begetting took place in the past, the tense suggests John is more interested 'in the actual state of life or manner of being'[8] *in the present*, evident by the way he ties it to the idea of doing what is right (see below).

Moreover, the verb in verse 29 is passive, which means that the new birth is not something we can conjure up ourselves but something that has been done for us. Just as we had no part to play in the decision regarding our physical birth – our parents decided that for us – so it is in the divine scheme of things, spiritual birth is the sole prerogative of God. In other words, being born into God's family is uniquely and exclusively a divine activity (cf. John 1:13) – God always takes the initiative in bringing men and women, boys and girls, into his household.

But the burning question for John is this: how can we tell if someone has been truly *born of God*? How do we know who really *is* and who is not a child of God? Well, family characteristics – you do what your parents do, of course, you behave as they behave. The 'proof' of being *born of God* is set within the wider context of verse 29 which is introduced by a conditional clause to demonstrate that the child who does what is right has truly experienced the new birth. John writes: *if you know that he is righteous, you know that everyone who does right has been born of [God]* (29). The one who is *righteous* is 'God' the Father and if we do what is right – that is, live and behave like him – we know we have been truly born of God. That is, 'a person's righteousness is . . . the *evidence* of . . . new birth, not the cause or condition of it'.[9] 'Doing' right is the ultimate *proof* of the fact that one is a child in God's household.

Careful note should be taken of John's emphasis upon *doing* (Gk *poieō*)[10] in verse 29, a verb which recurs repeatedly throughout the

---

[7] Cf. 3:9 (twice); 4:7; 5:1, 4, 18 (twice).

[8] Matthew Vellanickal, *The Divine Sonship of Christians in the Johannine Writings*, AnBib. 72 (Rome: Biblical Institute Press, 1977), p. 230.

[9] Stott, *Epistles of John*, p. 118.

[10] See Yarbrough, *1–3 John*, p. 18, for this usage as well as the incidence of this verb and other terms. John's pragmatism reminds me of some of my students who are from Missouri, the so-called 'Show-Me State' – they have no time for those who theorize about the fact that they know how to do something. No, they want proof you actually can *do* what you are talking about!

first epistle.[11] A theology that is remote from everyday living would not be the theology of John, or any other New Testament author for that matter. The apostle is no theological couch-potato as far the Christian life is concerned; rather he is very pragmatic – actions, not words, are what counts in John's book – he is more concerned with the practical side of being a part of God's family. In other words, it is not enough to merely *experience* the new birth, it is equally (if not more) important to show *evidence* of it. Orthodoxy must always lead to orthopraxy. We do that best when our righteous deeds emulate our heavenly Father. Martin Luther, the sixteenth-century reformer, said a similar thing many centuries later: 'Good works do not make a good man (i.e., a Christian), but *a good man* (i.e. a Christian) *does good works*.'[12] The apostle John would whole-heartedly agree.

2. Children who are loved by the Father (3:1)

Love is a Verb is the title of several books which have appeared in bookshops in recent years. In a day when the language of love has been emptied of any real meaning and significance and is often rede-fined by actors and filmmakers who 'play' at love in Hollywood, these titles highlight the importance of *expressing* love rather than merely saying 'I love you'. John gives the subject of love more discussion than any other book in the New Testament – 'agape is used . . . thirty-one times . . . in his epistles'.[13] But again the apostle is less concerned about a theoretical notion of love than he is with love's evidence. Several times in the letter we are told 'God is love' (e.g. 4:8) which, for John, defines the very essence and character of who God *is*, but love is also a divinely functional characteristic and describes what God *does*, as S. S. Smalley points out: '"Love" in John defines the *nature* and *activity* of God.'[14] Moreover, who God *is* and what God has *done* are often brought together at important points in this first epistle, as in 1 John 3:16: 'This is how we know what [God's] love is: Jesus Christ laid down his life for us'; again, 'This is how God showed his love among us: He sent his one and only Son into the world that we might live in him' (4:9). Love

[11] 1:6, 10; 2:17, 29; 3:4 (twice), 7, 8, 9, 10; 5:2, 10.
[12] Martin Luther, 'The Freedom of a Christian', in *Martin Luther: Selections from his Writings*, ed. with an intro. by John Dillenberger (New York: Doubleday, 1962), p. 69.
[13] Ceslaus Spicq, *Agape in the New Testament: St. John*, vol. 3 (St. Louis/ London: Herder Books Co., 1966), p. 103.
[14] S. S. Smalley, *1, 2, 3 John*, WBC 51 (Waco: Word, 1984), p. 49.

does – and certainly as far as divine love is concerned 'love is a verb'.

This is a point we need to keep before us as we approach 3:1 which focuses on the expression of God's love. John writes: *See what great love the Father has lavished on us that we should be called the children of God. And that is what we are!* (TNIV). The verse begins in a very striking manner by using what linguists call an 'attention-grabbing word', 'See'/'Behold',[15] which although it is in the form of a command and therefore not something we can take or leave, nevertheless points forward to the significance of the statement which follows and the point the writer really wants us to grasp, namely *how great is the love the Father has lavished on us, that we should be called the children of God*. What the apostle wants his readers to understand is the quality of God's love, evident by his choice of a most unusual word *potapos*,[16] an adjective modifying the noun 'love', meaning 'what sort of' (love). In the New Testament this word 'always refers to a . . . distinct and . . . unusual category'.[17] Originally *potapos* meant 'of what country' highlighting the fact that the love John is describing is extraterrestrial, a love which is different to anything we can associate with on this planet – a love which is literally 'out of this world'! The same word is used in Mark 13:1, for example, when Jesus' disciples saw the temple building and were so astonished they said to him: 'Look, Teacher! What (*potapoi*) massive stones! What (*potapoi*) magnificent buildings!' The quality of the construction was not something they had ever seen before.

But this word can also mean 'how great' and in this context also stresses the *extent* of that love, a reading which finds support from the clause which follows: *that we should be called the children of God*, which here is a further delineation of the magnitude of the love of the father for his children.[18] Thus, John is registering his astonishment at the *quality* and the *size* of the father's love for his

[15] Other attention-getting words include, 'Truly, truly', as in Jesus' statement: 'Truly, truly I say unto you, whoever hears my word and believes him who sent me, has everlasting life' (John 5:24, ESV). Such words often introduce an important statement but could easily be left out as the rest of the text makes complete sense without them. Such words are there for a purpose – they immediately get our attention and focus on the statement that follows.

[16] This word occurs only six times in the whole of the New Testament (Matt. 8:27; Mark 13:1 [twice]; Luke 1:29; 7:39; 2 Pet. 3:11.

[17] Spicq, *Agape*, p. 109.

[18] This means taking the clause in question not as purpose but as a further explanation of the main clause, 'How great is the Father's love...'; see Colin G. Kruse, *The Letters of John*, PNTC (Leicester: Apollos, 2002), p. 114, n 109; *contra* Yarbrough, *1–3 John*, p. 175.

children, for it can never be fully fathomed or comprehended precisely because its derivation is not human but divine.

John's reminder to the church of God's love is important for us too because sometimes God's children can be plagued with a lack of assurance. One thing Christians need to be continually reminded of as well as to remind one another is that God loves us unconditionally. Moreover, as we have noted, God does not simply tell us of his love but he has shown he loves us by sending his only Son to die on our behalf. We do God an immense disservice if we fail to realize we are loved by God, as John Owen, the puritan reminds us: 'The greatest sorrow and burden you can lay on the Father, the greatest unkindness you can do to him, is *not* to believe that he loves you'.[19] The importance of the latter was emphasized in a sermon by the prince of preachers, Charles Spurgeon:

> I once knew a good woman who was the subject of many doubts, and when I got to the bottom of her doubt, it was this: she knew she loved Christ, but she was afraid he did not love her. 'Oh!' I said, 'that is a doubt that will never trouble me; never, by any possibility, because I am sure of this, that the heart is so corrupt, naturally, that love to God never did get there without God's putting it there.' You may rest quite certain, that if you love God, it is a fruit, and not a root. *It is the fruit of God's love to you*, and did not get there by the force of any goodness in you. You may conclude, with absolute certainty, that God loves you if you love God.[20]

We would do well to linger long over the fact that *you* and *I* are children, cherished by God.

3. Children of God: a new name and identity (3:1)

The introductory clause *Behold how great is the love* not only stresses the quality and the greatness with which the children of God are loved but also emphasizes the *way* that they are loved for the 'kind of love God demonstrates is active and creative love, which "calls" us the children of God'.[21] The 'calling' here signifies the entering into a relationship whereby John's readers are described

[19] John Owen, *Communion with God*, ed. R. J. K. Law (Edinburgh: Banner of Truth, 1981), p. 13 (emphasis added).
[20] Charles Spurgeon, sermon no. 762: 'The Relationship of Marriage'.
[21] Marianne Meye Thompson, *1–3 John*, IVPNTC (Downers Grove/Leicester: IVP, 1992), p. 88.

as 'children of God'. This is nothing less than a procreative act[22] by God the Father[23] as noted in both the Gospel and letters of John (John 1:13; 1 John 3:1) where the identity of being 'children of God' is a resulting status of having been 'born of God'.

But 'calling' also includes 'naming' and the name of a person in the ancient world was of great significance: it was the means by which an individual was identified and, most important at the time, enabled them to trace their origin and derivation to the one to whom they belonged. One's identity in antiquity was inextricably linked to one's parents in general and the father in particular: 'what you had done' (i.e. achieved honour) was less important in the ancient world than 'the one to whom you belonged' (i.e., ascribed honour) and there is no greater honour than being a child of God in this most honourable of all households. This is particularly emphasized in the phrase 'children *of God*' which denotes *relationship*,[24] thereby underscoring the Christian's identity and belonging to the new family of God. Thus, if you are a Christian, your identity is not a plumber, bricklayer, nurse, clerk or doctor (that's what you *do*), but is first and foremost a child of God, namely who you *are*. This distinction is further highlighted by John a few verses later by the juxtaposition of the believer's filial relationship alongside another much more sinister filial association, the one divine ('the children of God', *ta tekna tou theou*) and the other devilish ('the children of the devil', *ta tekna tou diabolou*, 3:10). This parallelism of the 'children of God' and the 'children of the devil' was one we noted in chapter 6 and is only found in the Johannine literature. One's name is one of the many markers of identity which John uses to demonstrate how the human race is divided into two diametrically opposite camps.[25] What John says is stark and candid because there is no *via media*: either one's identity is tied up to a relationship with God or it is tied up to a relationship with the evil one. There is no third party or filial relationship other than these. And in order to underscore this new identity of being *children of God*, John adds: *And that is what we are!*[26] This, as Howard Marshall rightly points out, is 'no legal

---

[22] Yarbrough, *1–3 John*, p. 175.

[23] The Greek word order is significant as 'Father' is at the end of the clause which reads: 'Behold how great the love he has given to us, the Father'. The word 'Father' is at the end for emphasis.

[24] This is more technically called a genitive of relationship; see Daniel B. Wallace, *Greek Grammar Beyond the Basics: An Exegetical Syntax of the New Testament* (Grand Rapids: Zondervan, 1996), pp. 83–84.

[25] See 'John, Letters of', in *DBI*, pp. 456–458 for others.

[26] The phrase 'and we are' is omitted by some Greek manuscripts but it has better external attestation and should therefore be retained.

fiction',[27] for the believer's filial relationship to God is every bit as real and present possession as any biological relationship between sons and daughters and their parents today. In brief, we *are* God's children and 'members of his household: not only in name, but also in fact'.[28] This is for real!

4. Children honoured by God but dishonoured in the world (3:1)

Having described his readers as children who belong to God John proceeds to tell them that it is because of this[29] that the world does not recognize them (3:1). The word *world* is a typically Johannine one in the Gospel and the first letter, describing those who are diametrically opposed to God.[30] Thus, in the Gospel, Jesus' coming into the world resulted in the rejection of the Son of God (and because of Jesus' close association with God, the rejection of his Father as well): 'He was in the world and the world did not recognize him' (John 1:10). Similarly, in the epistle *the reason the world does not know [recognize] us is that it did not know [recognize] him* (1), Jesus.[31] This is not surprising given that the world is a diabolical (3:8, 10, Gk *diabolos*, 'devil') domain whose standards run counter to everything that the children of God are and stand for. In other words, although John's readers are now the children upon whom 'God ascribes the honour of God's own household'[32] such honour is not given to them by outsiders nor is it understood by the prevailing culture of his day. And Christians today are often misunderstood, sometimes treated with disdain and not regarded very highly in the eyes of the world. Nevertheless, they are looking forward to the day when they will be vindicated and seen for who they really are (cf. 3:2) – the children of God.

---

[27] I. Howard Marshall, *The Epistles of John*, NICNT (Grand Rapids: Eerdmans, 1978), p. 170.

[28] Smalley, *John*, p. 142.

[29] The prepositional phrase 'because of this' points backwards rather than forwards.

[30] Marshall, *Epistles of John*, p. 144.

[31] Although the rejection refers to Christ the Father cannot be excluded; see Martin M. Culy, *I, II, III John: A Handbook on the Greek Text* (Waco: Baylor Press, 2004), p. 68.

[32] David A. deSilva, *Honour, Patronage, Kinship and Purity: Unlocking New Testament Culture* (Downers Grove: IVP, 2000), p. 73.

5. Children living between the 'now' and the 'not yet' (3:2)

The reality of the believers' filial relationship to God continues to be John's focus and in verse 2 he affectionately calls them *Beloved* [*Dear friends*], which serves the purpose of reminding them of the Father's love *and* the apostle's love for them. By also including himself in the statement *we are children of God*, John demonstrates that he is putting into practice 'his own ethical demand to love within the brotherhood'.[33] Addressing the community as 'beloved' together with the phrase *we are children of God* accentuates the present reality of his readers' new familial disposition with God. But this relationship of sonship has not yet been fully consummated, its completion still lies ahead in the future, as John goes on to point out: *we shall be like him, for we shall see him as he is* (2b). This 'now/ not yet' is part of the eschatological tension between the present and the future aspects of being the children of God, a tension which we noted, for example, in the writings of the apostle Paul (cf. Rom. 8:15, 23) as regards our adoption as God's children.[34] In other words, sonship has a retrospective and a prospective dimension which recognizes what has already been accomplished but looks forward to what has yet to take place.[35]

Again, like Paul (cf. 1 Thess. 5:5) John discusses sonship within the context of the second coming of the Son of God. The climax of his readers' filial relationship is tied to the return of Jesus Christ the Son of God, a matter about which he is in no shadow of a doubt as the latter half of verse 2 makes clear: *we know that when he [Christ] does*[36] *appear we shall be like him for we shall see him as he really is* (author's translation). John links the sure and certain return of the Son of God with what will be in the future, even though he does not spell out the finer details of how it will actually come about. Nevertheless, when that happens a transformation will take place for God's offspring. But what happens between now and then? We now turn to this question.

---

[33] Smalley, *1, 2, 3 John*, p. 144.

[34] See chapter 7.

[35] Sinclair B. Ferguson, 'The Reformed Doctrine of Sonship', in Nigel M. de. S. Cameron and Sinclair B. Ferguson (eds.), *Pulpit and People: Essays in Honour of William Still on his 75th Birthday* (Edinburgh: Rutherford House, 1986), p. 87.

[36] In the original language this statement may appear to throw doubt on the return of Christ. This does not do justice to the use of the language here, for what is at stake here is not the *event* of Christ's second coming but the *timing* of his appearing – Jesus will come again; see Culy, *I, II, III John*, p. 63.

6. Children with a moral responsibility to live holy lives (3:3)

As noted earlier, chapter 3 begins with God's love, but divine love acts and always demands appropriate action and an appropriate response. Having emphasized the fact that his readers live in the intervening period between the 'now' and the 'not yet', John exhorts them to conduct themselves as God's children. In other words, there is a focus on obedience and the responsibility to behave as members of God's family, a moral obligation to act in accordance with those who profess to belong to the household of God. This ethical emphasis becomes all the more urgent when it is seen against the return of Jesus the Son, as it is here. John repeatedly demands validity of his readers to show that religious experience must be matched by action, lest they engage in nothing more than self-deception. Judith Lieu rightly points out that the child who has been 'born of God *does or does not*[37] live in a certain manner.

It is worth reflecting on how this moral aspect is one that pervades the biblical theme of sonship. For example, earlier Israel as son under the old covenant was expected to be holy (Deut. 14:1–2) and Jesus the Son of God demonstrated repeatedly his obedience to the Father and by so doing provided a model of filial excellence to follow (Matt. 4:1–11). And we have also observed how the New Testament writers, such as the apostle Paul, use the believer's filial relationship to God (e.g., Rom. 8:13–14) to call God's children to obedience by putting to 'death the misdeeds of the body'. John is no different and adds to this thrust, which connects sonship with ethics and the need to act responsibly by making good moral choices. Purity and holiness of life demonstrate the reality of one's filial relationship to God and when it is clearly visible it is powerful signal to an unbelieving world, to those who do not profess any allegiance to God or the church.[38]

There are two main points which John makes in regard to his readers so conducting themselves, namely, *Christocentric* and *personal*.

After describing the certainty of the return of Christ (*we know that when he appears*, 3:2), John goes on to exhort his readers with the Christocentric announcement that everyone who has this hope *in him purify themselves, just as he is pure* (3, TNIV). The comparative statement here at the end of verse 3 (*just as he is pure*) is the goal

---

[37] Judith Lieu, *The Theology of the Johannine Epistles* (Cambridge: Cambridge University Press: 1991), p. 50.

[38] deSilva, *Honor, Patronage, Kinship and Purity*, p. 294.

or the moral example toward which the children of God are striving – they are to be holy just as Jesus Christ the Son of God is holy. Living a godly life and endeavouring to live as Jesus lived not only sets God's spiritual offspring apart from the surrounding culture of the day but it is also pleasing to their heavenly Father, and John's remarks reflect the normal social expectation in antiquity, namely, that children were to obey and honour their parents.[39]

The second reason for such conduct is *anthropological* or *personal*; there is an onus and a moral responsibility on the child of God to purify *himself*. The verb *purify* has a clear ethical overtones and is in the present continuous tense, indicating a process as opposed to a once-and-for-all action. Elsewhere in the letter John makes it clear that 'the blood of Jesus, his Son, purifies us from all sin' (1:7), but sanctification is a two-sided coin and by using the reflexive pronoun (*himself*) the apostle emphasizes the moral duty for the child of God to play a role in their own sanctification. The significance of all this in the light of the return of the Son of God is that holiness is focused on the character of Christ and his person, which brings an accompanying personal responsibility on the children of God to do everything they can to live differently to the world.

7. Children who love their Father *and* their brothers and sisters (5:1–2)

We move towards the end of the letter to look at some further expectations of God's children. As we do, it is worth pointing out how unbelievers sometimes have a point when they look at the church and see division and disunity as well as a lack of love between those who profess to be Christians, members of God's family. As a result, they do not want anything to do with the church, and who could blame them? The Christian song of another era 'And they'll know we are Christians by our love by our love, Yes, they'll know we are Christians by our love' is one piece of evidence of a changed life and John addresses this aspect from two perspectives, loving the Father and loving one another as siblings in Christ.

a. Loving the Father (5:1–2)

Having already shown how God the Father has clearly demonstrated his love towards us in concrete and tangible ways, supremely

---

[39] Peter Balla, *The Child-Parent Relationship in the New Testament and its Environment* (Tübingen: Mohr Siebeck, 2003), p. 224.

in the giving of his Son to die, it is not surprising that God's children are to show love towards their Father in return. Moreover, it is interesting how loving one's parent was a stereotypical attitude in the ancient world – every child was supposed to reciprocate by loving their mother and father in return.[40] For example, one ancient writer tells us that 'parents love their children as soon as they are born' and 'children love their parents . . . when . . . they have acquired understanding'.[41] John is working with these assumptions when he makes the point that in the spiritual realm such love is the evidence one has been born of God: *Everyone who believes that Jesus is the Christ is born of God, and everyone who loves the father loves his child as well.* Earlier in the letter John states that children love the Father because the Father first loved them: 'we love [him] because he first loved us' (4:19). This is not to say that God needs our love, for there is perfect unity and love within the Godhead between Father, Son and Holy Spirit. Nevertheless, reciprocating the Father's love is a measure of our gratitude for the immeasurable grace and love which he has lavished upon us. Such love, moreover, is not to be reduced or confined to piety of speech or mere words, but should instead be more concrete and visible, just as we noted earlier how the Father's love was tangibly demonstrated toward us in the giving of his Son Jesus to die on our behalf. In other words, God's love is not something for the believer merely to reflect upon, but a love that is to be imitated and reproduced in our lives. Interestingly, ancient writers contemporaneous to John's day recognized how in the physical realm children could never fully repay their biological parents for all they had done for them. As God's children, we can never hope to 'repay' our heavenly Father either, but it should not prevent us from endeavouring to deepen our love for God and our appreciation for all he has done in sending his Son Jesus to die on our behalf.

b. Loving our brothers and sisters in Christ (5:1b)

Golf's Ryder Cup, between Europe and the United States, is called after Sam Ryder but it is seldom noted that it was Abe Mitchell who taught Ryder the game of golf and whose figure it is that adorns the top of the cup. The relationship between the two men was more than one of mere friendship, and as the slogan for the 2010 competi-

---

[40] See Trevor J. Burke, *Family Matters: a Socio-Historical Study of Kinship Metaphors in 1 Thessalonians*, JSNTS 247 (London: T&T Clark, 2003), pp. 52–57, 67–68, 76–77, and 89–93.

[41] This is from Aristotle's *Nichomachean Ethics*, 8.11.2.

tion in Wales put it, the Ryder Cup is 'A Tournament Forged on Brotherhood'.

When God brings us into his family, there is the vertical relationship of being his children but we are also on the horizontal level brothers and sisters to one another tasked with the responsibility to love one another. John makes this point clear in 5:1: *Everyone who believes that Jesus is the Christ is born of God and everyone who loves the father loves* his child *as well*. 'To love God's child' is tantamount to loving our brothers and sisters in the Lord. In fact, these two ideas are related not only here but elsewhere in the letter: 'If we say we love God yet hate a brother or sister, we are liars. For if we do not love a fellow believer, whom we have seen, we cannot love God, whom we have not seen' (4:20, TNIV). John's statements compare favourably to contemporary writers of the first century who also tell us that sibling love is evidence of love for one's parents: 'Now, as regards parents, brotherly love is of such a sort that to love one's brother is forthwith proof of love for mother and father.'[42]

As we noted, brotherly relations are frequently mentioned in this letter;[43] indeed, the Greek term for 'brother' *adelphos* 'is a compound word (*a* = "from" and *delphus* = "womb") and conveys the idea of coming from the same womb'.[44] Brothers and sisters in the natural realm were to love one another precisely because they shared a common parentage. In the Christian family, God has birthed us as his spiritual offspring and one way we show our gratitude to God is through loving our brothers and sisters in Christ. Love between siblings, moreover, is the authentic sign of being born into God's household, as John explains: 'We know that we have passed from death to life because we love our brothers and sisters' (3:14).

In the ancient world, there was no closer relationship than that between a brother and sister because it was natural for siblings to 'feel affection for each other'.[45] So close was this relationship that a brother and a sister were 'not to let a stone come between them'.[46] Here Plutarch, writing in the first century, clearly shows there was a closeness and an intimacy between siblings. If this was so in the physical realm, how much more should it be the case in the spiritual or Christian family? – brothers and sisters in Christ should demonstrate love for one another. John, moreover, does not want his readers to merely talk about sibling love or to give mental consent to

---

[42] Plutarch, *Frat. Amor.* 6.480F.

[43] E.g., 3:16; 4:20 (twice), 21; 5:16.

[44] Sinclair B. Ferguson, *Children of the Living God* (Edinburgh: Banner of Truth, 1989), p. 54.

[45] Plutarch, *Frat. Amor.* 5.480B.

[46] Ibid., 19.490D.

it; rather, as he writes elsewhere, it must be expressed in tangible and concrete ways. John knows nothing of cerebral Christianity – those who are Christian only from the neck up, who claim their hearts have been changed but whose hands and feet fail to support their empty words. Earlier he had described sibling love in more concrete terms as follows: 'If anyone has material possessions and sees his brother in need but has no pity on him, how can the love of God be in him?' (3:17). As God's spiritual offspring, we are to remain sensitive to the needs of brothers and sisters within the household of God (and of those who are outside the Christian community too) who may be going through difficult times. This is how Christians in the early New Testament church lived where, for example, believers pooled their resources from time to time so as to make them available to any needy person in the family of God, the church (cf. Acts 4:34). A Christian philosopher named Aristides in the early second century also paints the following powerful description of the economic caring and sharing that existed among brothers and sisters in the church:

> They walk in all humility and kindness, and falsehood is not found among them, and they love one another. They despise not the widow, and grieve not the orphan. He that hath, distributeth liberally to him that hath not. If they see a stranger, they bring him under their roof and rejoice over him, as it were their own *brother: for they call themselves brethren*, not after the flesh, but after the spirit and in God; but when one of their number passes away from the world, and any of them see him, then he provides for his burial according to his ability; and if they hear of any of the number is imprisoned or oppressed for the name of their Messiah, all of them provide for his needs . . . And if there is among them a man that is poor and needy, and they have not an abundance of necessaries, they fast two or three days that they may supply the needy with their necessary food.[47]

If this is so, what could sibling love really look like and how is it to be demonstrated in the church today? It might take the form of something as simple as writing an email to a Christian friend whom you know is going through a tough time. Better still, why not go further and write them a letter? Perhaps I should tell you why from first-hand experience. When you write a letter you have to go and find some paper, then compose the letter, search for an envelope

---

[47] Quoted in Ron J. Sider, *Rich Christians in an Age of Hunger: Moving from Affluence to Generosity* (Nashville: Nelson, 2005), p. 85 (emphasis added).

and when all this is done you then have to physically go out and purchase a stamp in order to post it. It takes more time, thought and energy than sending an email. Receiving a letter is a little like receiving a gift which you unwrap and then savour every word which the sender has written – something I have often experienced when serving in Nigeria and the Fiji Islands thousands of miles from home. Many times my wife and I received correspondence[48] from family, friends and church members, who wrote to encourage us in one way or another.

One powerful expression of sibling love I heard of recently was in a church here in Chicago where a member became quite ill and had to have dialysis on a weekly basis. Over time she became so sick that she needed to have a kidney transplant in order to live. In the USA such operations cost a lot of money and trying to find a donor who would be a perfect match for the recipient would not be easy. And, to compound matters, if one could be found, there is a high risk of rejection by the recipient, not to mention other complications of infection, etc. The church began to pray for this seriously ill sister in Christ, and after much prayer another member of the congregation, another Christian sister, came forward and was willing to donate one of her healthy kidneys. The necessary laboratory checks were carried out for compatibility and the donor was found to be a perfect match! Prior to moving ahead the donor was counselled about the operation, especially regarding the fact that in operations of this kind the donor can have a longer period of recovery than the recipient. She decided to go ahead to donate a part of her body – a healthy kidney – in order to save the life of another member in her church family. Here was a member of a local church – and two members not related by birth in the natural realm – demonstrating true sibling love!

I am not suggesting we all go out and immediately begin to give parts of our bodies away, though in these days of organ donation this may be an area in which Christians could give some serious thought to! What it does mean, however, is that each of us has a responsibility to heed the biblical injunction given by the apostle Paul in Romans 12:1: 'Therefore I urge you, brothers and sisters, in view of God's mercy, to offer *your bodies*[49] as living sacrifices, holy and pleasing to God – this is true worship' (TNIV). Evidently Paul here is not merely thinking here of worship within the context of a building on one day of the week, but of worship as a way of life. In other words, every part of our body, our hearts and hands,

[48] This was just prior to the internet revolution and email.
[49] The word Paul uses means our 'whole self' and not just our physical body.

lips and legs, every member, should daily be offered to God and to one another. Such worship is not only sacrificial, holy and pleasing to God but is also rational, as Paul says, because it involves the mind. When this happens those outside the church, the household of God, will be able to say, as recorded by Tertullian: 'See how these Christians love each other!'

However, sometimes this does not happen and Christian talk is not matched by the Christian's walk, which is exemplified in the well known hymn 'Onward Christian Soldiers' below – the first verse is the original which has been re-written and given a different spin in the second stanza that follows:

> Like a mighty army
>   Moves the church of God;
> Brothers, we are treading
>   where the saints have trod:
> We are not divided,
>   all one body we,
> One in hope and doctrine,
>   One in charity.[50]

> Like a mighty tortoise
>   moves the church of God.
> *Brothers*, we are treading
>   where we've always trod.
> We are all divided,
>   not one body we,
> very strong in doctrine,
>   *weak in charity*.

If we were to truly grasp the importance of loving God as our Father as well as loving one another as brothers and sisters in Christ, what a powerful signal this would send to an unbelieving world.

Summary

Set against a context of schism, John's pastoral strategy is to protect this community by reminding the believers of their new sense of belonging as God's children in order to strengthen the filial bonds within. John describes salvation as being born of God, born into a new family, whose members are called to live righteously as their

---

[50] Hymn: 'Onward Christian soldiers', Sabine Baring-Gould (1834–1924).

Father is righteous. God the Father, moreover, has lavished his love upon us and given us a new identity as the children *of God* with the expectation to honour him, though we are dishonoured in a world that is antagonistic to everything that is Christian. There is also the tension between being God's children 'now' and the full consummation of our sonship lying ahead (the 'not yet'). In the intervening period, holiness is to exemplify our lives, which includes reciprocating the love which our Father has lavished on us as his children as well as loving our brothers and sisters in Christ.

Revelation 21:3–8
12. God's sons and daughters, home at last!

As we have considered the biblical theme of sonship we have been on a journey where there have been many highs and many lows as well as unexpected twists and turns along the road. We have visited various places and landscapes, for example, Egypt where God saved his 'son' Israel from slavery before taking the nation through the wilderness into the Promised Land. We have also been to Jerusalem, to the palace, where a king was sworn in as 'son' and where he was promised a dynasty, 'a house' that would never end. Babylon was another location – perhaps a surprising one for us but not for God – where prodigal son Israel had been exiled and from where he eventually returned. Bethlehem was another stop along the way where a very unique Son was born, Jesus, the son of Israel's God, who stands in the Davidic line, triumphing over and fulfilling the promises where all the previous sons before him had failed. We followed this Son to the River Jordan (baptism), into the desert where he was tempted, and to the mountaintop (transfiguration) before heading on to the capital Jerusalem, the location where he died and was resurrected and appointed as 'Son of God with power'. And through God's Son, we as God's sons and daughters are also part of this unfolding drama, and are now being led, trained and disciplined, and called to grow in likeness to the Son with whom we are in solidarity.

We now come to the climax of our narrative of sonship – the final scene, if you like – and appropriately we turn to the last book of the Bible, Revelation, and the penultimate chapter. It is fitting that we consider this book, for the word 'Revelation' is the Greek word *apokalypsis* which means 'unveiling' and what is revealed here – albeit in sometimes mysterious and symbolic language – is another world, the final destiny to which every child of God is heading, their heavenly home.

Revelation 21:7 will be the focus of our attention, which is the last reference to the believer's filial relationship to God in Scripture, and the only time it is mentioned in Revelation. The verse reads: *He who overcomes will inherit all this, and I will be his God and he will be my son.* This reference, moreover, is located in a speech (21:3–8) which has been described as capturing 'in a nut-shell the meaning of the entire book of Revelation'.[1] Revelation 21:7 begins with an initial reference to the one *who overcomes* and raises the important question of understanding this phrase and the book against the historical context in which it was written, for while Revelation is a hybrid as far as genre is concerned – a mixture of apocalyptic (1:1) and prophecy (1:3) – it is also in part a letter (e.g., 1:4–8; 2 – 3) and letters have concrete historical circumstances against which they must be read and grasped. Two contexts have usually been advanced: the latter part of the reign of Nero (54–68 AD) or the latter part of the reign of Domitian (81–96), with the majority of commentators coming down in favour of the second. Whichever period is in view, the reality for John (who himself has been forcibly exiled to the island of Patmos) and his readers is that both are currently experiencing social pressure and persecution. Thus, the book as a whole and certainly John's words in 21:7 are an exhortation for this community to 'dig in' and persevere if they are ever to reach the safe haven of heaven.

What will heaven be like? In trying to conceive of this, C. S. Lewis once asked a friend this very question: 'David, could you define heaven for me?' This friend, who like Lewis shared a love for Oxford and their native Ulster, attempted to do so when the latter 'soon interrupted [his] theological meanderings. "My friend, you're much too complicated; an honest Ulsterman should know better. Heaven is Oxford lifted and placed in the middle of County Down."'[2]

I am sure absolutely certain that heaven will be even more glorious than this, a point made clear by the magnificent description and the language used of the new Jerusalem in Revelation 21, which stands in stark contrast with the previous seventh scene and its emphasis on judgment in Revelation 20. Revelation 21 is a picture of new beginnings and while commentators differ over many interpretative issues in this passage, it is important that we keep on track with our theme. Revelation was not written to satisfy its readers'

---

[1] J. Ramsey Michaels, *Revelation*, IVPNTC (Downers Grove: IVP, 1997), p. 235.

[2] See David Bleakley, *C. S. Lewis: At Home in Ireland* (Bangor: Strandtown Press, 1998), p. 53.

curiosity but to encourage and prepare them for eternity. There are three main points which are made in reference to sonship.

1. Sons and daughters for whom relationship will be everything! (21:3, 7)

The book of Revelation is like a rich fruit cake that could be sliced and looked at from many different angles. One way to look at it is from the perspective of a number of different relationships.[3] For example, there is the relationship between the inhabitants in the new Jerusalem whose names are acknowledged before God (3:5), which assumes some degree of recognition and the retention of individuality. Another relationship is the one between the saints and the angels (Rev. 7:10–11), but the primary association and most personal one is that between God and his people, described by the author in parent-child terminology in 21:7: *I will be his God and he will be my son*.[4]

But the filial description here is not the first time familial language is used in the speech because God's parental care had already been hinted at in an earlier verse and in covenantal terms with the reference to *his people* (3). This general language, however, is eclipsed by the more personal and familial terminology of *my son* and is an unmistakable indication of our association with God and the affection with which he cherishes us as his children. The intimacy of the relationship, moreover, is heightened by the personal pronouns of *I*, *my*, *his*, and *he*, which portray a beautiful picture of God's children enjoying warm, unbroken and satisfying fellowship with God the Father and his Son.

Sonship, being God's children, then, as we have noted throughout our biblical story is only and always about *relationship* – it began in a garden with Adam 'the son of God'[5] and now comes to a glorious climax in heaven, New Jerusalem. And as John describes what is actually beyond all language and thought in human language, he is clear on one thing, that relationship is fundamental and it 'leaves us' as G. B. Caird, states 'with the . . . indelible impression *that heaven is belonging to the family of God*.'[6]

---

[3] Lois K. Fuller Dow, *Images of Zion: Biblical Antecedents for the New Jerusalem* (Phoenix: Sheffield Press, 2010), p. 202. This is an excellent and very readable discussion of all the issues.

[4] Ibid.

[5] Luke 3:38.

[6] G. B. Caird, *A Commentary on the Revelation of St. John*, Harper's New Testament Commentaries (New York: Harper and Row, 1966), p. 267.

2. Sons and daughters who will one day suffer no more! (21:4–8)

John and his readers were experiencing ridicule, social pressure and persecution, but while suffering may be their present lot, heaven is described in terms of an absence of all forms of adversity, which will one day be a thing of the past. Verse 4 states: *He will wipe away every tear from their eyes. There will be no more death or mourning or crying or pain, for the older order of things has passed away.*

Imagine again for a moment what heaven could possibly be like. Perhaps for some of God's children this might mean the release from a broken heart as a result of a loved one who suddenly and unexpectedly died. For others, it may mean freedom from an ailment or a chronic illness – physical or mental – which has plagued them for many years and for which they have not had the resources to pay for an operation or for treatment to alleviate it. For many in the Majority World, I suspect it will mean release from grinding poverty and the impact of globalization to which the West has contributed with our insatiable greed for greater profit and more possessions. In this regard, and as I write, I have a very vivid picture in my mind's eye of a scene that unfolded some twenty-three years ago in a street in Kano, Nigeria where we had just arrived – of a legless man scuttling across the street swinging his arms and torso from side to side to get to the other side. I suspect heaven will mean wholeness for such a man. Or perhaps it will mean the liberation from a deep hurt, an aching pain you've carried for many decades as a result of a broken relationship. The difficulties and struggles which all of us as God's children face are different and making sense of them is not always easy, nor are we always fully able to comprehend why they occur. John Bunyan, the seventeenth-century English puritan writer, knew his own share of suffering when he was imprisoned on two separate occasions for preaching about Christ. In order to try and make sense of the ambiguities, sorrows, and pains of the Christian life, and while he was still in prison, he wrote his allegory *The Pilgrim's Progress* depicting the Christian life, which he likened to a journey from the 'City of Destruction' to the 'Heavenly City'. Writing this book and reflecting on his own experiences proved to be a comfort and means of reassurance to Bunyan and to countless millions of Christians down through the centuries. Whatever our circumstances as God's children, heaven awaits and we have the assurance of freedom from all kinds of suffering, when there will be no more death, no more mourning, no more crying, no more pain. All these will be a thing of the past because the old order has gone and the new age will have begun.

But in the meantime, between now and then, John reminds his congregation that adversity will continue and that they need to persevere and endure. He sounds this note at the beginning of 21:7 with the phrase *the one who overcomes*, which suggests there are still obstacles to surmount and struggles to deal with. These adversities, moreover, are personally focused, as the singular expression 'everyone'[7] makes clear. John also sets his readers the twin alternatives or responses they can make in the light of the persecution which they are presently undergoing – they will either be 'conquerors' (7) or 'cowards' (8). In discussing these, the important subtheme of suffering is raised once again in the context of sonship, an experience which earlier 'sons', namely Israel and Jesus the Son of God, underwent. It is a vivid reminder to his readers that the final consummation of sonship will not be easily entered into.

John specifically writes that the son or daughter who overcomes will receive an inheritance, the two themes noted earlier in respect of Israel, Jesus and believers. The inheritance here is not a physical idea but is more personal, relational and spiritual, because the salvation blessings which Jesus the Son has secured for us through his death on the cross which are mentioned in Revelation 2 – 3 (e.g., 2:7) are repeated in Revelation 21 – 22 (e.g., 22:2).[8] All these and more the children of God will have a share in. But the deliberate use of the singular filial expression *son* brings clearly to mind 2 Samuel 7:14 (and Ps. 89: 26–29) and the promise made of a coming son of David who would reign forever, Jesus, the Son. Now such promises are fulfilled by those who are 'in Jesus' (Rev. 1:9) and God's sons and daughters inherit what Christ the Son inherits (cf. 5:12–13; 11:15), for the inheritance will '*apply to all believers*, who are included in the *household of God*'.[9]

In contrast to those who are 'conquerors' (7), however, is another possible response which John's readers could make in the face of adversity and persecution, namely to act like 'cowards' (8). Evidently, not all of John's readers in Asia will inherit, a point borne out by the exclusivity of the conclusion of the speech where we find a comprehensive list of those who will not be included: *But the cowardly, the unbelieving, the vile, the murderers, the sexually immoral, those who practice magic arts, the idolaters and all liars – their place will be in the fiery lake of burning sulphur. This is the second death* (8).

---

[7] The (substantive) participle is in the singular.
[8] G. K. Beale, *The Book of Revelation,* NIGTC (Grand Rapids: Eerdmans, 1999), p. 1058.
[9] Ibid., p. 1057.

In the context of suffering and persecution, the purpose of verses 6–8 is to exhort true Christians to persevere through hardship and to inherit the fullness of God's blessings. 'Those who deny Christ', as Robert Mounce points out, by falling prey to the allurements of this world 'have no inheritance in the family of God'.[10] But those of God's children who endure to the end will be saved, and when that day comes all kinds of suffering as we now know them will indeed be finally over!

3. Sons and daughters who will bask forever in the presence of the Father and the Son (21:3)

Nothing else can take the place of a person being with us – ask anyone who has lost a loved one and they will invariably tell you it is the physical presence of the one who has died which they miss so much. An email, a telephone call, a letter or a picture can never take the place of the presence of a person right there beside us.

But for God's children who endure to the end, we can look forward to enjoying the blissful presence of the Father and the Son forever, as well as being reunited with loved ones who have died in the Lord. As John seeks to describe New Jerusalem, he underscores this point of being in God's presence (*'with them'*) no less than three times: *Now the dwelling of God is with men, and he will live with them. They will be his people, and God himself will be with them and be their God* (3). As we think of God being with us, a number of Old Testament texts immediately spring to mind, including the prophecy of Ezekiel which points forward to a time when God says: 'Son of man, this is the place of my throne and the place for the soles of my feet. This is where *I will live among the people of Israel for ever.*'[11]

Being in God's presence is a point also made in John's Gospel[12] in respect of Jesus, who promised that his disciples would be with him when he returned a second time. In John 13 – 17, the so-called Farewell Discourse, when Jesus was about to experience the greatest challenge to his earthly ministry, the cross, he addressed his disciples in the upper room. Ironically, instead of Jesus' disciples comforting him, Jesus is the one who comes alongside his disciples with the following words of encouragement:

[10] Robert H. Mounce, *The Book of Revelation*, NICNT (Grand Rapids: Eerdmans, 1979), p. 374.

[11] Ezek. 43:7. Beale, *Revelation*, p. 1046.

[12] I am assuming common authorship for the Gospel of John and Revelation.

Do not let your hearts be troubled. Trust in God; trust also in me. In my Father's house are many rooms; if it were not so, I would have told you. I am going there to prepare a place for you. And if I go and prepare a place for you, *I will come back and take you to* be *with me* that you also may be where I am.[13]

While the phrase 'the Father's house' has been taken by some as a reference to the extended family which in Israelite society provided security for people, D. A. Carson has rightly pointed out that the phrase 'the father's house' had earlier been used in the Gospel linking the temple and *heaven* as both being *God's presence*.[14] Jesus here tells his disciples how he will go via the cross to secure salvation for them (and us), but when he returns he will take us to be *with him*. God's children will one day bask in the welcoming presence of the Father and the Son.

The idea of God being present with his people at different times is an important one throughout Scripture, beginning as far back as Genesis 39:2 with Joseph, and climaxing in the coming of Jesus Christ, 'Immanuel' (i.e., 'God with us', Matt. 1:23). Here in Revelation the promise of 'God with us', the final state as it is sometimes called – and of being in his presence – will be permanent, unbroken and forever. We are not there yet, but as children of God we are heavenward-bound. When that new day dawns, as it most certainly will, we will know the uncontainable thrill, the unspeakable joy of being with the God who brought us into filial relationship with himself in the first instance, and of being reunited with those who have gone before, as we are caught up into his happy presence, a united household of sons and daughters. Then we will know the reality of what the psalmist David wrote so many centuries ago:

> Surely goodness and love will follow me
>   all the days of my life.
> And *I will dwell in the house of the* LORD *forever*.[15]

Only then, will the story of sonship be complete and the journey for all of God's children finally over, and we will be home – home at last!

---

[13] John 14:1–2, emphasis added.
[14] Donald A. Carson, *The Farewell Discourse and Final Prayer of Jesus: An Exposition of John 14–17* (Grand Rapids: Baker, 1980), pp. 21–22.
[15] Ps. 23:6.

Study guide

HOW TO USE THIS STUDY GUIDE

The aim of this study guide is to help you get to the heart of what Trevor has written and challenge you to apply what you learn to your own life. The questions have been designed for use by individuals or by small groups of Christians meeting, perhaps for an hour or two each week, to study, discuss and pray together. When used by a group with limited time, the leader should decide beforehand which questions are most appropriate for the group to discuss during the meeting and which should perhaps be left for group members to work through by themselves or in smaller groups during the week.

PREVIEW. Use the guide and the contents pages as a map to become familiar with what you are about to read, your 'journey' through the book.

READ. Look up the Bible passages as well as the text.

ANSWER. As you read look for the answers to the questions in the guide.

DISCUSS. Even if you are studying on your own try to find another person to share your thoughts with.

REVIEW. Use the guide as a tool to remind you what you have learned. The concluding comment sections at the end of each chapter will also be useful. The best way of retaining what you learn is to write it down in a notebook or journal.

APPLY. Translate what you have learned into your attitudes and actions, considering your relationship with God, your personal life, your family life, your working life, your church life, your role as a citizen and your world-view.

Introduction: Sonship as a biblical metaphor (pp. 17–34)

1. What evidence is there that the Bible is a book of images and motifs and how does sonship differ from many of these (pp. 17–18)?
2. What danger should be avoided in a study of sonship and why is it 'a mistake of some magnitude' (p. 18)?
3. Why is the metaphor of sonship an unusual one with which to describe anyone (pp. 18–19)?
4. In what contexts do we find the expression 'son' in Scripture (pp. 19–20)?
5. Can a study of 'sonship' be justified in an age of sexual equality (p. 10 and pp. 20–21)?
6. In what sense does sonship function as an *inclusio* to the biblical canon (p. 22)?
7. How does the account of Adam's creation throw light on (a) the image and likeness of God and (b) the role of Jesus as Son (pp. 23–24)?
8. In what ways is sonship developed as a metaphor of salvation in (a) the exodus account, (b) John's Gospel and (c) the Pauline epistles (pp. 24–26)?
9. What is meant by describing sonship as essentially 'a functional category in the Bible' and how was that worked out in the life of Israel (pp. 27–28)?
10. What new doctrinal emphasis shapes the concept of filial moral responsibility in the New Testament (pp. 28–29)?
11. What three interlocking themes are addressed in Romans 8:17–25 and what implications do they have for us (pp. 29–30)?
12. Where is the evidence that God is 'a relentlessly relational Being' (pp. 30–31)?

'Christianity is not about a philosophy, a code of practice, or a religion, but a relationship' (p. 31).

---

13. In what ways is today's world 'increasingly fractured' (p. 31)?
14. Is there a danger in emphasizing the Bible as the word of God and if so how can it be avoided (pp. 31–32)?
15. What are the implications of a filial relationship with God on a horizontal level and how can they be worked out in practice (pp. 32–34)?

PART 1. SONSHIP IN THE OLD TESTAMENT

Exodus 4:22–23
1. A son is born: Israel (pp. 37–52)

1. 'Israel is my firstborn son.' In what ways is this a first in the Hebrew Bible (p. 37)?
2. What gives this brief statement its theological weight (pp. 38–39)?
3. What parallels are there between the life experiences of Moses and the people of Israel (pp. 39–40)?
4. Why is it significant that Israel is called a *firstborn son* (pp. 40–41)?
5. What is the irony in the name Israel (p. 41)?
6. What is James I Cook's understanding of Israel's sonship and what arguments can be brought against it (pp. 41–44)?
7. What are (a) the similarities and (b) the differences between sonship and covenant (pp. 44–45)?
8. In what sense is the '*lex talionis*' worked out in the contest between Yahweh and Pharaoh (pp. 46–47)?
9. What is the central question in the encounter between Yahweh and Pharaoh and how is it emphasized by the structure of Exodus 4:22–23 (pp. 47–48)?
10. Where do the themes of these verses recur in the New Testament (pp. 48–49)?
11. What evidence is there that sonship is not a static relationship but a developing one (pp. 49–51)?
12. What are the salvific aspects of sonship (a) negatively and (b) positively (pp. 51–52)?

Deuteronomy 1:31; 8:5; 14:1–2; 32:1–43
2. A son heading home (pp. 53–68)

1. In what way does the message of Deuteronomy resonate with contemporary society (p.53)?
2. In what three ways is the command to 'remember' applied in Deuteronomy 1:31 (pp. 54–58)?
3. What aspect of the father-son relationship is highlighted in Deuteronomy 8:5 (p. 58)?
4. 'If the lessons from the past are to do any good they must be heeded so as not to be repeated' (p. 59). What lessons from the past are relevant in your life?
5. What are the two aspects of the verb 'discipline' (pp. 59–60)?
6. What significant shift takes place when we turn to Deuteronomy 14:1–2 and what are its implications (pp. 60–61)?

7. Was the prohibition, 'Do not cut yourselves or shave the front of your heads for the dead' a meaningless ritual (p. 61)? Is there anything in contemporary society that might be an equivalent?
8. What is the distinction between positional and progressive holiness (pp. 62–63)?
9. What 'long distance history' is anticipated in Deuteronomy 32:1–43 (p. 63)?
10. What charges are brought against God's people in Deuteronomy 32:5–6 (pp. 64–65)?
11. How does God as Father respond to the people's behaviour (pp. 65–67)?

'The question of whether God suffers (the impassibility of God), moreover, is not only a philosophical one to discuss but also impacts all people, especially those Christians who have been tragically torpedoed into grief. But God as parent is also caught up in the drama of adversity' (p. 66).

---

2 Samuel 7
3. A son sworn in: the king (pp. 69–80)

1. How do commentators rate the significance of 2 Samuel 7 (p. 70)?
2. What words 'dominate the landscape in this chapter' and why are they significant (p. 71)?
3. In what way was God's plan different from David's (pp. 72–73)?
4. What 'important literary feature' is evident in verses 8–11 and what lesson can we learn from it (pp. 73–80)?
5. Why is verse 14 'a capstone verse' (pp. 74–75)?
6. Why was it important for the king to comply with God's will (pp. 75–76)?
7. How do God's promises to David compare with (a) his dealings with Saul and (b) the coming of Jesus (p. 77)?
8. Which key words in this chapter tie verses 5–17 and verses 18–29 together (p. 78)?
9. What three words does Brueggemann use to define the sequence of David's prayer and what insights do they give us into David's response to God (pp. 78–80)?

Hosea 11:1–11; Isaiah 1:2–4
4. A prodigal son returns home (pp. 81–95)

1. Reflect on the place of home and family in your own experience (p. 81).
2. What was the historical context of Hosea's prophecy and what metaphors did he use to convey his message (p. 82)?
3. Which four verbs describe God's fatherly role towards Israel in the past and how are they expounded (pp. 83–85)?
4. In what two ways did Israel respond to God's fatherly care (pp. 86–88)?
5. How does Hosea's tone change at chapter 11 verse 5 and what occasioned the change (p. 88)?
6. Why are verses 8–9 'arguably the most poignant words in Scripture' (pp. 88–90)?

'If heartache could be placed on a scale of suffering, we might put the rebuff of a stranger at the bottom followed next by the upset of a clash between friends, but at the very top must surely be the stinging, jilting pain of a parent-child estrangement alongside the deep wound of a betrayal in marriage. In this prophecy, God is portrayed as experiencing both' (p. 89).

---

7. How is the prodigal son syndrome reflected in 21st century society (pp. 90–91)?
8. What factors mitigate against future hope and how does Hosea counter them (pp. 91–92)?
9. Where do other Old Testament prophets reflect the message of restoration in Hosea (pp. 93–94)?
10. What aspect of the father-son relationship gave hope to Israel (p. 94)?

PART 2. SONSHIP IN THE NEW TESTAMENT

Luke 2:6–7; 1:32–36; Matthew 2:13–18; 3:13–17; 4:1–11; Luke 9:28–36; Matthew 27:33–54; Romans 1:3–4
5. Jesus the Son of God (pp. 99–119)

1. Why is the Old Testament background crucial for the New Testament teaching on sonship (p. 99)?
2. What significance do Luke and Paul attribute to the timing of Jesus' birth (pp. 100–101)?

3. What twin themes emerge in Gabriel's announcement to Mary and how are they developed later in the New Testament (pp. 101–102)?
4. What significance would be attached to the title 'Son of God' in New Testament times and why in the light of that are the circumstances of Jesus' birth so surprising (pp. 102–103)?
5. Is Matthew's quotation of Hosea 11:1 'an example of illegitimate transfer' (pp. 104–105)?

'In this the most Jewish of Gospels, Jesus is the true Son of God Israel never proved to be. Jesus as Son is the new Israel of God, the one who rights all the wrongs of all the previous sons of God who had failed so miserably' (p. 105).

---

6. Why is the juxtaposition of baptism and temptation theologically important (pp. 106–107)?
7. 'A truly Trinitarian event.' Why is this an appropriate description of Jesus' baptism (pp. 107–108)?
8. How did Satan tempt Jesus and how did Jesus resist him (pp. 108–111)?
9. What features of the transfiguration narrative shed light on Jesus' mission and link to Old Testament events (pp. 111–112)?
10. What significance should be attached to the triple taunts of the bystanders at the cross (pp. 113–114)?
11. Why should Romans 1:2–4 not be 'allowed to fall off the front of the letter' (pp. 114–118)?
12. 12 In what ways can Romans 1:3–4 be interpreted and which do you find most persuasive (pp. 117–118)?

John 1:14, 18; 5:16–30; 1:12–13; 3:1–10; 8:31–58; 11:51–52; 20:21–23
6. The Son of God and the children of God (pp. 120–138)

1. What two main reasons are identified for including the fourth Gospel in a study of sonship (pp. 120–121)?
2. What distinction does John make in his writings between Jesus and believers and is this reflected elsewhere in the New Testament (pp. 121–122)?
3. What is the meaning of *monogenēs* and how should it be translated (pp. 122–123)?
4. Why is the combination of *monogenēs* and *theos* in John 1:18 unusual and what does it imply (pp. 123–124)?

5. What three features of John 5:16–30 illuminate the filial identity and credentials of Jesus (pp. 124–128)?
6. What two emphases are outlined in John 1:12–13 and how does John relate them (pp. 128–129)?
7. Are regeneration and adoption the same thing and how does the encounter with Nicodemus develop the theme of new birth (pp. 129–131)?
8. What question is dealt with in John 8:31–58 and how is it answered (pp. 131–133)?
9. In what way does ecclesiology figure in John's overall theology (pp. 133–136)?
10. How are sonship and mission connected in John's Gospel (pp. 136–137)?

'For Jesus the test of true belonging and, more importantly, of divine sonship is more ethically than physically rooted; it is not a matter of merely claiming descent but of conduct and lifestyle' (p. 132).

Romans 8:3, 12–25; Ephesians 1:5; Galatians 4:4
7. Adopted sons and daughters empowered by the Spirit (pp. 139–160)

1. What is the meaning and significance of *huiothesia* and where is it used in the New Testament (p. 140)?
2. How are the theological terms justification and adoption related and how are they different (pp. 140–141)?
3. What is the role of God the Father in adoption (pp. 141–144)?
4. What is the role of the Son in adoption (pp. 144–145)?
5. What is the role of the Spirit in adoption (pp. 145–148)?
6. How should the expression 'Spirit of adoption' be understood (pp. 147–148)?
7. What does Paul mean by the believer's inheritance and how is it related to God's Old Testament promises (pp. 148–149)?
8. What is meant by being led by the Spirit and how is the Old Testament language reinterpreted by Paul (pp. 150–151)?
9. What two aspects of the Spirit's leading does Paul emphasize (pp. 151–153)?
10. What grammatical features of Romans 8:12–17 are noteworthy and how should the verb 'to bear witness to/with' be understood (pp. 153–155)?
11. What are the immediate results of adoption (pp. 155–159)?

12. Does Paul's teaching on adoption in Romans 8 help us to understand suffering (pp. 155–159)?

Ephesians 1:4–6; 2:1–10; 4:11–16
8. Children of wrath who become strong and stable sons and daughters of God (pp. 161–176)

1. How does the term *nēpioi* differ from *tekna* and *huioi* (p. 162)?
2. What features characterize the opening of Ephesians and what conclusions can we draw from them (pp. 162–163)?
3. What is the background to Paul's use of *huiothesia* in Ephesians 1:5 (pp. 163–164)?
4. What further features of adoption are evident in this verse (pp. 164–166)?

'It is a useful and instructive practice for us as Christians, in order to appreciate what God has done in our lives, to sometimes look over our shoulder into the past to see where we once were. This also helps to orientate us in the present and move forward into the future' (p. 166).

---

5. How does Paul describe the Christian's past in Ephesians 2 and what significance does filial language have in this description (pp. 166–168)?
6. Is it legitimate to say that God the Father is guilty of 'cosmic child abuse' (pp. 168–169)?
7. How is the concept of sonship developed in Ephesians 4:11–16 (p. 170)?
8. What two aspects of growth are important and how does Paul describe them (pp. 170–172)?
9. Where else in the New Testament is the theme of Ephesians 4:14 reflected (pp. 172–174)?
10. What would you identify as 'unnecessary or unhealthy "growth"' in the Christian life (pp. 174–175)?
11. What non-filial imagery does Paul use to illustrate growth to maturity (p. 175)?

1 Thessalonians 1:9–10; 4:16; 5:1–11
9. Sonship and the second coming of God's Son (pp. 177–189)

1. Why has eschatology been given more emphasis than ecclesiology in the study of 1 Thessalonians and what evidence is there for a community focus (pp. 177–179)?

2. What reasons can be given for Paul's heavy use of familial terms in this letter (pp. 179–180)?
3. What implications can we deduce from the view that 1 Thessalonians is Paul's earliest letter (p. 180)?
4. How do the verbs 'turned', 'serve' and 'wait' encapsulate the good news preached by Paul (pp. 180–183)?
5. In what contexts does Paul link wider Christological themes with the sonship of Jesus (pp. 182–183)?
6. What is the appropriate Christian response to death and bereavement (pp. 183–184)?

'Christians who die in the Lord are not hopeless but rather are hopeful where hope typically in the New Testament understanding does not convey the idea of uncertainty but of confident assurance of being physically raised at the last day when Jesus comes again in glory' (p. 184).

---

7. What mistake should be avoided in connection with the second coming of Christ (pp. 184–185)?
8. What is meant by the expressions *sons of the light* and *sons of the day* and what practical implications follow (pp. 185–187)?
9. Would Gentiles have found it more difficult than Jews to adopt a Christian lifestyle (pp. 187–188)?

Hebrews 1:1–13; 3:5–6; 2:10–18; 12:1–13
10. A sermon on sonship (pp. 190–205)

1. What quality which we find in Hebrews is unparalleled elsewhere in the New Testament and what does it tell us about the nature of the book (pp. 190–191)?
2. On what grounds can sonship be claimed to be the dominant theme of the epistle (pp. 191–193)?
3. Why was it necessary to emphasize Jesus' superiority to the angels and does it have resonance today (pp. 193–194)?
4. What conclusions should be drawn from the author's quotations from the Old Testament (pp. 194–195)?
5. What are the similarities and dissimilarities between Jesus and Moses (pp. 195–196)?
6. What grammatical feature links the sonship of Jesus with that of believers (p. 196)?
7. What parallels does the author of Hebrews draw between the sonship of Jesus and that of believers (pp. 197–198)?

239

8. What was unique about the sufferings of Jesus (pp. 198–199)?
9. What grammatical features signal the shift from chapter 11 to chapter 12 (p. 199)?
10. Are the sufferings described in verses 4–6 a result of the readers' sins (p. 200)?
11. What four factors are we encouraged to remember during times of suffering (pp. 200–205)?

'When suffering is understood from the divine perspective as something permitted by God, then it is seen not as proof of his rejection but rather as a sign of his affection and warm embrace' (p. 203).

---

1 John 2:29 – 3:3; 5:1–12
11. Children born and loved by God and called to love each other (pp. 206–223)

1. What five observations are made about those who had seceded from the Johannine community (p. 206)?
2. What was John's twofold pastoral plan (pp. 206–207)?
3. In what way does John differentiate between the relationship of Jesus as son and that of believers as children and is it important (pp. 207–208)?
4. What features of John's use of *gennaō* add to our understanding of new birth (pp. 208–209)?
5. What significance should we draw from John's use of *poieō* in his first epistle (pp. 209–210)?
6. In what two ways is love defined by John (pp. 210–211)?
7. How does John express the quality and extent of God's love (pp. 211–212)?
8. What does the 'calling' of God signify (pp. 212–214)?
9. What does John mean when he talks about the world in this context (p. 214)?
10. What themes in Paul's writings appear also in 1 John 3 (p. 215)?
11. What two main points does John make in connection with the moral responsibility to live holy lives (pp. 216–217)?
12. How far is it possible for us to reciprocate God's love for us (pp. 217–218)?
13. How was love between Christian brothers and sisters shown in the early church and how might it be demonstrated in the church today (pp. 218–222)?

Revelation 21:3–8
12. God's sons and daughters, home at last! (pp. 224–230)

1. Take time to review the theme so far, summarized here (p. 224).
2. Where do we find the last reference to the believer's filial relationship to God in Scripture (pp. 224–225)?
3. What is the context in which Revelation was written and how does that help us to understand its meaning (p. 225)?
4. What different relationships are explored in Revelation (p. 226)?
5. Does Revelation 21 give us a further perspective on the issue of suffering (pp. 227–229)?
6. In what ways does John underline the importance of being in God's presence (pp. 229–230)?

The Bible Speaks Today: Old Testament series

The Message of Genesis 1 – 11
The dawn of creation
David Atkinson

The Message of Genesis 12 – 50
From Abraham to Joseph
Joyce G. Baldwin

The Message of Exodus
The days of our pilgrimage
Alec Motyer

The Message of Leviticus
Free to be holy
Derek Tidball

The Message of Numbers
Journey to the promised land
Raymond Brown

The Message of Deuteronomy
Not by bread alone
Raymond Brown

The Message of Judges
Grace abounding
Michael Wilcock

The Message of Ruth
The wings of refuge
David Atkinson

The Message of Samuel
Personalities, potential, politics and power
Mary Evans

The Message of Chronicles
One church, one faith, one Lord
Michael Wilcock

The Message of Ezra and Haggai
Building for God
Robert Fyall

The Message of Nehemiah
God's servant in a time of change
Raymond Brown

The Message of Esther
God present but unseen
David G. Firth

The Message of Job
Suffering and grace
David Atkinson

The Message of Psalms
1 – 72
Songs for the people of God
Michael Wilcock

The Message of Psalms
73 – 150
Songs for the people of God
Michael Wilcock

The Message of Proverbs
Wisdom for life
David Atkinson

The Message of Ecclesiastes
A time to mourn, and a time to dance
Derek Kidner

The Message of the Song of Songs
The lyrics of love
Tom Gledhill

The Message of Isaiah
On eagles' wings
Barry Webb

The Message of Jeremiah
Against wind and tide
Derek Kidner

The Bible Speaks Today: New Testament series